# Foundations

## *of*

# Game Engine Development

# Foundations

## *of*

# Game Engine Development

VOLUME 1

# MATHEMATICS

by Eric Lengyel

**Terathon Software LLC**
*Lincoln, California*

**Foundations of Game Engine Development**
**Volume 1: Mathematics**

ISBN-13: 978-0-9858117-4-7

Fourth printing

**Published by Terathon Software LLC**
www.terathon.com

**Series website:** foundationsofgameenginedev.com

**About the cover:** The cover image is a scene from a game entitled *The 31st*, developed with the Tombstone Engine. Artwork by Javier Moya Pérez.

# Contents

# Preface

This book provides a detailed introduction to the mathematics used by modern game engine programmers. The first three chapters cover the topics of linear algebra (vectors and matrices), transforms, and geometry in a conventional manner common to many other textbooks on the subject. This is done to provide a familiarity with the usual approach so that it's easy to make connections to similar expositions of the same topics elsewhere in the literature. Along the way, we will make several attempts to foreshadow the discussion of a manifestly more elegant and more correct mathematical model that appears in the fourth chapter. The last quarter of the book endeavors to provide a deeper understanding of many of the concepts discussed earlier by introducing Grassmann algebra and geometric algebra. Knowledge of these branches of mathematics also allows us to convey intuition and provide details in the first three chapters that are difficult to find anywhere else.

One of the goals of this book is to give practical engineering advice. This is accomplished through many short code listings appearing throughout the book showing how the mathematics we've discussed is implemented inside real-world game engines. To avoid filling pages with code listings that are illustratively redundant, some data structures or functions referenced in various places have intentionally been left out. This happens only when the form and behavior of the missing code is obvious. For example, Chapter 1 includes code listings that define a data structure and operations corresponding to a three-dimensional vector, but it doesn't show similar code for a four-dimensional vector, even though it's used by other code listings later in the book, because it would be largely identical. The complete library of code is available on the website cited below.

We assume that the reader has a solid understanding of basic trigonometry, a working knowledge of the C++ language, and some familiarity with standard floating-point numbers. A bit of calculus appears in Chapter 3, but a full grasp of this isolated usage is not essential to the rest of the book. Otherwise, all of the mathematics that we cover is built from the ground up. Advanced readers possessing a thorough knowledge of linear algebra may wish to skip much of the first two chapters. However, we recommend that all readers take a look at Chapter 3 before proceeding to the final chapter because Chapter 4 assumes a familiarity with the notation and conceptual details discussed in Chapter 3.

Important equations and key results appearing in the text are boxed with a blue outline. This is intended both to highlight the most valuable information and to make it easier to find when using the book as a reference.

Each chapter concludes with a set of exercises, and many of those exercises ask for a short proof of some kind. The exercises are designed to provide additional educational value, and while many of them have easy solutions, others are a little trickier. To ensure that getting stuck doesn't deprive any reader of a small but interesting mathematical revelation, the answers to all of the exercises are provided on the website cited below.

This book is the first volume in a series that covers a wide range of topics related to game engine development. The official website for the *Foundations of Game Engine Development* series can be found at the following address:

foundationsofgameenginedev.com

This website contains information about all of the books in the series, including announcements, errata, code listings, and answers to exercises.

## Acknowledgements

The first volume was made possible by a successful crowdfunding campaign, and the author owes a debt of gratitude to the hundreds of contributors who supported the *Foundations of Game Engine Development* series before even a single word was written. Special thanks go to the following people in particular for showing extra support by making contributions that exceed the cost of a copy of the book.

Alexandre Abreu
Luis Alvarado
Kelvin Arcelay
Daniel Archard
Robert Beckebans
Andrew Bell
Andreas Bergmeier
Marco Bouterse
Lance Burns
Daniel Carey
Bertrand Carre
Ignacio Castano Aguado
Søren Christensen
Daniel Collin
Vicente Cuellar
Courtois Damien
Paul Demeulenaere
François Devic
Jean-Francois Dube
Ashraf Eassa
Wolfgang Engel
Fredrik Engkvist
Brandon Fogerty
Jean-François F Fortin
Nicholas Francis
Marcus Fritzsch
Taylor Gerpheide
Nicholas Gildea

Trevor Green
Nicolas Guillemot
Mattias Gunnarsson
Aaron Gutierrez
Timothy Heldna
Andres Hernandez
Hauke Hildebrandt
James Huntsman
Martin Hurton
François Jaccard
Martijn Joosten
Tonci Jukic
Tim Kane
Soufiane Khiat
Hyuk Kim
Youngsik Kim
Christopher Kingsley
Kieron Lanning
Kwon-il Lee
Jean-Baptiste Lepesme
William Leu
Shaochun Lin
Yushuo Liu
Yunlong Ma
Brook Miles
Javier Moya Pérez
Michael Myles
Dae Myung

Norbert Nopper
Nikolaos Patsiouras
Georges Petryk
Ian Prest
Mike Ramsey
Darren Ranalli
Steen Rasmussen
Guarneri Rodolphe
Yuri Kunde Schlesner
Bill Seitzinger
Michael D. Shah
Brian Sharp
Sean Slavik
Daniel Smith
Soufi Souaiaia
Tiago Sousa
Aaron Spehr
Justin Squirek
Tim Stewart
Runar Thorstensen
Joel de Vahl
Lars Viklund
Ken Voskuil
Shawn Walker-Salas
Ian Whyte
Graham Wihlidal

# Chapter **1**

# Vectors and Matrices

Vectors and matrices are basic mathematical building blocks in the field of linear algebra. They show up in the development of game engines practically everywhere and are used to describe a wide array of concepts ranging from simple points to projective coordinate transformations. The importance of acquiring a strong intuition for vector mathematics and mastering the fundamental calculations that are involved cannot be overstated because a great number of game engine topics inescapably depend on these skills. With this in mind, we begin at the earliest possible starting point and build from the ground up with a thorough introduction that assumes only an existing proficiency in trigonometry on the part of the reader.

## 1.1 Vector Fundamentals

Traditionally, basic numerical quantities arising in geometry, physics, and many other fields applied to virtual simulations fall into two broad categories called scalars and vectors. A *scalar* is a quantity such as distance, mass, or time that can be fully described using a single numerical value representing its size, or its *magnitude*. A *vector* is a quantity that carries enough information to represent a direction in space in addition to a magnitude, as described by the following examples.

- The difference between two points contains information about both the distance between the points, which is the magnitude of the vector, and the direction that you would need to go to get from one point to the other along a straight line.
- The velocity of a projectile at a particular instant is given by both its speed (the magnitude) and the direction in which it is currently travelling.

■   A force acting on an object is represented by both its strength (the magnitude) and the direction in which it is applied.

In *n* dimensions, a direction and magnitude are described by *n* numerical coordinates, and these are called the *components* of a vector. When we want to write down the complete value of a vector, we often list the components inside parentheses. For example, a three-dimensional vector **v** having components 1, 2, and 3 is written as

$$\mathbf{v} = (1, 2, 3). \tag{1.1}$$

We follow the common practice of writing vectors in bold to distinguish them from scalars, which are written in italic. We identify an individual component of a vector **v** by writing a zero-based subscript such that $v_0$ means the first component, $v_1$ means the second component, and so on. Notice that we write the vector itself in italic in these cases because the component that we're talking about is a scalar quantity. Using this notation, an *n*-dimensional vector **v** can be written as

$$\mathbf{v} = (v_0, v_1, \ldots, v_{n-1}). \tag{1.2}$$

Beginning with a subscript of zero for the first component is a departure from the usual convention in purely mathematical circles, where the subscript for the first component is typically one. However, zero-based indices are a much better fit for the way in which computers access individual fields in data structures, so we use the zero-based convention in this book to match the values that would actually be used when writing code.

The meaning of a vector's components depends on the coordinate system in which those components are expressed. It is usually the case that we are working in Cartesian coordinates, and this being the case, the numbers making up a three-dimensional vector are called the *x*, *y*, and *z* components because they correspond to distances measured parallel to the *x*, *y*, and *z* axes. (In two dimensions, the third component doesn't exist, and we have only the *x* and *y* components.)

In addition to numerical subscripts, we can identify the components of a vector **v** using labels that correspond to the coordinate axes. In three dimensions, for example, we often write

$$\mathbf{v} = (v_x, v_y, v_z), \tag{1.3}$$

where it's understood that each subscript is to be interpreted only as a label and not as a variable that represents an index. If we want to equate the components to their values, then using the example in Equation (1.1), we can write them as

$$v_x = 1 \qquad v_y = 2 \qquad v_z = 3. \tag{1.4}$$

Four-dimensional space is a setting in which a great deal of mathematics is done in the course of game engine development, as will be discussed frequently in the chapters that follow this one. The first three components of a four-dimensional vector are still called $x$, $y$, and $z$, but we have run out of letters in the alphabet beyond that, so the universally accepted practice is to call the fourth component $w$. The fourth component is sometimes called a "weight" value, so it's especially convenient that $w$ happens to be the letter closest to $x$, $y$, and $z$.

It may be tempting to think of one-dimensional vectors as no different than scalars since a member of either set is represented by a single numerical value. Ordinarily, there is no need to make a distinction between the two, but you should be aware of the fact that algebraic structures exist in which values are composed of both scalars and one-dimensional vectors. Some of these structures will be discussed in Chapter 4.

It becomes a bit cumbersome to write out the words "two-dimensional", "three-dimensional", and "four-dimensional" every time it's necessary to state a number of dimensions, so throughout the rest of this book, we shall use the shorthand notation 2D, 3D, and 4D in many instances.

The definition of a simple data structure holding the components of a 3D vector is shown in Listing 1.1. The structure is named `Vector3D`, and it has floating-point members named x, y, and z that can be accessed directly. A constructor taking three values can be used to initialize the vector, and this is useful for implementing the vector operations that are discussed below. A default constructor is explicitly included so that it's possible to declare a vector object without performing any initialization. (This is necessary because default constructors are not implicitly generated when other constructors are present.) The structure also includes two overloaded bracket operators, enabling access to the components using zero-based indices, consisting of one operator for non-constant objects, which can be used for component assignment, and one operator for constant objects. Note that these operators do not check that the index is in the valid range of $[0, 2]$, so using an index outside of this range will cause memory outside of the data structure to be accessed erroneously.

## 1.2  Basic Vector Operations

For vectors to be of any practical use, we need to be able to perform calculations with them, and to know what calculations to perform with vectors, we first need to associate some physical meaning with them. This is often done by visualizing

**Listing 1.1.** This is the definition of a simple data structure holding the components of a 3D vector. Structures for vectors of different dimensionality are similar.

```
struct Vector3D
{
    float       x, y, z;

    Vector3D() = default;

    Vector3D(float a, float b, float c)
    {
        x = a;
        y = b;
        z = c;
    }

    float& operator [](int i)
    {
        return ((&x)[i]);
    }

    const float& operator [](int i) const
    {
        return ((&x)[i]);
    }
};
```

a vector as a line segment having an arrowhead at one end, as illustrated in Figure 1.1. The orientation of the line segment and the end on which the arrowhead appears represent the vector's direction, and the length of the line segment represents the vector's magnitude. We use the term *arrow* after this point to mean the combination of a line segment and an arrowhead.

It's important to realize that a vector by itself does not have any specific location in space. The information it possesses is merely an oriented magnitude and nothing more. If we draw a vector as an arrow in one place, and we draw another arrow with the same direction and length somewhere else, then they both represent the exact same vector. A vector can be used to represent a point that does have a location in space by thinking of the vector as a relative offset from a given origin.

**Figure 1.1.** A vector can be visualized as a line segment having an arrowhead at one end.

### 1.2.1  Magnitude and Scalar Multiplication

When we need to express the magnitude of a vector $\mathbf{v}$, we place two vertical bars on either side to make it appear as $\|\mathbf{v}\|$. The magnitude of an $n$-dimensional vector is calculated with the formula

$$\|\mathbf{v}\| = \sqrt{\sum_{i=0}^{n-1} v_i^2}\,, \tag{1.5}$$

which is just the Pythagorean theorem in $n$ dimensions. In three dimensions, we can expand the summation and write

$$\|\mathbf{v}\| = \sqrt{v_x^2 + v_y^2 + v_z^2}\,, \tag{1.6}$$

where we are now using the labels $x$, $y$, and $z$ instead of the numerical subscripts 0, 1, and 2 to designate the different components. Note that the magnitude can never be negative because each term in the summation is a squared quantity.

The vector whose components are all zero is called the *zero vector*, and it is the only vector for which the magnitude is zero. The zero vector is sometimes represented by a bold zero as in

$$\mathbf{0} = (0, 0, \ldots, 0). \tag{1.7}$$

The magnitude of a vector can be changed by multiplying it by a scalar value. When we multiply a vector $\mathbf{v}$ by a scalar $t$, we simply write them side by side, and we apply the multiplication to each of the components to obtain

$$t\mathbf{v} = (tv_0, tv_1, \ldots, tv_{n-1}). \tag{1.8}$$

Scalar multiplication is a commutative operation, meaning that it doesn't matter on which side we multiply by $t$ because it's always the case that $t\mathbf{v} = \mathbf{v}t$. In the formula for the magnitude of $t\mathbf{v}$, the value $t^2$ now appears in each term of the summation, so it can be factored out and removed from the radical as $|t|$. Thus, multiplying a vector $\mathbf{v}$ by a scalar $t$ changes the magnitude of $\mathbf{v}$ by a factor of $|t|$. This property can be written as

$$\|t\mathbf{v}\| = |t|\,\|\mathbf{v}\|, \tag{1.9}$$

demonstrating that the absolute value of a scalar quantity can always be pulled out of the expression for evaluating a magnitude.

As shown in Figure 1.2, scalar multiplication produces a vector with a new magnitude but with a direction that is parallel to the original vector. When the scalar is positive, the new vector still points in the same direction as the original, but when the scalar is negative, the new vector points in the opposite direction. A negated vector, written $-\mathbf{v}$, is one that has been multiplied by the scalar $-1$. In this case, the direction is reversed, but the magnitude is not changed.

A vector that has a magnitude of one is called a *unit vector*. Unit vectors are particularly important because they are able to provide directional information without a magnitude when a meaningful size of some kind is not necessary. Any nonzero vector can be turned into a unit vector by dividing it by its magnitude. The magnitude is a scalar quantity, and when we say that we're dividing a vector by a scalar $t$, we really mean that we're multiplying by the scalar's reciprocal, $1/t$. Thus, a nonzero vector $\mathbf{v}$ can be turned into a unit vector $\hat{\mathbf{v}}$ using the formula

$$\hat{\mathbf{v}} = \frac{\mathbf{v}}{\|\mathbf{v}\|}. \tag{1.10}$$

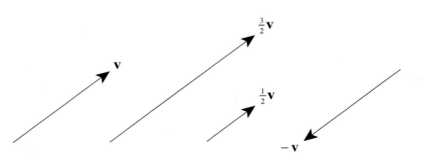

**Figure 1.2.** Scalar multiplication changes the magnitude of a vector while keeping the direction parallel to that of the original vector. If the scalar is negative, then the new vector points in the opposite direction.

The hat written above the **v** on the left side of this equation is a common way of indicating that the vector has *unit length*, or a magnitude of one. The process of setting a vector's magnitude to one is called *normalization*, and a unit vector that has been produced by this process is often referred to as *normalized*. To avoid confusion, you should be aware that this is not related to a type of vector called a *normal vector*, which is a concept described in Chapter 3.

In Listing 1.2, functions that implement scalar multiplication and division are added to the `Vector3D` data structure as overloaded operators. A special function is provided for vector negation by overloading the unary minus operator. This code also includes a function that calculates the magnitude of a vector and another function that divides by the magnitude in order to normalize a vector.

**Listing 1.2.** This code adds scalar multiplication and division to the `Vector3D` data structure. It also includes functions that calculate the magnitude of a vector and produce the normalized version of a vector. (Note that the `Normalize()` function can be implemented more efficiently by using a reciprocal square root function, if one is available, with scalar multiplication instead of division.)

```
struct Vector3D
{
    Vector3D& operator *=(float s)
    {
        x *= s;
        y *= s;
        z *= s;
        return (*this);
    }

    Vector3D& operator /=(float s)
    {
        s = 1.0F / s;
        x *= s;
        y *= s;
        z *= s;
        return (*this);
    }
};

inline Vector3D operator *(const Vector3D& v, float s)
{
    return (Vector3D(v.x * s, v.y * s, v.z * s));
```

```
}

inline Vector3D operator /(const Vector3D& v, float s)
{
    s = 1.0F / s;
    return (Vector3D(v.x * s, v.y * s, v.z * s));
}

inline Vector3D operator -(const Vector3D& v)
{
    return (Vector3D(-v.x, -v.y, -v.z));
}

inline float Magnitude(const Vector3D& v)
{
    return (sqrt(v.x * v.x + v.y * v.y + v.z * v.z));
}

inline Vector3D Normalize(const Vector3D& v)
{
    return (v / Magnitude(v));
}
```

## 1.2.2 Addition and Subtraction

Vectors can be added and subtracted by applying these operations componentwise. That is, for two $n$-dimensional vectors $\mathbf{a}$ and $\mathbf{b}$, we have

$$\mathbf{a} + \mathbf{b} = \left( a_0 + b_0, a_1 + b_1, \ldots, a_{n-1} + b_{n-1} \right) \tag{1.11}$$

and

$$\mathbf{a} - \mathbf{b} = \left( a_0 - b_0, a_1 - b_1, \ldots, a_{n-1} - b_{n-1} \right). \tag{1.12}$$

Vector addition and scalar-vector multiplication exhibit many of the same basic algebraic properties as ordinary numbers due to the componentwise nature of the operations. These properties are summarized in Table 1.1, and their proofs are obvious enough to be omitted here.

The effect of adding two vectors $\mathbf{a}$ and $\mathbf{b}$ can be visualized by drawing the vector $\mathbf{a}$ anywhere and then placing the beginning of the vector $\mathbf{b}$ at the end of the

| Property | Description |
|---|---|
| $(\mathbf{a}+\mathbf{b})+\mathbf{c} = \mathbf{a}+(\mathbf{b}+\mathbf{c})$ | Associative law for vector addition. |
| $\mathbf{a}+\mathbf{b} = \mathbf{b}+\mathbf{a}$ | Commutative law for vector addition. |
| $(st)\mathbf{a} = s(t\mathbf{a})$ | Associative law for scalar-vector multiplication. |
| $t\mathbf{a} = \mathbf{a}t$ | Commutative law for scalar-vector multiplication. |
| $t(\mathbf{a}+\mathbf{b}) = t\mathbf{a}+t\mathbf{b}$ | Distributive laws for scalar-vector multiplication. |
| $(s+t)\mathbf{a} = s\mathbf{a}+t\mathbf{a}$ | |

**Table 1.1.** These are the basic properties of vector addition and scalar-vector multiplication. The letters $\mathbf{a}$, $\mathbf{b}$, and $\mathbf{c}$ represent vectors of the same dimensionality, and the letters $s$ and $t$ represent scalar values.

vector $\mathbf{a}$ where its arrowhead is drawn. The vector $\mathbf{a}+\mathbf{b}$ is then drawn as the arrow beginning where $\mathbf{a}$ begins and ending where $\mathbf{b}$ ends, as illustrated in Figure 1.3(a). Because the addition operation applied to the individual components is commutative, the sum $\mathbf{b}+\mathbf{a}$ produces the same vector as $\mathbf{a}+\mathbf{b}$, and placing the beginning of the vector $\mathbf{a}$ at the end of the vector $\mathbf{b}$ gives the same result, as shown in Figure 1.3(b).

The difference between two vectors $\mathbf{a}$ and $\mathbf{b}$ can be visualized in much the same way as their sum, except that in the case of $\mathbf{a}-\mathbf{b}$, the vector $\mathbf{b}$ is negated before its beginning is placed at the end of the vector $\mathbf{a}$. We simply reverse the direction of the vector being subtracted, as shown in Figure 1.4.

In Listing 1.3, functions that implement vector addition and subtraction are added to the `Vector3D` data structure as overloaded operators.

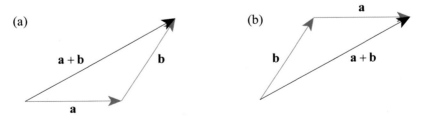

**Figure 1.3.** (a) The sum of two vectors $\mathbf{a}$ and $\mathbf{b}$ is visualized by placing the beginning of $\mathbf{b}$ at the end of $\mathbf{a}$ and drawing a new vector $\mathbf{a}+\mathbf{b}$ that begins where $\mathbf{a}$ begins and ends where $\mathbf{b}$ ends. (b) Reversing the roles of the two vectors produces the same result because vector addition is commutative.

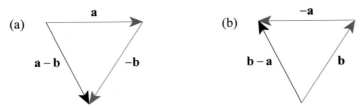

**Figure 1.4.** The difference of two vectors **a** and **b** is visualized by adding the negation of the second vector to the first. (a) The difference **a** − **b** is given by **a** + (−**b**). (b) The difference **b** − **a** is equal to the negation of **a** − **b** and thus points in the opposite direction with the same magnitude.

**Listing 1.3.** This code adds vector addition and subtraction to the `Vector3D` data structure.

```cpp
struct Vector3D
{
    Vector3D& operator +=(const Vector3D& v)
    {
        x += v.x;
        y += v.y;
        z += v.z;
        return (*this);
    }

    Vector3D& operator -=(const Vector3D& v)
    {
        x -= v.x;
        y -= v.y;
        z -= v.z;
        return (*this);
    }
};

inline Vector3D operator +(const Vector3D& a, const Vector3D& b)
{
    return (Vector3D(a.x + b.x, a.y + b.y, a.z + b.z));
}

inline Vector3D operator -(const Vector3D& a, const Vector3D& b)
{
    return (Vector3D(a.x - b.x, a.y - b.y, a.z - b.z));
}
```

## 1.3 Matrix Fundamentals

A *matrix* is a mathematical object composed of a set of numerical quantities arranged in a two-dimensional array of rows and columns. When a matrix has $n$ rows and $m$ columns, we say that its size is $n \times m$, which is read "$n$ by $m$". If it's the case that $n = m$, then we say the matrix is a *square* matrix. The numbers that make up a matrix $\mathbf{M}$ are called its *entries*, and using a $2 \times 3$ matrix as an example, we write them inside brackets as in

$$\mathbf{M} = \begin{bmatrix} 1 & 2 & 3 \\ 4 & 5 & 6 \end{bmatrix}. \tag{1.13}$$

As with vectors, we write the letter representing a matrix in bold, and although not an established convention, we use uppercase letters for matrices and lowercase letters for vectors in this book to make it easier to distinguish between the two. An individual entry of a matrix $\mathbf{M}$ is identified by writing two zero-based subscripts such that the first subscript represents the row index, and the second subscript represents the column index. The symbol $M_{ij}$ means the entry appearing in the $i$-th row and $j$-th column. Sometimes, a comma may be inserted between the indices for clarity. Using this notation, an $n \times m$ matrix $\mathbf{M}$ can be written as

$$\mathbf{M} = \begin{bmatrix} M_{00} & M_{01} & \cdots & M_{0,(m-1)} \\ M_{10} & M_{11} & \cdots & M_{1,(m-1)} \\ \vdots & \vdots & \ddots & \vdots \\ M_{(n-1),0} & M_{(n-1),1} & \cdots & M_{(n-1),(m-1)} \end{bmatrix}. \tag{1.14}$$

The entries $M_{ii}$, where the row index and column index are equal to each other, are called the *diagonal* entries of the matrix $\mathbf{M}$, and they are said to reside on the *main diagonal* of the matrix. The main diagonal starts with the upper-left entry and continues downward and to the right. The entries $M_{ij}$ for which $i \neq j$ are called the *off-diagonal* entries of the matrix $\mathbf{M}$. Any matrix for which all of the off-diagonal entries are zero is called a *diagonal matrix*. For example, the matrix

$$\begin{bmatrix} 3 & 0 & 0 \\ 0 & 8 & 0 \\ 0 & 0 & 4 \end{bmatrix} \tag{1.15}$$

is a diagonal matrix because the only nonzero entries appear on the main diagonal. Note that some or all of the entries on the main diagonal itself could be zero, and the matrix would still be considered to be a diagonal matrix.

The *transpose* of a matrix $\mathbf{M}$ is the matrix denoted by $\mathbf{M}^{\mathrm{T}}$ whose rows are equal to the columns of $\mathbf{M}$, or equivalently, whose columns are equal to the rows of $\mathbf{M}$. If the matrix $\mathbf{M}$ has size $n \times m$, then the matrix $\mathbf{M}^{\mathrm{T}}$ has size $m \times n$, and its entries are given by $M_{ij}^{\mathrm{T}} = M_{ji}$. The transpose of a matrix can be thought of as the reflection of its entries across the main diagonal. As an example, the transpose of the matrix $\mathbf{M}$ shown in Equation (1.13) is given by

$$\mathbf{M}^{\mathrm{T}} = \begin{bmatrix} 1 & 4 \\ 2 & 5 \\ 3 & 6 \end{bmatrix}. \tag{1.16}$$

If a matrix $\mathbf{M}$ is equal to its transpose $\mathbf{M}^{\mathrm{T}}$, meaning that it's always the case that $M_{ij} = M_{ji}$, then it is called a *symmetric matrix* because all of the entries above and right of the main diagonal are the same as the entries below and left of the main diagonal, with the row and column indices reversed, as in the example

$$\begin{bmatrix} 1 & 5 & -3 \\ 5 & 4 & 2 \\ -3 & 2 & 0 \end{bmatrix}. \tag{1.17}$$

A matrix must be square in order to be symmetric, and every diagonal matrix is automatically symmetric.

If the entries of a transpose $\mathbf{M}^{\mathrm{T}}$ are equal to the negations of the same entries in the matrix $\mathbf{M}$, meaning that it's always the case that $M_{ij}^{\mathrm{T}} = -M_{ij}$, then the matrix $\mathbf{M}$ is called an *antisymmetric matrix* or a *skew-symmetric matrix*. Note that for this to be the case, all of the entries on the main diagonal must be zero as in the example

$$\begin{bmatrix} 0 & 1 & -4 \\ -1 & 0 & 7 \\ 4 & -7 & 0 \end{bmatrix}. \tag{1.18}$$

A special type of antisymmetric matrix is mentioned in the discussion of the cross product later in this chapter.

An $n$-dimensional vector can be regarded as an $n \times 1$ matrix or as a $1 \times n$ matrix, and as such, is called a *column vector* or a *row vector*, respectively. While many textbooks make no meaningful distinction between these two types of matrices and casually use the transpose operation to convert from one to the other, there is an important difference between the two that is addressed later in this book. For now, we need only to choose either column vectors or row vectors as our convention and stick to it. The mathematics works the same way no matter which one we select, and both conventions appear in various technologies used in 3D rendering, but the tradition in the more mathematically-oriented literature has been to write a vector as a matrix having a single column. We follow the same rule in this book so that a vector $\mathbf{v}$ is written as

$$\mathbf{v} = (v_0, v_1, \ldots, v_{n-1}) = \begin{bmatrix} v_0 \\ v_1 \\ \vdots \\ v_{n-1} \end{bmatrix}. \tag{1.19}$$

A comma-separated list of $n$ components is equivalent to an $n \times 1$ matrix containing the same numbers in the same order. If we apply the transpose operation to $\mathbf{v}$, then we get the row vector

$$\mathbf{v}^{\mathrm{T}} = \begin{bmatrix} v_0 & v_1 & \ldots & v_{n-1} \end{bmatrix}, \tag{1.20}$$

which despite its horizontal layout, is different from the comma-separated list of components. It is sometimes convenient for us to create row vectors at this point by using the transpose operation, but you should be aware that doing so actually changes the meaning of the vector. This will be discussed in Chapter 4, at which point the transpose operations that we currently use become unnecessary.

It is frequently useful to treat a matrix as an array of column vectors or row vectors. For example, suppose that $\mathbf{a}$, $\mathbf{b}$, and $\mathbf{c}$ are 3D column vectors. Then we can construct a $3 \times 3$ matrix $\mathbf{M}$ by making those vectors the columns of the matrix and writing it as

$$\mathbf{M} = \begin{bmatrix} \mathbf{a} & \mathbf{b} & \mathbf{c} \end{bmatrix}. \tag{1.21}$$

When matrices are used to transform from one coordinate system to another in Chapter 2, treating the columns of a matrix as a set of vectors will become particularly meaningful.

The matrices that arise in game engines are very often $3 \times 3$ or $4 \times 4$ in size. Listing 1.4 shows the definition of a structure named `Matrix3D` that holds the entries of a $3 \times 3$ matrix in a two-dimensional array. It has two nontrivial constructors, one that takes floating-point parameters for all nine matrix entries and another that takes 3D vector parameters that become the three columns of the matrix.

We have a choice about the order in which we store matrix entries in memory because we could have consecutive entries grouped along the rows, or we could have them grouped along the columns. This choice is independent of whether we use column vectors or row vectors as our mathematical convention, but there is an advantage to keeping the entries together in such a way that vectors can be referenced inside the matrix without having to copy entries. Since we have already decided to use column vectors, we want to store matrices such that consecutive entries run down each column. This gives us the ability to extract column vectors for free by simply computing the memory address at which each column begins. In this case, the indices of the entries, viewed as a flat one-dimensional array, are given by the illustrative matrix

$$\begin{bmatrix} 0 & 3 & 6 \\ 1 & 4 & 7 \\ 2 & 5 & 8 \end{bmatrix}. \tag{1.22}$$

This arrangement of entries in memory is called *column-major order*, as opposed to the *row-major order* that we would be using had we chosen to group consecutive entries by row.

In order to implement column-major storage order in a two-dimensional array, we need to make the first array index the column number and the second array index the row number. This is the opposite of the mathematical notation that everybody uses, so instead of allowing direct access to the matrix entries, we make those private and provide overloaded parentheses operators that take two indices in the familiar row-column order. As with the Vector3D structure, the operators defined for the Matrix3D structure do not check whether the indices are in the $[0, 2]$ range, so care must be exercised by the calling code to ensure that accesses stay within bounds.

The code in Listing 1.4 also includes overloaded bracket operators that access entire columns of a $3 \times 3$ matrix as 3D vectors. Suppose that m is a Matrix3D object. Then m[0], m[1], and m[2] are references to Vector3D objects occupying the same memory as the first, second, and third columns of the matrix.

**Listing 1.4.** This is the definition of a simple data structure holding the entries of a $3 \times 3$ matrix. The $(i, j)$ entry of a matrix is accessed by using operator (), and the $j$-th column is accessed as a 3D vector by using operator []. Structures for matrices of different size are similar.

```
struct Matrix3D
{
    private:

        float       n[3][3];
```

```
public:

    Matrix3D() = default;

    Matrix3D(float n00, float n01, float n02,
             float n10, float n11, float n12,
             float n20, float n21, float n22)
    {
        n[0][0] = n00; n[0][1] = n10; n[0][2] = n20;
        n[1][0] = n01; n[1][1] = n11; n[1][2] = n21;
        n[2][0] = n02; n[2][1] = n12; n[2][2] = n22;
    }

    Matrix3D(const Vector3D& a, const Vector3D& b, const Vector3D& c)
    {
        n[0][0] = a.x; n[0][1] = a.y; n[0][2] = a.z;
        n[1][0] = b.x; n[1][1] = b.y; n[1][2] = b.z;
        n[2][0] = c.x; n[2][1] = c.y; n[2][2] = c.z;
    }

    float& operator ()(int i, int j)
    {
        return (n[j][i]);
    }

    const float& operator ()(int i, int j) const
    {
        return (n[j][i]);
    }

    Vector3D& operator [](int j)
    {
        return (*reinterpret_cast<Vector3D *>(n[j]));
    }

    const Vector3D& operator [](int j) const
    {
        return (*reinterpret_cast<const Vector3D *>(n[j]));
    }
};
```

# 1.4  Basic Matrix Operations

Like vectors, matrices can be added and subtracted entrywise, and they can be multiplied by scalars. These operations require little explanation, and they are rarely encountered in game engine development, so we spend only a brief moment on those before moving on to the much more important operation of multiplying matrices by other matrices.

## 1.4.1  Addition, Subtraction, and Scalar Multiplication

Two matrices of the same size can be added or subtracted by simply adding or subtracting corresponding entries. That is, for $n \times m$ matrices $\mathbf{A}$ and $\mathbf{B}$, we can write

$$\left( \mathbf{A} + \mathbf{B} \right)_{ij} = A_{ij} + B_{ij} \tag{1.23}$$

and

$$\left( \mathbf{A} - \mathbf{B} \right)_{ij} = A_{ij} - B_{ij}. \tag{1.24}$$

A matrix $\mathbf{M}$ is multiplied by a scalar $t$ by applying the multiplication to every entry of the matrix, which we can write as

$$\left( t\mathbf{M} \right)_{ij} = t M_{ij}. \tag{1.25}$$

The basic properties of matrix addition and scalar-matrix multiplication are summarized in Table 1.2. These are the same properties that are listed for vectors in Table 1.1, which is unsurprising because vectors can be regarded as matrices having a single column.

## 1.4.2  Matrix Multiplication

Matrix multiplication is one of the most frequently used algebraic operations in game engine development. It is primarily applied to the transformation of geometric objects such as directions, points, and planes from one coordinate system to another, which is an important topic discussed at many places throughout the rest of this book. Here, we introduce the purely computational aspects of matrix multiplication and describe some of their fundamental properties.

Two matrices can be multiplied together if and only if the number of columns in the first matrix is equal to the number of rows in the second matrix. The result is a new matrix having the same number of rows as the first matrix and the same

| Property | Description |
|---|---|
| $(\mathbf{A}+\mathbf{B})+\mathbf{C}=\mathbf{A}+(\mathbf{B}+\mathbf{C})$ | Associative law for matrix addition. |
| $\mathbf{A}+\mathbf{B}=\mathbf{B}+\mathbf{A}$ | Commutative law for matrix addition. |
| $(st)\mathbf{A}=s(t\mathbf{A})$ | Associative law for scalar-matrix multiplication. |
| $t\mathbf{A}=\mathbf{A}t$ | Commutative law for scalar-matrix multiplication. |
| $t(\mathbf{A}+\mathbf{B})=t\mathbf{A}+t\mathbf{B}$ | Distributive laws for scalar-matrix multiplication. |
| $(s+t)\mathbf{A}=s\mathbf{A}+t\mathbf{A}$ | |

**Table 1.2.** These are the basic properties of matrix addition and scalar-matrix multiplication. The letters $\mathbf{A}$, $\mathbf{B}$, and $\mathbf{C}$ represent matrices of the same size, and the letters $s$ and $t$ represent scalar values.

number of columns as the second matrix. That is, if $\mathbf{A}$ is an $n\times p$ matrix, and $\mathbf{B}$ is a $p\times m$ matrix, then the product $\mathbf{AB}$ is an $n\times m$ matrix. Note that the order of multiplication cannot generally be reversed. The product $\mathbf{BA}$ does not exist in this example unless $n=m$. Also, matrix multiplication is not generally commutative, so when both products do exist, it's *not* true that $\mathbf{AB}=\mathbf{BA}$ except in special situations.

When an $n\times p$ matrix $\mathbf{A}$ is multiplied by a $p\times m$ matrix $\mathbf{B}$, the $(i,j)$ entry of the matrix product $\mathbf{AB}$ is given by the formula

$$(\mathbf{AB})_{ij}=\sum_{k=0}^{p-1} A_{ik}B_{kj}. \tag{1.26}$$

The calculation of the $(i,j)$ entry of the matrix $\mathbf{AB}$ involves only row $i$ of the matrix $\mathbf{A}$ and only column $j$ of the matrix $\mathbf{B}$, which both contain $p$ entries that are multiplied together and summed. An example of this calculation is illustrated in Figure 1.5, where a $2\times 3$ matrix is multiplied by a $3\times 2$ matrix to produce a $2\times 2$ matrix.

One of the most common matrix products arising in game engine development is a $3\times 3$ matrix $\mathbf{M}$ multiplied by a $3\times 1$ column vector $\mathbf{v}$. The result is a new $3\times 1$ column vector that has possibly been rotated to a new orientation or scaled in some way. The components of the transformed vector are calculated by applying Equation (1.26) three times with $i=0,1,2$. The value of $j$ is always zero because $\mathbf{v}$ has only one column. The full product $\mathbf{Mv}$ can be written as

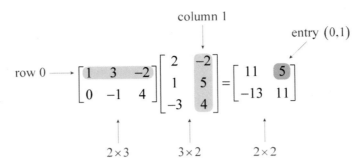

**Figure 1.5.** A $2 \times 3$ matrix is multiplied by a $3 \times 2$ matrix to produce a $2 \times 2$ matrix. The parts highlighted in blue are the entries that participate in the calculation of the $(0,1)$ entry of the product, highlighted in green. The entries in row 0 of the first matrix are multiplied by the corresponding entries in column 1 of the second matrix and summed, yielding the calculation $1 \cdot (-2) + 3 \cdot 5 + (-2) \cdot 4 = 5$.

$$\mathbf{Mv} = \begin{bmatrix} M_{00} & M_{01} & M_{02} \\ M_{10} & M_{11} & M_{12} \\ M_{20} & M_{21} & M_{22} \end{bmatrix} \begin{bmatrix} v_x \\ v_y \\ v_z \end{bmatrix} = \begin{bmatrix} M_{00}v_x + M_{01}v_y + M_{02}v_z \\ M_{10}v_x + M_{11}v_y + M_{12}v_z \\ M_{20}v_x + M_{21}v_y + M_{22}v_z \end{bmatrix}. \quad (1.27)$$

Upon taking a closer look at the right side of Equation (1.27), we see that the matrix-vector product $\mathbf{Mv}$ is a linear combination of the columns of $\mathbf{M}$, and the coefficients are the components of $\mathbf{v}$. If we write $\mathbf{M} = \begin{bmatrix} \mathbf{a} & \mathbf{b} & \mathbf{c} \end{bmatrix}$, then we have

$$\boxed{\mathbf{Mv} = v_x \mathbf{a} + v_y \mathbf{b} + v_z \mathbf{c}.} \quad (1.28)$$

This is particularly illuminating if we consider the unit vectors parallel to the coordinate axes. If $\mathbf{v} = (1, 0, 0)$, then $\mathbf{Mv} = \mathbf{a}$; if $\mathbf{v} = (0, 1, 0)$, then $\mathbf{Mv} = \mathbf{b}$; and if $\mathbf{v} = (0, 0, 1)$, then $\mathbf{Mv} = \mathbf{c}$. The columns of $\mathbf{M}$ tell us exactly how the $x$, $y$, and $z$ axes are reoriented in a new coordinate system established through multiplication by $\mathbf{M}$. This is the key concept within the topic of coordinate transformations, which is covered in Chapter 2.

Functions that implement multiplication of $3 \times 3$ matrices by other $3 \times 3$ matrices and by 3D vectors are shown in Listing 1.5. Both functions are overloaded operators that take a reference to a Matrix3D object as the first parameter and either a Matrix3D object or a Vector3D object as the second parameter. Because it's a practical thing to do for matrices of this size, the code attains maximum speed by explicitly computing every term for each entry of the products without using any loops.

**Listing 1.5.** This code adds matrix-matrix and matrix-vector multiplication to the `Matrix3D` data structure.

```
Matrix3D operator *(const Matrix3D& A, const Matrix3D& B)
{
    return (Matrix3D(A(0,0) * B(0,0) + A(0,1) * B(1,0) + A(0,2) * B(2,0),
                     A(0,0) * B(0,1) + A(0,1) * B(1,1) + A(0,2) * B(2,1),
                     A(0,0) * B(0,2) + A(0,1) * B(1,2) + A(0,2) * B(2,2),
                     A(1,0) * B(0,0) + A(1,1) * B(1,0) + A(1,2) * B(2,0),
                     A(1,0) * B(0,1) + A(1,1) * B(1,1) + A(1,2) * B(2,1),
                     A(1,0) * B(0,2) + A(1,1) * B(1,2) + A(1,2) * B(2,2),
                     A(2,0) * B(0,0) + A(2,1) * B(1,0) + A(2,2) * B(2,0),
                     A(2,0) * B(0,1) + A(2,1) * B(1,1) + A(2,2) * B(2,1),
                     A(2,0) * B(0,2) + A(2,1) * B(1,2) + A(2,2) * B(2,2)));
}


Vector3D operator *(const Matrix3D& M, const Vector3D& v)
{
    return (Vector3D(M(0,0) * v.x + M(0,1) * v.y + M(0,2) * v.z,
                     M(1,0) * v.x + M(1,1) * v.y + M(1,2) * v.z,
                     M(2,0) * v.x + M(2,1) * v.y + M(2,2) * v.z));
}
```

Some of the basic properties of matrix multiplication are listed in Table 1.3. Most of these are easily proven, but the last property stating that $(\mathbf{AB})^T = \mathbf{B}^T \mathbf{A}^T$ is not quite as obvious. Suppose that $\mathbf{A}$ is an $n \times p$ matrix and $\mathbf{B}$ is a $p \times m$ matrix. The $(i, j)$ entry of $(\mathbf{AB})^T$ is the $(j, i)$ entry of $\mathbf{AB}$, and after swapping the indices $i$ and $j$ in Equation (1.26), we can write

$$(\mathbf{AB})^T_{ij} = (\mathbf{AB})_{ji} = \sum_{k=0}^{p-1} A_{jk} B_{ki}. \tag{1.29}$$

The summand on the right side of the equation is just the product between two numbers, so we can reverse the order of the factors. We can also replace each factor by the entry of the corresponding transpose matrix with the indices reversed to get

$$\sum_{k=0}^{p-1} A_{jk} B_{ki} = \sum_{k=0}^{p-1} B^T_{ik} A^T_{kj}. \tag{1.30}$$

The right side of this equation is now precisely the definition of the $(i, j)$ entry of the product $\mathbf{B}^T \mathbf{A}^T$.

| Property | Description |
|---|---|
| $(\mathbf{AB})\mathbf{C} = \mathbf{A}(\mathbf{BC})$ | Associative law for matrix multiplication. |
| $\mathbf{A}(\mathbf{B}+\mathbf{C}) = \mathbf{AB}+\mathbf{AC}$ | Distributive laws for matrix multiplication. |
| $(\mathbf{A}+\mathbf{B})\mathbf{C} = \mathbf{AC}+\mathbf{BC}$ | |
| $(t\mathbf{A})\mathbf{B} = \mathbf{A}(t\mathbf{B}) = t(\mathbf{AB})$ | Scalar factorization for matrices. |
| $(\mathbf{AB})^{\mathrm{T}} = \mathbf{B}^{\mathrm{T}}\mathbf{A}^{\mathrm{T}}$ | Product rule for matrix transpose. |

**Table 1.3.** These are the basic properties of matrix multiplication. The letters $\mathbf{A}$, $\mathbf{B}$, and $\mathbf{C}$ represent matrices, and the letter $t$ represents a scalar value.

## 1.5 Vector Multiplication

There are a number of ways to multiply two vectors together. The most obvious is to apply the multiplication componentwise, and this is what happens in all modern shading languages when the multiplication operator appears in the code. However, this has very little physical significance and is mainly used for multiplying colors together. When vectors are being used to represent quantities with some geometric meaning, the most constructive methods of multiplication are two operations known as the dot product and the cross product. We provide defining formulas for these products here and discuss their properties and applications. In Chapter 4, we will demonstrate that these formulas can actually be derived from a more fundamental principle.

### 1.5.1 Dot Product

The *dot product* between two $n$-dimensional vectors $\mathbf{a}$ and $\mathbf{b}$ is a scalar quantity given by the formula

$$\mathbf{a} \cdot \mathbf{b} = \sum_{i=0}^{n-1} a_i b_i. \tag{1.31}$$

The corresponding components of the two vectors are multiplied together and summed. This product gets its name from the notation $\mathbf{a} \cdot \mathbf{b}$ in which a dot is placed between the two vectors participating in the product. Because it produces a scalar quantity, the dot product is also known as the *scalar product*.

In three dimensions, the dot product can be written as

$$\mathbf{a} \cdot \mathbf{b} = a_x b_x + a_y b_y + a_z b_z, \tag{1.32}$$

and this is the most common form in which the dot product is calculated. The implementation of the `Dot()` function in Listing 1.6 uses this formula to compute the dot product between two `Vector3D` data structures.

If the vectors $\mathbf{a}$ and $\mathbf{b}$ are regarded as column matrices, then the dot product can also be expressed as

$$\mathbf{a} \cdot \mathbf{b} = \mathbf{a}^{\mathrm{T}} \mathbf{b} = \begin{bmatrix} a_0 & a_1 & \cdots & a_{n-1} \end{bmatrix} \begin{bmatrix} b_0 \\ b_1 \\ \vdots \\ b_{n-1} \end{bmatrix}, \tag{1.33}$$

which produces a $1 \times 1$ matrix having a single entry whose value is given by the sum in Equation (1.31). There is significance to the fact that this is the product of a row vector and a column vector, and this is a topic that will be discussed in Chapter 4.

Comparing the definition of the dot product with the formula for vector magnitude given by Equation (1.5), we see that the dot product of a vector with itself produces the squared magnitude of that vector. We use the special notation $v^2$ in place of the dot product $\mathbf{v} \cdot \mathbf{v}$ or the squared magnitude $\|\mathbf{v}\|^2$ for its conciseness. All three expressions have the same meaning. When squared, it is a common convention to write the letter representing a vector in italic because the result of the dot product of a vector with itself is a scalar quantity.

A few basic properties of the dot product are listed in Table 1.4, and each one is easily verified. Of particular importance is that the dot product is commutative, meaning that the order of the factors doesn't matter. This is different from the cross product, discussed next, which changes sign when its factors are reversed.

Although not at all obvious from its definition, the dot product between two vectors $\mathbf{a}$ and $\mathbf{b}$ satisfies the equality

**Listing 1.6.** This code implements the dot product between two `Vector3D` data structures.

```
inline float Dot(const Vector3D& a, const Vector3D& b)
{
    return (a.x * b.x + a.y * b.y + a.z * b.z);
}
```

| Property | Description |
|---|---|
| $\mathbf{a} \cdot \mathbf{b} = \mathbf{b} \cdot \mathbf{a}$ | Commutative law for the dot product. |
| $\mathbf{a} \cdot (\mathbf{b} + \mathbf{c}) = \mathbf{a} \cdot \mathbf{b} + \mathbf{a} \cdot \mathbf{c}$ | Distributive law for the dot product. |
| $(t\mathbf{a}) \cdot \mathbf{b} = \mathbf{a} \cdot (t\mathbf{b}) = t(\mathbf{a} \cdot \mathbf{b})$ | Scalar factorization for the dot product. |

**Table 1.4.** These are the basic properties of the dot product. The letters $\mathbf{a}$, $\mathbf{b}$, and $\mathbf{c}$ represent vectors of the same dimensionality, and the letter $t$ represents a scalar value.

$$\mathbf{a} \cdot \mathbf{b} = \|\mathbf{a}\| \|\mathbf{b}\| \cos \theta, \tag{1.34}$$

where $\theta$ is the planar angle between the directions of $\mathbf{a}$ and $\mathbf{b}$ if they were to be drawn as arrows starting at the same location. This equality represents the main application of the dot product, and it provides a computationally cheap way to determine how much two vectors are parallel to each other or perpendicular to each other. If $\mathbf{a}$ and $\mathbf{b}$ are both unit vectors (i.e., they both have a magnitude of one), then $\mathbf{a} \cdot \mathbf{b}$ is always in the range $[-1, 1]$ because in this case $\mathbf{a} \cdot \mathbf{b} = \cos \theta$, and the range of the cosine function is $[-1, 1]$.

Assuming the magnitudes of $\mathbf{a}$ and $\mathbf{b}$ remain the same, the dot product $\mathbf{a} \cdot \mathbf{b}$ attains its largest positive value when $\mathbf{a}$ and $\mathbf{b}$ are parallel and point in the same direction. When $\mathbf{a}$ and $\mathbf{b}$ are parallel and point in opposite directions, $\mathbf{a} \cdot \mathbf{b}$ attains its largest negative value. If $\mathbf{a}$ and $\mathbf{b}$ are perpendicular, then $\mathbf{a} \cdot \mathbf{b}$ is zero no matter what the magnitudes of $\mathbf{a}$ and $\mathbf{b}$ are. In general, the dot product is positive when the angle between the vectors is less than 90 degrees and negative when the angle is greater than 90 degrees, as illustrated in Figure 1.6. Loosely speaking, the dot product provides a measure of how much one vector is like another.

When $\mathbf{a} \cdot \mathbf{b} = 0$, the vectors $\mathbf{a}$ and $\mathbf{b}$ are said to be *orthogonal*, and this term is used even if one of the vectors being multiplied together is the zero vector. Orthogonality is a concept that includes the geometric state of two vectors being perpendicular to each other, but it also has a more abstract meaning in different settings that are not explored in this book.

The trigonometric relationship stated by Equation (1.34) can be understood by considering a triangle having two sides formed by drawing vectors $\mathbf{a}$ and $\mathbf{b}$ from the same starting location, as shown in Figure 1.7. The third side of the triangle is then given by the vector $\mathbf{a} - \mathbf{b}$, drawn between the ending locations of $\mathbf{a}$ and $\mathbf{b}$. For the angle $\theta$ between $\mathbf{a}$ and $\mathbf{b}$, the law of cosines states that

$$(\mathbf{a} - \mathbf{b})^2 = a^2 + b^2 - 2\|\mathbf{a}\| \|\mathbf{b}\| \cos \theta. \tag{1.35}$$

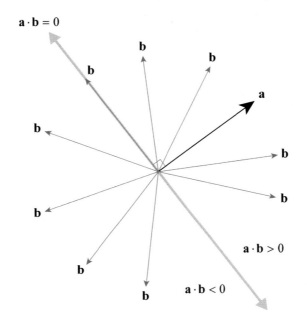

**Figure 1.6.** The dot product **a** · **b** is positive when the angle between vectors **a** and **b** is less than 90 degrees, and it is negative when the angle is greater than 90 degrees. The dot product is zero when **a** and **b** are perpendicular.

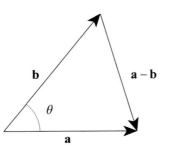

**Figure 1.7.** The equality **a** · **b** = ‖**a**‖‖**b**‖ cos θ follows from the law of cosines applied to the triangle having sides **a** and **b**.

The squared magnitude on the left side of the equation is equivalent to the dot product $(\mathbf{a} - \mathbf{b}) \cdot (\mathbf{a} - \mathbf{b})$, which can be expanded as

$$(\mathbf{a} - \mathbf{b}) \cdot (\mathbf{a} - \mathbf{b}) = a^2 - \mathbf{a} \cdot \mathbf{b} - \mathbf{b} \cdot \mathbf{a} + b^2. \tag{1.36}$$

The $a^2$ and $b^2$ terms cancel the same terms on the right side of Equation (1.35), and due to commutativity, the two dot products are equal. We can thus write

$$-2(\mathbf{a} \cdot \mathbf{b}) = -2 \|\mathbf{a}\| \|\mathbf{b}\| \cos \theta, \tag{1.37}$$

from which Equation (1.34) follows immediately.

## 1.5.2 Cross Product

The *cross product* between two 3D vectors $\mathbf{a}$ and $\mathbf{b}$ is another 3D vector given by the formula

$$\mathbf{a} \times \mathbf{b} = \left( a_y b_z - a_z b_y, a_z b_x - a_x b_z, a_x b_y - a_y b_x \right). \tag{1.38}$$

Each component of the result involves products of the *other two* components of the vectors being multiplied together. For example, the $z$ component of the cross product is calculated using the $x$ and $y$ components of the input vectors. A way to remember the formula for the cross product is to realize that the subscripts for $\mathbf{a}$ and $\mathbf{b}$ used in the positive term of each component of the product are the next two letters in the sequence $x \to y \to z$, *with wraparound*, and the subscripts are simply reversed for the negative term. The next two letters for the $x$ component are $y$ and $z$, the next two letters for the $y$ component are $z$ and $x$ (because $x$ follows $z$ after wrapping), and the next two letters for the $z$ component are $x$ and $y$.

As with the dot product, the cross product gets its name from the notation $\mathbf{a} \times \mathbf{b}$ in which a cross is placed between the two vectors participating in the product. Because it produces a vector quantity, the cross product is also known as the *vector product*. The implementation of the `Cross()` function in Listing 1.7 uses Equation (1.38) to compute the cross product between two `Vector3D` data structures.

The cross product $\mathbf{a} \times \mathbf{b}$ can also be expressed as a matrix product by forming a special $3 \times 3$ antisymmetric matrix denoted by $[\mathbf{a}]_\times$ and multiplying it by the column vector $\mathbf{b}$. The matrix $[\mathbf{a}]_\times$ is defined as

$$[\mathbf{a}]_\times = \begin{bmatrix} 0 & -a_z & a_y \\ a_z & 0 & -a_x \\ -a_y & a_x & 0 \end{bmatrix}, \tag{1.39}$$

**Listing 1.7.** This code implements the cross product between two `Vector3D` data structures.

```
inline Vector3D Cross(const Vector3D& a, const Vector3D& b)
{
    return (Vector3D(a.y * b.z - a.z * b.y,
                     a.z * b.x - a.x * b.z,
                     a.x * b.y - a.y * b.x));
}
```

and when multiplied by **b**, it gives us

$$\mathbf{a} \times \mathbf{b} = [\mathbf{a}]_\times \mathbf{b} = \begin{bmatrix} 0 & -a_z & a_y \\ a_z & 0 & -a_x \\ -a_y & a_x & 0 \end{bmatrix} \begin{bmatrix} b_x \\ b_y \\ b_z \end{bmatrix} = \begin{bmatrix} -a_z b_y + a_y b_z \\ a_z b_x - a_x b_z \\ -a_y b_x + a_x b_y \end{bmatrix}. \quad (1.40)$$

The matrix formulation can sometimes make the proofs of vector identities easier, and this is demonstrated for a common identity later in this section.

It's important to emphasize that the cross product is defined only for three dimensions, whereas the dot product is defined for all numbers of dimensions. This limitation is a consequence of the fact that the cross product is actually a subtle misinterpretation of a more general and more algebraically sound operation called the *wedge product*, which will be a central concept in Chapter 4. However, use of the cross product is well established throughout science and engineering, and its properties are well understood, so we provide a conventional introduction to it here under the notice that a more elegant presentation of the underlying nature of the mathematics appears later in this book.

If two vectors **a** and **b** are parallel, either because they point in the same direction or they point in opposite directions, then the cross product **a** × **b** is zero no matter what the magnitudes of **a** and **b** are. Because they are parallel, one of the vectors can be written as a scalar multiple of the other, so we can say that **b** = $t$**a** for some scalar $t$. The fact that the cross product is zero then becomes obvious when **b** is replaced by $t$**a** in the definition to get

$$\mathbf{a} \times (t\mathbf{a}) = (a_y t a_z - a_z t a_y, a_z t a_x - a_x t a_z, a_x t a_y - a_y t a_x) = (0, 0, 0). \quad (1.41)$$

When two vectors **a** and **b** are not parallel, the cross product **a** × **b** is a new vector that is perpendicular to both **a** and **b**. This is evident if we calculate the dot products **a** · (**a** × **b**) and **b** · (**a** × **b**) because both of them are always zero, as exemplified by

$$\mathbf{a} \cdot (\mathbf{a} \times \mathbf{b}) = a_x a_y b_z - a_x a_z b_y + a_y a_z b_x - a_y a_x b_z + a_z a_x b_y - a_z a_y b_x, \quad (1.42)$$

in which each pair of like-colored terms cancels. The vectors $\mathbf{a}$ and $\mathbf{b}$, not being parallel, establish a plane to which the cross product $\mathbf{a} \times \mathbf{b}$ is perpendicular, and we have two choices as to what direction the vector $\mathbf{a} \times \mathbf{b}$ actually points. If we are looking at the plane from a position not lying in the plane itself, then $\mathbf{a} \times \mathbf{b}$ could point toward us, or it could point away from us. The correct direction is determined by the *handedness* of the coordinate system.

As shown in Figure 1.8, there are two possible configurations for the three coordinate axes, and they are called *left-handed* and *right-handed* because the positive $z$ axis points in the direction of the left or right thumb when the fingers of the same hand curl around the $z$ axis in the direction from the positive $x$ axis to the positive $y$ axis. The same rule is applied to the cross product $\mathbf{a} \times \mathbf{b}$ with the vectors $\mathbf{a}$ and $\mathbf{b}$ assuming the roles of the $x$ and $y$ axes and the vector $\mathbf{a} \times \mathbf{b}$ assuming the role of the $z$ axis. Because $\mathbf{a}$ and $\mathbf{b}$ are not required to be perpendicular, we need to stipulate that the fingers curl from $\mathbf{a}$ to $\mathbf{b}$ in the direction of the smallest angle between them. The universal convention in scientific fields is that the underlying coordinate system is always right-handed, and thus the rule for determining the direction in which $\mathbf{a} \times \mathbf{b}$ points is called the *right-hand rule*. When the fingers of the right hand are held such that they curl in the direction of the smallest angle beginning with $\mathbf{a}$ and ending with $\mathbf{b}$, then the right thumb points in the direction of $\mathbf{a} \times \mathbf{b}$. This is illustrated in Figure 1.9, where it also becomes apparent that reversing the order of the vectors causes the cross product to point in the opposite direction.

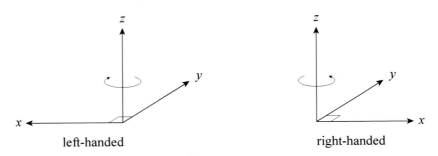

left-handed                                         right-handed

**Figure 1.8.** In a left-handed or right-handed coordinate system, the left or right thumb points in the direction of the positive $z$ axis when the fingers of the same hand curl around the $z$ axis in the direction from the positive $x$ axis to the positive $y$ axis.

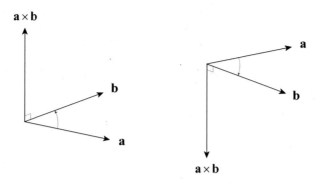

**Figure 1.9.** In a right-handed coordinate system, the cross product follows the right-hand rule. When the fingers of the right hand curl in the direction of the smallest angle from the vector **a** to the vector **b**, the right thumb points in the direction of **a** × **b**.

The magnitude of the cross product between two vectors **a** and **b** satisfies the equality

$$\|\mathbf{a} \times \mathbf{b}\| = \|\mathbf{a}\| \|\mathbf{b}\| \sin \theta, \tag{1.43}$$

where $\theta$ is the planar angle between the directions of **a** and **b** if they were to be drawn as arrows starting at the same location. This can be proven by first squaring the cross product to obtain

$$\begin{aligned}
(\mathbf{a} \times \mathbf{b})^2 &= (a_y b_z - a_z b_y)^2 + (a_z b_x - a_x b_z)^2 + (a_x b_y - a_y b_x)^2 \\
&= a_y^2 b_z^2 + a_z^2 b_y^2 + a_z^2 b_x^2 + a_x^2 b_z^2 + a_x^2 b_y^2 + a_y^2 b_x^2 \\
&\quad - 2(a_y a_z b_y b_z + a_z a_x b_z b_x + a_x a_y b_x b_y).
\end{aligned} \tag{1.44}$$

All of this factors nicely if we add $a_x^2 b_x^2 + a_y^2 b_y^2 + a_z^2 b_z^2$ at the beginning and subtract it back at the end. We can then write

$$\begin{aligned}
(\mathbf{a} \times \mathbf{b})^2 &= (a_x^2 + a_y^2 + a_z^2)(b_x^2 + b_y^2 + b_z^2) - (a_x b_x + a_y b_y + a_z b_z)^2 \\
&= a^2 b^2 - (\mathbf{a} \cdot \mathbf{b})^2.
\end{aligned} \tag{1.45}$$

(This equation is known as *Lagrange's identity*.) By substituting $a^2 b^2 \cos^2 \theta$ for the squared dot product, we have

$$(\mathbf{a} \times \mathbf{b})^2 = a^2 b^2 (1 - \cos^2 \theta) = a^2 b^2 \sin^2 \theta, \tag{1.46}$$

and taking square roots finishes the proof.

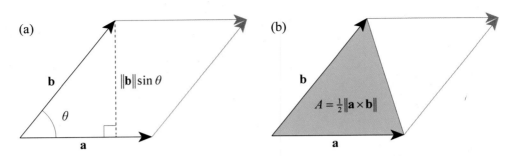

**Figure 1.10.** (a) The equality $\|\mathbf{a} \times \mathbf{b}\| = \|\mathbf{a}\|\|\mathbf{b}\|\sin\theta$ shows that magnitude of the cross product $\mathbf{a} \times \mathbf{b}$ is equal to the area of the parallelogram having sides $\mathbf{a}$ and $\mathbf{b}$. (b) The area $A$ of a triangle having sides $\mathbf{a}$ and $\mathbf{b}$ is half the area of the parallelogram and is thus half of the magnitude of the cross product $\mathbf{a} \times \mathbf{b}$.

As shown in Figure 1.10(a), the trigonometric relationship stated by Equation (1.43) means that the cross product $\mathbf{a} \times \mathbf{b}$ has a magnitude equal to the area of the parallelogram having sides $\mathbf{a}$ and $\mathbf{b}$. The length of the base of the parallelogram is $\|\mathbf{a}\|$, and the height of the parallelogram is $\|\mathbf{b}\|\sin\theta$. If we split the parallelogram in half by making a cut along the line connecting the ends of $\mathbf{a}$ and $\mathbf{b}$ as shown in Figure 1.10(b), then we create two congruent triangles that both have half the area of the parallelogram. Thus, the area of a triangle having sides $\mathbf{a}$ and $\mathbf{b}$ is given by half of the magnitude of the cross product $\mathbf{a} \times \mathbf{b}$. More generally, the area $A$ of a triangle having vertices at the points $\mathbf{p}_0$, $\mathbf{p}_1$, and $\mathbf{p}_2$ is given by

$$A = \tfrac{1}{2}\left\|\left(\mathbf{p}_1 - \mathbf{p}_0\right) \times \left(\mathbf{p}_2 - \mathbf{p}_0\right)\right\|. \tag{1.47}$$

Several properties of the cross product are listed in Table 1.5. The first one states that $\mathbf{a} \times \mathbf{b} = -\mathbf{b} \times \mathbf{a}$, and this is called the *anticommutative* property of the cross product. When the order of the vectors multiplied together in the cross product is reversed, the result is a vector that is negated. This effect can be seen by reversing the roles of $\mathbf{a}$ and $\mathbf{b}$ in the definition of the cross product given by Equation (1.38). We also mentioned this property earlier in the discussion of the right-hand rule. If the order of the vectors is reversed, then the right hand would have to be turned upside down for the fingers to curl in the proper direction matching the order of the input vectors, so the resulting cross product points in the opposite direction.

Table 1.5 includes a property that involves the multiplication of three vectors using the cross product, and it is called the *vector triple product*. This property is an identity that lets us rewrite the cross products of three vectors $\mathbf{a}$, $\mathbf{b}$, and $\mathbf{c}$ as

| Property | Description |
|---|---|
| $\mathbf{a} \times \mathbf{b} = -\mathbf{b} \times \mathbf{a}$ | Anticommutativity of the cross product. |
| $\mathbf{a} \times (\mathbf{b} + \mathbf{c}) = \mathbf{a} \times \mathbf{b} + \mathbf{a} \times \mathbf{c}$ | Distributive law for the cross product. |
| $(t\mathbf{a}) \times \mathbf{b} = \mathbf{a} \times (t\mathbf{b}) = t(\mathbf{a} \times \mathbf{b})$ | Scalar factorization for the cross product. |
| $\mathbf{a} \times (\mathbf{b} \times \mathbf{c}) = \mathbf{b}(\mathbf{a} \cdot \mathbf{c}) - \mathbf{c}(\mathbf{a} \cdot \mathbf{b})$ | Vector triple product. |
| $(\mathbf{a} \times \mathbf{b})^2 = a^2 b^2 - (\mathbf{a} \cdot \mathbf{b})^2$ | Lagrange's identity. |

**Table 1.5.** These are the basic properties of the cross product. The letters **a**, **b**, and **c** represent 3D vectors, and the letter $t$ represents a scalar value.

$$\mathbf{a} \times (\mathbf{b} \times \mathbf{c}) = \mathbf{b}(\mathbf{a} \cdot \mathbf{c}) - \mathbf{c}(\mathbf{a} \cdot \mathbf{b}). \tag{1.48}$$

The mnemonic "bac minus cab" is often used to remember the way in which the cross products are transformed into a difference of the input vectors **b** and **c** multiplied by the dot products of the other two input vectors. If we move the parentheses in Equation (1.48) so that the cross product $\mathbf{a} \times \mathbf{b}$ is calculated first, then we have

$$(\mathbf{a} \times \mathbf{b}) \times \mathbf{c} = -\mathbf{c} \times (\mathbf{a} \times \mathbf{b}) = \mathbf{c} \times (\mathbf{b} \times \mathbf{a}) \tag{1.49}$$

after a couple applications of the anticommutative property. Thus, changing the order of the cross products in the vector triple product has the same effect as exchanging the vectors **a** and **c** in Equation (1.48), from which we can conclude

$$(\mathbf{a} \times \mathbf{b}) \times \mathbf{c} = \mathbf{b}(\mathbf{a} \cdot \mathbf{c}) - \mathbf{a}(\mathbf{c} \cdot \mathbf{b}). \tag{1.50}$$

This highlights the fact that the cross product is not generally an associative operation. The exception is the case in which $\mathbf{a} = \mathbf{c}$, where it is true that

$$\mathbf{a} \times (\mathbf{b} \times \mathbf{a}) = (\mathbf{a} \times \mathbf{b}) \times \mathbf{a}. \tag{1.51}$$

The nonassociativity of the cross product raises an alarm that something isn't quite right, and this is an issue that will be cleared up in Chapter 4.

One possible proof of the vector triple product identity makes use of the antisymmetric matrix introduced by Equation (1.39). If we replace the cross products in Equation (1.48) with the equivalent matrix products, then we have

$$\mathbf{a} \times (\mathbf{b} \times \mathbf{c}) = [\mathbf{a}]_{\times}([\mathbf{b}]_{\times}\mathbf{c}) = ([\mathbf{a}]_{\times}[\mathbf{b}]_{\times})\mathbf{c}, \tag{1.52}$$

where the associativity of matrix multiplication allows us to move the parentheses. After multiplying the two antisymmetric matrices together, we can write the vector triple product as

$$[\mathbf{a}]_\times [\mathbf{b}]_\times \mathbf{c} = \begin{bmatrix} -a_y b_y - a_z b_z & a_y b_x & a_z b_x \\ a_x b_y & -a_x b_x - a_z b_z & a_z b_y \\ a_x b_z & a_y b_z & -a_x b_x - a_y b_y \end{bmatrix} \begin{bmatrix} c_x \\ c_y \\ c_z \end{bmatrix}. \quad (1.53)$$

The $3 \times 3$ matrix in this equation almost looks like the matrix product $\mathbf{ba}^{\mathrm{T}}$, if only the diagonal entries had the form $a_k b_k$. Fortunately, we can add and subtract a term of this form to each of the diagonal entries to get

$$[\mathbf{a}]_\times [\mathbf{b}]_\times \mathbf{c} = \left( \begin{bmatrix} a_x b_x & a_y b_x & a_z b_x \\ a_x b_y & a_y b_y & a_z b_y \\ a_x b_z & a_y b_z & a_z b_z \end{bmatrix} - \begin{bmatrix} \mathbf{a} \cdot \mathbf{b} & 0 & 0 \\ 0 & \mathbf{a} \cdot \mathbf{b} & 0 \\ 0 & 0 & \mathbf{a} \cdot \mathbf{b} \end{bmatrix} \right) \begin{bmatrix} c_x \\ c_y \\ c_z \end{bmatrix}, \quad (1.54)$$

and now we can simplify and reassociate the matrix products to arrive at

$$[\mathbf{a}]_\times [\mathbf{b}]_\times \mathbf{c} = \mathbf{ba}^{\mathrm{T}} \mathbf{c} - (\mathbf{a} \cdot \mathbf{b}) \mathbf{c}$$
$$= \mathbf{b}(\mathbf{a} \cdot \mathbf{c}) - \mathbf{c}(\mathbf{a} \cdot \mathbf{b}). \quad (1.55)$$

## 1.5.3 Scalar Triple Product

The *scalar triple product* of three vectors $\mathbf{a}$, $\mathbf{b}$, and $\mathbf{c}$ is the scalar quantity produced by multiplying two of the vectors together using the cross product and then multiplying by the third vector using the dot product, as in $(\mathbf{a} \times \mathbf{b}) \cdot \mathbf{c}$. It turns out that it doesn't matter where the cross product goes and where the dot product goes, and the scalar triple product gives the same result as long as the vectors are multiplied together in the same order with wraparound. As such, the special notation $[\mathbf{a}, \mathbf{b}, \mathbf{c}]$, without any specific multiplication symbols, is often used to represent the scalar triple product, and we can write

$$\boxed{[\mathbf{a}, \mathbf{b}, \mathbf{c}] = (\mathbf{a} \times \mathbf{b}) \cdot \mathbf{c} = (\mathbf{b} \times \mathbf{c}) \cdot \mathbf{a} = (\mathbf{c} \times \mathbf{a}) \cdot \mathbf{b}.} \quad (1.56)$$

If the order of the input vectors is reversed, then the scalar triple product is negated to give us

$$[\mathbf{c}, \mathbf{b}, \mathbf{a}] = (\mathbf{c} \times \mathbf{b}) \cdot \mathbf{a} = (\mathbf{b} \times \mathbf{a}) \cdot \mathbf{c} = (\mathbf{a} \times \mathbf{c}) \cdot \mathbf{b} = -[\mathbf{a}, \mathbf{b}, \mathbf{c}]. \quad (1.57)$$

This accounts for all six possible permutations of the vectors $\mathbf{a}$, $\mathbf{b}$, and $\mathbf{c}$.

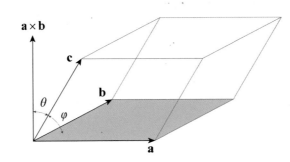

**Figure 1.11.** The scalar triple product $(\mathbf{a} \times \mathbf{b}) \cdot \mathbf{c}$ yields the volume of the parallelepiped spanned by the vectors $\mathbf{a}$, $\mathbf{b}$, and $\mathbf{c}$. The area of the base is given by $\|\mathbf{a} \times \mathbf{b}\|$, and the height is given by $\|\mathbf{c}\| \sin \varphi$. Because $\varphi$ and $\theta$ are complementary angles, the height is also given by $\|\mathbf{c}\| \cos \theta$, so the dot product $(\mathbf{a} \times \mathbf{b}) \cdot \mathbf{c}$ is equal to the area of the base multiplied by the height.

Suppose that the vectors $\mathbf{a}$, $\mathbf{b}$, and $\mathbf{c}$ form the edges of a parallelepiped as shown in Figure 1.11. We already know that the cross product $\mathbf{a} \times \mathbf{b}$ has a magnitude equal to the area of the parallelogram spanned by $\mathbf{a}$ and $\mathbf{b}$ that forms the base of the parallelepiped. The height is given by $\|\mathbf{c}\| \sin \varphi$, where $\varphi$ is the angle between the vector $\mathbf{c}$ and the plane containing the base. Because the angle $\theta$ between the vectors $\mathbf{a} \times \mathbf{b}$ and $\mathbf{c}$ is complementary to $\varphi$, we know that $\sin \varphi = \cos \theta$. The cosine function suggests that we take the dot product between $\mathbf{a} \times \mathbf{b}$ and $\mathbf{c}$ to get

$$(\mathbf{a} \times \mathbf{b}) \cdot \mathbf{c} = \|\mathbf{a} \times \mathbf{b}\| \|\mathbf{c}\| \cos \theta = \|\mathbf{a} \times \mathbf{b}\| \|\mathbf{c}\| \sin \varphi, \qquad (1.58)$$

and we now have, on the right side of the equation, the area of the base multiplied by the height. We conclude that the scalar triple product $(\mathbf{a} \times \mathbf{b}) \cdot \mathbf{c}$ yields a value equal to the volume of the parallelepiped spanned by the vectors $\mathbf{a}$, $\mathbf{b}$, and $\mathbf{c}$. Changing the order of the vectors simply causes the volume to be calculated from a different perspective with a possible change in sign due to the orientation of the vectors participating in the cross product.

## 1.6 Vector Projection

We learned early in this chapter that vectors can be added together to form new vectors, but situations arise in which we need to perform the opposite task. Given a particular vector, we might want to find two or more other vectors with specific alignments that add up to our original vector. This is a process called *decomposing* a vector into its separate components.

The most straightforward decomposition involves breaking a vector into pieces that are aligned to the coordinate axes. The letters **i**, **j**, and **k** are commonly used to represent unit vectors aligned to the positive $x$, $y$, and $z$ axes, and they are thus defined as

$$\mathbf{i} = (1, 0, 0)$$
$$\mathbf{j} = (0, 1, 0)$$
$$\mathbf{k} = (0, 0, 1). \tag{1.59}$$

If we wanted to decompose a 3D vector **v** into components parallel to the coordinate axes, then we could write

$$\mathbf{v} = v_x \mathbf{i} + v_y \mathbf{j} + v_z \mathbf{k} \tag{1.60}$$

by simply picking out each component of **v** and multiplying it by the unit vector for the corresponding axis. We would like to develop something more general than this, however, so we need to find a way to write the same thing without referring to the actual $x$, $y$, and $z$ coordinates of **v**. The way to accomplish this is to realize that each coordinate is equal to the magnitude of **v** multiplied by the cosine of the angle that **v** makes with the corresponding axis. This means that $v_x = \mathbf{v} \cdot \mathbf{i}$, $v_y = \mathbf{v} \cdot \mathbf{j}$, and $v_z = \mathbf{v} \cdot \mathbf{k}$, so we can rewrite Equation (1.60) as

$$\mathbf{v} = (\mathbf{v} \cdot \mathbf{i}) \mathbf{i} + (\mathbf{v} \cdot \mathbf{j}) \mathbf{j} + (\mathbf{v} \cdot \mathbf{k}) \mathbf{k}. \tag{1.61}$$

This is illustrated in two dimensions in Figure 1.12. Each component of Equation (1.61) is called the *projection* of **v** onto one of the vectors **i**, **j**, and **k** parallel to the coordinate axes.

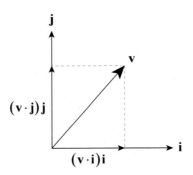

**Figure 1.12.** The vector **v** is projected onto vectors **i** and **j** parallel to the $x$ and $y$ axes. The component of **v** parallel to **i** is given by $(\mathbf{v} \cdot \mathbf{i}) \mathbf{i}$, and the component of **v** parallel to **j** is given by $(\mathbf{v} \cdot \mathbf{j}) \mathbf{j}$.

In general, we can use the dot product to project any vector **a** onto any other nonzero vector **b** using the formula

$$\mathbf{a}_{\parallel\mathbf{b}} = \frac{\mathbf{a}\cdot\mathbf{b}}{b^2}\mathbf{b}. \qquad (1.62)$$

The notation $\mathbf{a}_{\parallel\mathbf{b}}$ indicates the component of the vector **a** that is parallel to the vector **b**, and Equation (1.62) gives us the *projection* of **a** onto **b**. (The alternative notation $\text{proj}_\mathbf{b}\,\mathbf{a}$ is sometimes used in other texts for the projection of **a** onto **b**, and it has the same meaning as $\mathbf{a}_{\parallel\mathbf{b}}$.) Here, the word "component" means part of the decomposition of the vector **a** without referring to any particular coordinate. The division by $b^2$ accounts for the possibility that **b** is not a unit vector. We divide by the magnitude of **b** once for the dot product and again so that the projection points in the direction of the unit vector $\mathbf{b}/\|\mathbf{b}\|$. Note that if the dot product $\mathbf{a}\cdot\mathbf{b}$ is negative, then $\mathbf{a}_{\parallel\mathbf{b}}$ is still parallel to **b** but points in the opposite direction.

The projection of **a** onto **b** can be expressed as the matrix product

$$\mathbf{a}_{\parallel\mathbf{b}} = \frac{1}{b^2}\mathbf{b}\mathbf{b}^{\text{T}}\mathbf{a}. \qquad (1.63)$$

The product $\mathbf{b}\mathbf{b}^{\text{T}}$ yields a symmetric matrix that can be multiplied by the vector **a** to perform the projection. In three dimensions, we have

$$\mathbf{a}_{\parallel\mathbf{b}} = \frac{1}{b^2}\begin{bmatrix} b_x^2 & b_x b_y & b_x b_z \\ b_x b_y & b_y^2 & b_y b_z \\ b_x b_z & b_y b_z & b_z^2 \end{bmatrix}\begin{bmatrix} a_x \\ a_y \\ a_z \end{bmatrix}. \qquad (1.64)$$

The matrix in this equation is an example of an *outer product*. In general, the outer product between two vectors **u** and **v** is written as $\mathbf{u}\otimes\mathbf{v}$, and it produces a matrix for which the $(i, j)$ entry is equal to $u_i v_j$ as in

$$\mathbf{u}\otimes\mathbf{v} = \mathbf{u}\mathbf{v}^{\text{T}} = \begin{bmatrix} u_x \\ u_y \\ u_z \end{bmatrix}\begin{bmatrix} v_x & v_y & v_z \end{bmatrix} = \begin{bmatrix} u_x v_x & u_x v_y & u_x v_z \\ u_y v_x & u_y v_y & u_y v_z \\ u_z v_x & u_z v_y & u_z v_z \end{bmatrix}. \qquad (1.65)$$

If we subtract the projection $\mathbf{a}_{\parallel\mathbf{b}}$ from the original vector **a**, then we get the part that's perpendicular to the vector **b** because we've removed everything that is parallel to **b**. The perpendicular part of the decomposition is called the *rejection* of **a** from **b** and is written

$$\mathbf{a}_{\perp \mathbf{b}} = \mathbf{a} - \mathbf{a}_{\parallel \mathbf{b}} = \mathbf{a} - \frac{\mathbf{a} \cdot \mathbf{b}}{b^2}\mathbf{b}.$$                                      (1.66)

The notation $\mathbf{a}_{\perp \mathbf{b}}$ indicates the component of the vector $\mathbf{a}$ that is perpendicular to the vector $\mathbf{b}$. Of course, it is always the case that $\mathbf{a}_{\parallel \mathbf{b}} + \mathbf{a}_{\perp \mathbf{b}} = \mathbf{a}$.

As shown in Figure 1.13, the projection of $\mathbf{a}$ onto $\mathbf{b}$ and the rejection of $\mathbf{a}$ from $\mathbf{b}$ form the sides of a right triangle in which $\mathbf{a}$ is the hypotenuse. Clearly, $(\mathbf{a}_{\parallel \mathbf{b}})^2 + (\mathbf{a}_{\perp \mathbf{b}})^2 = a^2$, and basic trigonometry tells us

$$\|\mathbf{a}_{\parallel \mathbf{b}}\| = \|\mathbf{a}\|\cos\theta$$
$$\|\mathbf{a}_{\perp \mathbf{b}}\| = \|\mathbf{a}\|\sin\theta,$$                                      (1.67)

where $\theta$ is the angle between $\mathbf{a}$ and $\mathbf{b}$. The presence of the sine function in the magnitude of the rejection suggests that there is another formula for the rejection that involves the cross product, and this is explored in Exercise 5.

In Listing 1.8, functions named `Project()` and `Reject()` implement the projection and rejection operations for the `Vector3D` data structure. Faster versions of these functions can be implemented by omitting the division by $b^2$ for cases when the caller knows that the vector $\mathbf{b}$ has unit length.

One of the primary applications of vector projection is a process called *orthogonalization* in which each member in a set of vectors is modified so that it is perpendicular, or orthogonal, to all of the other vectors. If we have only two nonparallel vectors $\mathbf{a}$ and $\mathbf{b}$, then they can be made into an orthogonal set by either replacing $\mathbf{a}$ with $\mathbf{a}_{\perp \mathbf{b}}$ or by replacing $\mathbf{b}$ with $\mathbf{b}_{\perp \mathbf{a}}$. In both cases, we are subtracting

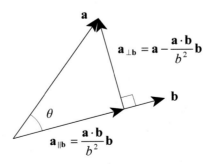

**Figure 1.13.** The projection $\mathbf{a}_{\parallel \mathbf{b}}$ of $\mathbf{a}$ onto $\mathbf{b}$ and the rejection $\mathbf{a}_{\perp \mathbf{b}}$ of $\mathbf{a}$ from $\mathbf{b}$ form the sides parallel and perpendicular to the vector $\mathbf{b}$, respectively, of a right triangle in which the vector $\mathbf{a}$ forms the hypotenuse.

**Listing 1.8.** This code implements projection and rejection operations for the `Vector3D` data structure.

```
inline Vector3D Project(const Vector3D& a, const Vector3D& b)
{
    return (b * (Dot(a, b) / Dot(b, b)));
}

inline Vector3D Reject(const Vector3D& a, const Vector3D& b)
{
    return (a - b * (Dot(a, b) / Dot(b, b)));
}
```

away the projection of one vector onto the other vector so that the parallel component is removed, leaving only the perpendicular component.

We mentioned that two *nonparallel* vectors **a** and **b** could be made orthogonal. If **a** and **b** happened to be parallel, then $\mathbf{a}_{\perp\mathbf{b}}$ and $\mathbf{b}_{\perp\mathbf{a}}$ would both be the zero vector because there is no component of either that is perpendicular to the other. Technically, the zero vector is orthogonal to any other vector, but it's not a very useful result. Being nonparallel means that one vector cannot be written as a scalar multiple of the other. This concept can be extended to a greater number of vectors, and it is known generally as *linear independence*. A set of vectors $\{\mathbf{v}_1, \mathbf{v}_2, \ldots, \mathbf{v}_n\}$ is linearly independent if there do *not* exist scalars $a_1, a_2, \ldots, a_n$ such that

$$a_1\mathbf{v}_1 + a_2\mathbf{v}_2 + \cdots + a_n\mathbf{v}_n = \mathbf{0}. \tag{1.68}$$

This is a concise way of stating that no one vector $\mathbf{v}_i$ can be written as a sum of scalar multiples of all the other vectors in the set. Linear independence means that every vector in the set has a component that is not possessed by any of the other vectors. Consequently, a linearly independent set of $n$-dimensional vectors can have at most $n$ members because after that many, we have run out of orthogonal directions.

Suppose we have a set of $n$ linearly independent vectors $\{\mathbf{v}_1, \mathbf{v}_2, \ldots, \mathbf{v}_n\}$. The general procedure for producing a set of mutually orthogonal vectors $\{\mathbf{u}_1, \mathbf{u}_2, \ldots, \mathbf{u}_n\}$ is called the *Gram-Schmidt process*. It works by first setting $\mathbf{u}_1 = \mathbf{v}_1$ and then considering each additional vector $\mathbf{v}_i$ with $i = 2, \ldots, n$, one at a time. The vector $\mathbf{v}_i$ is made perpendicular to the vectors that have already been orthogonalized by subtracting away its projection onto every $\mathbf{u}_k$ with $k < i$, as done with the formula

$$\mathbf{u}_i = \mathbf{v}_i - \sum_{k=1}^{i-1} (\mathbf{v}_i)_{\parallel \mathbf{u}_k} = \mathbf{v}_i - \sum_{k=1}^{i-1} \frac{\mathbf{v}_i \cdot \mathbf{u}_k}{\mathbf{u}_k^2} \mathbf{u}_k. \qquad (1.69)$$

For example, a set of three vectors $\{\mathbf{v}_1, \mathbf{v}_2, \mathbf{v}_3\}$ is orthogonalized by using the calculations

$$\mathbf{u}_1 = \mathbf{v}_1$$
$$\mathbf{u}_2 = \mathbf{v}_2 - (\mathbf{v}_2)_{\parallel \mathbf{u}_1}$$
$$\mathbf{u}_3 = \mathbf{v}_3 - (\mathbf{v}_3)_{\parallel \mathbf{u}_1} - (\mathbf{v}_3)_{\parallel \mathbf{u}_2}. \qquad (1.70)$$

It is a common requirement that the vectors $\mathbf{u}_i$ be renormalized to unit length after the orthogonalization process by dividing each one by its magnitude. In this case, the process is called *orthonormalization*, and a typical example of its application is the adjustment of the columns of a $3 \times 3$ transformation matrix. If such a matrix has undergone repeated multiplication by other matrices, floating-point rounding errors tend to accumulate, and this causes the columns to become nonorthogonal to a significant degree. As will be discussed in Chapter 2, the columns of a transformation matrix correspond to the directions of the axes in a particular coordinate space, and we usually want all of them to be unit length and perpendicular to each other. Thus, the orthonormalization procedure is often used to enforce these requirements after a matrix has suffered a large number of limited-precision calculations.

## 1.7 Matrix Inversion

One of the main reasons that matrices appear so frequently in game engines is because they represent coordinate system transformations. That is, a matrix $\mathbf{M}$ describes how a vector, point, line, plane, or even another transformation can be moved from a coordinate system $A$ with its own origin and set of axes to another coordinate system $B$ with a different origin and set of axes. It is often necessary to be able to perform the reverse transformation from coordinate system $B$ back to coordinate system $A$, and to accomplish this, we must be able to find a matrix $\mathbf{M}^{-1}$, called the *inverse* of $\mathbf{M}$, that undoes the transformation performed by the matrix $\mathbf{M}$. In this section, we describe what an inverse matrix is, and we show how to compute the inverses of matrices having the typical sizes that arise in game engines.

### 1.7.1 Identity Matrices

The *identity matrix* $\mathbf{I}_n$ is the $n \times n$ matrix whose entries on the main diagonal are all ones and whose entries everywhere else are all zeros, which can be written as

$$\mathbf{I}_n = \begin{bmatrix} 1 & 0 & \cdots & 0 \\ 0 & 1 & \cdots & 0 \\ \vdots & \vdots & \ddots & \vdots \\ 0 & 0 & \cdots & 1 \end{bmatrix}.$$ (1.71)

When it's obvious what the size of the identity matrix is based on context (or it doesn't matter), the subscript $n$ is often omitted after the letter $\mathbf{I}$.

$\mathbf{I}_n$ is called the identity matrix because it has the property that $\mathbf{AI}_n = \mathbf{A}$ for all $r \times n$ matrices $\mathbf{A}$ with any number of rows $r$, and $\mathbf{I}_n \mathbf{B} = \mathbf{B}$ for all $n \times c$ matrices $\mathbf{B}$ with any number of columns $c$. This is easily verified by plugging the identity matrix into the formula for matrix multiplication given by Equation (1.26) as in

$$(\mathbf{IB})_{ij} = \sum_{k=0}^{n-1} I_{ik} B_{kj} = B_{ij}.$$ (1.72)

The only nonzero term in the summation is the one for which $k = i$, and because $I_{ii} = 1$, no change is made to $B_{ij}$. Multiplying a matrix by the identity matrix is analogous to multiplying an ordinary scalar by the number one.

We mention the identity matrix first because it's what allows us to define the inverse of a matrix. Inverses are defined only for square matrices, and the inverse of an $n \times n$ matrix $\mathbf{M}$ is a matrix denoted by $\mathbf{M}^{-1}$ having the property that $\mathbf{MM}^{-1} = \mathbf{I}_n$ and $\mathbf{M}^{-1}\mathbf{M} = \mathbf{I}_n$. An inverse does not always exist, and the rest of this section discusses how to determine whether it does exist, and if so, how it can be calculated.

## 1.7.2 Determinants

The *determinant* of an $n \times n$ matrix $\mathbf{M}$ is a scalar value that can be thought of as a sort of magnitude for $\mathbf{M}$. It is written as $\det(\mathbf{M})$ or $|\mathbf{M}|$. If we consider the $n$ columns or the $n$ rows of the matrix as a set of vectors, then the determinant is equal to the hypervolume of the $n$-dimensional parallelotope formed by those vectors, and it can be positive or negative depending on the orientation of the vectors. A matrix has an inverse if and only if its determinant is not zero.

The calculation of the determinant for an $n \times n$ matrix $\mathbf{M}$ requires that we sum over $n!$ terms corresponding to all of the possible permutations of the sequence $\{0, 1, 2, \ldots, n-1\}$. Each term has $n$ factors that are taken from the $n$ rows of the matrix $\mathbf{M}$, and each factor comes from a different column as specified by the permutation for the term to which the factor belongs. For example, the determinant of a $3 \times 3$ matrix has six terms corresponding to the six permutations of the sequence

$\{0, 1, 2\}$. These permutations are $\{0, 1, 2\}$, $\{1, 2, 0\}$, $\{2, 0, 1\}$, $\{0, 2, 1\}$, $\{1, 0, 2\}$, and $\{2, 1, 0\}$, and they supply the column indices for the three factors that make up each term. The row indices for these factors are always 0, 1, and 2. Thus, the determinant of a $3 \times 3$ matrix $\mathbf{M}$ is given by

$$\det(\mathbf{M}) = M_{00}M_{11}M_{22} + M_{01}M_{12}M_{20} + M_{02}M_{10}M_{21}$$
$$- M_{00}M_{12}M_{21} - M_{01}M_{10}M_{22} - M_{02}M_{11}M_{20}. \qquad (1.73)$$

This formula is implemented in Listing 1.9 for the `Matrix3D` data structure with terms grouped by their first factor.

Notice that the last three terms are negated. A permutation is either *even* or *odd*, and the terms corresponding to odd permutations are negated. Whether a permutation is even or odd depends on how many *transpositions* it requires to rearrange the original sequence into the order represented by the permutation, where a transposition means the exchange of two indices. The permutation $\{0, 1, 2\}$ is even because it doesn't change anything and thus requires zero transpositions. The permutations $\{1, 2, 0\}$ and $\{2, 0, 1\}$ are even because they each require two transpositions. The permutations $\{0, 2, 1\}$, $\{1, 0, 2\}$, and $\{2, 1, 0\}$ are odd because they each require only one transposition.

The determinant of a $1 \times 1$ matrix is simply the value of its single entry. The determinant of a $2 \times 2$ matrix has two terms representing the permutations $\{0, 1\}$ and $\{1, 0\}$ with zero transpositions and one transposition, respectively. Using the vertical bar notation, we can write the determinant of a $2 \times 2$ matrix as

$$\begin{vmatrix} a & b \\ c & d \end{vmatrix} = ad - bc. \qquad (1.74)$$

In general, we represent a particular permutation by a function $\sigma(k)$ that rearranges the indices in the range $[0, n-1]$ by mapping each original index to its permuted index. The set of all $n!$ such functions on $n$ indices is called the *symmetric*

**Listing 1.9.** This code calculates the determinant of a $3 \times 3$ matrix for the `Matrix3D` data structure.

```
float Determinant(const Matrix3D& M)
{
    return (M(0,0) * (M(1,1) * M(2,2) - M(1,2) * M(2,1))
          + M(0,1) * (M(1,2) * M(2,0) - M(1,0) * M(2,2))
          + M(0,2) * (M(1,0) * M(2,1) - M(1,1) * M(2,0)));
}
```

*group* $S_n$, and it includes one permutation called the *identity* permutation that maps each index to itself. The *sign* of a permutation, written $\text{sgn}(\sigma)$, is equal to $+1$ if $\sigma$ is even and $-1$ if $\sigma$ is odd. Using these definitions, the determinant of any $n \times n$ matrix $\mathbf{M}$ can be expressed as

$$\det(\mathbf{M}) = \sum_{\sigma \in S_n} \left( \text{sgn}(\sigma) \prod_{k=0}^{n-1} M_{k,\sigma(k)} \right). \tag{1.75}$$

This is known as the Leibniz formula for the determinant, and it highlights the fact that the determinant is derived from all possible combinations of the matrix entries such that no row or column index is repeated in any term.

Equation (1.75) can be implemented in a recursive manner using a method called *expansion by minors*. A *minor* of an $n \times n$ matrix $\mathbf{M}$ is the determinant of an $(n-1) \times (n-1)$ submatrix of $\mathbf{M}$ that excludes one row and one column of $\mathbf{M}$. We use the notation $\mathbf{M}_{\overline{ij}}$ to represent the submatrix of $\mathbf{M}$ that excludes row $i$ and column $j$. Whereas the notation $M_{ij}$ means the entry in row $i$ and column $j$, the overbar above the subscripts in $\mathbf{M}_{\overline{ij}}$ is interpreted as meaning "not" in the sense that the submatrix includes everything that is not in row $i$ or column $j$. The $(i, j)$ minor of a matrix $\mathbf{M}$ is the determinant given by $\left| \mathbf{M}_{\overline{ij}} \right|$.

Using expansion by minors, the determinant of an $n \times n$ matrix $\mathbf{M}$ is given by

$$\det(\mathbf{M}) = \sum_{j=0}^{n-1} M_{kj} (-1)^{k+j} \left| \mathbf{M}_{\overline{kj}} \right|, \tag{1.76}$$

where $k$ can be chosen to be any fixed row in the matrix. If a matrix is known to have a row containing a lot of zeros, then it would be advantageous to select that row for $k$ because doing so eliminates terms in the summation. Of course, this also means that if a matrix contains a row consisting entirely of zeros, then its determinant must also be zero.

Applying Equation (1.76) to a $3 \times 3$ matrix $\mathbf{M}$, the determinant calculation for a row choice of $k = 0$ is

$$\begin{aligned}
\det(\mathbf{M}) &= \sum_{j=0}^{n-1} M_{0,j} (-1)^{j} \left| \mathbf{M}_{\overline{0,j}} \right| \\
&= M_{00} \left| \mathbf{M}_{\overline{00}} \right| - M_{01} \left| \mathbf{M}_{\overline{01}} \right| + M_{02} \left| \mathbf{M}_{\overline{02}} \right| \\
&= M_{00} (M_{11} M_{22} - M_{12} M_{21}) - M_{01} (M_{10} M_{22} - M_{12} M_{20}) \\
&\quad + M_{02} (M_{10} M_{21} - M_{11} M_{20}).
\end{aligned} \tag{1.77}$$

This can be better visualized as

$$
\det\left(\mathbf{M}\right) = M_{00}\begin{vmatrix} M_{00} & M_{01} & M_{02} \\ M_{10} & M_{11} & M_{12} \\ M_{20} & M_{21} & M_{22} \end{vmatrix} - M_{01}\begin{vmatrix} M_{00} & M_{01} & M_{02} \\ M_{10} & M_{11} & M_{12} \\ M_{20} & M_{21} & M_{22} \end{vmatrix}
$$

$$
+ M_{02}\begin{vmatrix} M_{00} & M_{01} & M_{02} \\ M_{10} & M_{11} & M_{12} \\ M_{20} & M_{21} & M_{22} \end{vmatrix}, \tag{1.78}
$$

where the red lines have crossed out the parts of $\mathbf{M}$ that are excluded from each of the $2 \times 2$ determinants involved in the calculation. After multiplying this out completely and rearranging terms, we see that this is equivalent to the determinant given by Equation (1.73).

The determinant of a $4 \times 4$ matrix $\mathbf{M}$ is a sum of four terms containing determinants of $3 \times 3$ submatrices. $4 \times 4$ matrices arise frequently in game engines, but it's usually the case that the fourth row is simply $\begin{bmatrix} 0 & 0 & 0 & 1 \end{bmatrix}$, so it makes sense to use $k = 3$ in Equation (1.76) to take advantage of the zeros. This leaves only one $3 \times 3$ determinant to calculate, and it corresponds to the bottom-right entry, which is just the number one. Whether the determinant of each submatrix must be negated can be illustrated by a matrix containing alternating plus and minus signs as in

$$
\begin{bmatrix} + & - & + & - \\ - & + & - & + \\ + & - & + & - \\ - & + & - & + \end{bmatrix}. \tag{1.79}
$$

There is a plus sign in the position of the bottom-right entry, so the $3 \times 3$ determinant $|\mathbf{M}_{\overline{33}}|$, where the last row and last column are excluded, is not negated. This means that the determinant of a $4 \times 4$ matrix in which the fourth row is $\begin{bmatrix} 0 & 0 & 0 & 1 \end{bmatrix}$ is equal to the determinant of the upper-left $3 \times 3$ matrix. The applicability of this fact is discussed in Chapter 2.

Several of the basic properties of the determinant are listed in Table 1.6. The first property, that the determinant of the identity matrix is one, is a special case of the more general property that the determinant of a diagonal matrix is equal to the product of the entries on its main diagonal. This is a rather obvious consequence of the fact that there is only one term in Equation (1.75) that is nonzero, and it's the term for which $\sigma$ is the identity permutation.

More interestingly, the determinant of the transpose of a matrix $\mathbf{M}$ is equal to the determinant of $\mathbf{M}$. This is true because for each factor appearing in Equation (1.75) for the matrix $\mathbf{M}^{\mathrm{T}}$, we can write $M^{\mathrm{T}}_{k,\sigma(k)} = M_{\sigma(k),k}$ and then reorder the $n$ factors for each permutation $\sigma$ by applying the inverse permutation $\sigma^{-1}$ to get

$$\prod_{k=0}^{n-1} M_{\sigma(k),k} = \prod_{k=0}^{n-1} M_{k,\sigma^{-1}(k)}. \tag{1.80}$$

Since the set of permutations and the set of inverse permutations are equivalent, the sum in Equation (1.75) is taken over the same terms and produces the same result. The fact that $\det\left(\mathbf{M}^{\mathrm{T}}\right) = \det\left(\mathbf{M}\right)$ means that we can expand the determinant by minors along a column just as we previously did by a row. This gives us the alternative formula

$$\det\left(\mathbf{M}\right) = \sum_{i=0}^{n-1} M_{ik}\left(-1\right)^{i+k}\left|\mathbf{M}_{\overline{ik}}\right| \tag{1.81}$$

to Equation (1.76), where $k$ can be chosen to be any fixed column in the matrix. The determinant can be calculated by expanding by minors over any row or any column of a matrix, and we can choose whatever happens to be most convenient.

The product rule $\det\left(\mathbf{AB}\right) = \det\left(\mathbf{A}\right)\det\left(\mathbf{B}\right)$ listed in Table 1.6 tells us that the determinant of a matrix product is equal to the product of the determinants of the two matrices being multiplied together. It follows that $\det\left(\mathbf{A}^{-1}\right) = 1/\det\left(\mathbf{A}\right)$ because $\det\left(\mathbf{A}\right)\det\left(\mathbf{A}^{-1}\right) = \det\left(\mathbf{AA}^{-1}\right) = \det\left(\mathbf{I}\right) = 1$. We'll be able to see why the product rule is true in the discussion of elementary matrices below.

| Property | Description |
|---|---|
| $\det\left(\mathbf{I}_n\right) = 1$ | Determinant of the identity. |
| $\det\left(\mathbf{A}^{\mathrm{T}}\right) = \det\left(\mathbf{A}\right)$ | Determinant of a transpose matrix. |
| $\det\left(\mathbf{A}^{-1}\right) = 1/\det\left(\mathbf{A}\right)$ | Determinant of an inverse matrix. |
| $\det\left(\mathbf{AB}\right) = \det\left(\mathbf{A}\right)\det\left(\mathbf{B}\right)$ | Product rule for the determinant. |
| $\det\left(t\mathbf{A}\right) = t^n \det\left(\mathbf{A}\right)$ | Scalar factorization for the determinant. |

**Table 1.6.** These are the basic properties of the determinant. The letters $\mathbf{A}$ and $\mathbf{B}$ represent $n \times n$ matrices, and the letter $t$ represents a scalar value.

### 1.7.3 Elementary Matrices

The inverse of a matrix $\mathbf{M}$ can be found by systematically performing a sequence of basic operations on $\mathbf{M}$ until it has been transformed into the identity matrix. Each of these basic operations can be represented by an *elementary matrix*, and the product of all the elementary matrices corresponding to all the basic operations used to transform $\mathbf{M}$ into the identity provides us with the inverse of $\mathbf{M}$. The exact procedure is described below after we take a moment to discuss the types of elementary matrices and their properties.

There are three *elementary row operations*, named as such because they each affect one or two entire rows of a matrix, and the particular types perform the following modifications to a matrix $\mathbf{M}$.

(a)  Multiply one row of $\mathbf{M}$ by a nonzero scalar value.
(b)  Exchange two rows of $\mathbf{M}$.
(c)  Add a scalar multiple of one row of $\mathbf{M}$ to another row of $\mathbf{M}$.

Each elementary row operation can be applied to an $n \times n$ matrix $\mathbf{M}$ by multiplying it on the left by an elementary matrix $\mathbf{E}$ that is constructed by performing the same operation on the identity matrix $\mathbf{I}_n$. To multiply row $r$ by a scalar value $t$, the elementary matrix $\mathbf{E}$ has the following form, where the $(r, r)$ entry of the identity matrix has been replaced by $t$.

$$\mathbf{E} = \begin{bmatrix} 1 & \cdots & 0 & \cdots & 0 \\ \vdots & \ddots & \vdots & & \vdots \\ 0 & \cdots & t & \cdots & 0 \\ \vdots & & \vdots & \ddots & \vdots \\ 0 & \cdots & 0 & \cdots & 1 \end{bmatrix} \leftarrow \text{row } r \tag{1.82}$$

To exchange row $r$ and row $s$, the elementary matrix $\mathbf{E}$ has the following form, where the same rows have been exchanged in the identity matrix.

$$\mathbf{E} = \begin{bmatrix} 1 & \cdots & 0 & \cdots & 0 & \cdots & 0 \\ \vdots & \ddots & \vdots & & \vdots & & \vdots \\ 0 & \cdots & 0 & \cdots & 1 & \cdots & 0 \\ \vdots & & \vdots & \ddots & \vdots & & \vdots \\ 0 & \cdots & 1 & \cdots & 0 & \cdots & 0 \\ \vdots & & \vdots & & \vdots & \ddots & \vdots \\ 0 & \cdots & 0 & \cdots & 0 & \cdots & 1 \end{bmatrix} \begin{matrix} \\ \\ \leftarrow \text{row } r \\ \\ \leftarrow \text{row } s \\ \\ \ \end{matrix} \tag{1.83}$$

To add row $s$ multiplied by the scalar value $t$ to row $r$, the elementary matrix $\mathbf{E}$ has the following form, where the $(r, s)$ entry of the identity matrix has been replaced by $t$.

$$\mathbf{E} = \begin{bmatrix} 1 & \cdots & 0 & \cdots & 0 & \cdots & 0 \\ \vdots & \ddots & \vdots & & \vdots & & \vdots \\ 0 & \cdots & 1 & \cdots & t & \cdots & 0 \\ \vdots & & \vdots & \ddots & \vdots & & \vdots \\ 0 & \cdots & 0 & \cdots & 1 & \cdots & 0 \\ \vdots & & \vdots & & \vdots & \ddots & \vdots \\ 0 & \cdots & 0 & \cdots & 0 & \cdots & 1 \end{bmatrix} \begin{matrix} \\ \\ \leftarrow \text{row } r \\ \\ \leftarrow \text{row } s \\ \\ \\ \end{matrix} \qquad (1.84)$$

When an elementary row operation is applied to a matrix $\mathbf{M}$, it has a specific effect on the determinant of $\mathbf{M}$, described as follows.

(a) Multiplying a row of $\mathbf{M}$ by the scalar value $t$ causes the determinant of $\mathbf{M}$ to be multiplied by $t$.
(b) Exchanging two rows of $\mathbf{M}$ causes the determinant of $\mathbf{M}$ to be negated.
(c) Adding a scalar multiple of one row of $\mathbf{M}$ to another row of $\mathbf{M}$ does not change the determinant of $\mathbf{M}$.

When considering the Leibniz formula for the determinant given by Equation (1.75), it's immediately evident that multiplying a row by a scalar value $t$ also multiplies the determinant by $t$ because each term in the summation contains exactly one factor that is multiplied by $t$.

The fact that exchanging two rows negates the determinant can be demonstrated with an induction argument. First, note that the result is true for $2 \times 2$ matrices because

$$\begin{vmatrix} c & d \\ a & b \end{vmatrix} = cb - da = -(ad - bc) = \begin{vmatrix} a & b \\ c & d \end{vmatrix}. \qquad (1.85)$$

To observe the effect on an $n \times n$ matrix with $n \geq 3$, we can now assume that the result is true for matrices of all sizes smaller than $n \times n$. Let $\mathbf{B}$ be the matrix constructed by exchanging rows $r$ and $s$ in the $n \times n$ matrix $\mathbf{A}$. We can choose another row $k$ such that $k \neq r$ and $k \neq s$ and calculate the determinant of $\mathbf{B}$ with Equation (1.76) as

$$\det(\mathbf{B}) = \sum_{j=0}^{n-1} B_{kj} (-1)^{k+j} \left| \mathbf{B}_{\overline{kj}} \right|. \tag{1.86}$$

Each submatrix $\mathbf{B}_{\overline{kj}}$ appearing in the summation is an $(n-1) \times (n-1)$ matrix that has had two rows exchanged because neither row $r$ nor row $s$ is excluded from $\mathbf{B}$. Therefore, it must be the case that $\left| \mathbf{B}_{\overline{kj}} \right| = - \left| \mathbf{A}_{\overline{kj}} \right|$ by induction. Since every term is negated, we can conclude that $\det(\mathbf{B}) = -\det(\mathbf{A})$.

An important consequence of the fact that exchanging two rows of a matrix negates its determinant is that a matrix containing two identical rows must have a determinant equal to zero. This is true because exchanging those identical rows would negate the determinant, but the matrix doesn't change at all when those rows are exchanged, so the determinant must remain the same when negated and thus can only be zero. Because transposing a matrix does not change its determinant, it is also true that a matrix containing two identical columns must have a determinant equal to zero.

To see that the determinant does not change when a multiple of one row is added to another, we again consider Equation (1.76). Suppose that the matrix $\mathbf{B}$ is constructed by taking row $s$ from the matrix $\mathbf{A}$, multiplying it by the scalar $t$, and adding the result to row $r$. Choosing $k = r$, we have

$$\begin{aligned}
\det(\mathbf{B}) &= \sum_{j=0}^{n-1} B_{rj} (-1)^{r+j} \left| \mathbf{B}_{\overline{rj}} \right| \\
&= \sum_{j=0}^{n-1} (A_{rj} + t A_{sj})(-1)^{r+j} \left| \mathbf{A}_{\overline{rj}} \right| \\
&= \det(\mathbf{A}) + t \sum_{j=0}^{n-1} A_{sj} (-1)^{r+j} \left| \mathbf{A}_{\overline{rj}} \right|. \tag{1.87}
\end{aligned}$$

The last summation is equivalent to the determinant of the matrix $\mathbf{A}$ after being modified so that the entries in row $r$ are the same as the entries in row $s$. Because that matrix has two identical rows, its determinant must be zero, and we are left with $\det(\mathbf{B}) = \det(\mathbf{A})$.

For the three types of elementary row operations, the determinants of the corresponding elementary matrices are the values by which another matrix's determinant is multiplied when the row operation is applied. This is clear when you consider that each elementary matrix is the result of applying an elementary row operation to the identity matrix. Thus, if $\mathbf{E}$ is an elementary matrix, then $\det(\mathbf{EM}) = \det(\mathbf{E})\det(\mathbf{M})$ for any matrix $\mathbf{M}$, and this establishes the product rule listed in Table 1.6 when one of the matrices is an elementary matrix. That the product rule holds in general will be shown below.

### 1.7.4 Inverse Calculation

If it exists, the inverse of a matrix can be found through a process called *Gauss-Jordan elimination* in which elementary row operations are successively applied to the matrix until it is transformed into the identity matrix. This process is described here as a general method for calculating the inverse of a square matrix of any size. For matrices of small size, faster methods exist, and they are presented later in this section.

Let $\mathbf{M}$ be an $n \times n$ matrix, and let $\mathbf{M}'$ represent the current transformation of $\mathbf{M}$ after all of the previous operations in the process have been applied. The Gauss-Jordan elimination procedure for finding the matrix $\mathbf{M}^{-1}$ comprises the following steps for every column $k$ of the matrix, with $0 \leq k < n$.

A. Find the row $r$ with $r \geq k$ such that $M'_{rk}$ has the largest absolute value, and let $p = M'_{rk}$. If $p = 0$, then the inverse of $\mathbf{M}$ does not exist.
B. If $r \neq k$, then exchange rows $r$ and $k$ using elementary row operation (b).
C. Multiply row $k$ of $\mathbf{M}'$ (after the exchange in Step B) by $1/p$ using elementary row operation (a). This sets $M'_{kk} = 1$.
D. For each row $i$ with $0 \leq i < n$ and $i \neq k$, add row $k$ multiplied by $-M'_{ik}$ to row $i$ using elementary row operation (c). This sets every entry in column $k$ above and below row $k$ to zero.

Steps A and B are called *pivoting*, and they are sometimes necessary to ensure that a nonzero entry is moved to the main diagonal. Additionally, the numerical stability of the floating-point operations used throughout the process is increased by choosing the largest entry in each column because this causes the scalar factors used in Step D to be smallest $n-1$ possibilities.

After the above steps have been applied to every column of the matrix $\mathbf{M}$, we know that

$$\mathbf{E}_m \mathbf{E}_{m-1} \cdots \mathbf{E}_2 \mathbf{E}_1 \mathbf{M} = \mathbf{I}, \tag{1.88}$$

where the matrices $\mathbf{E}_1, \mathbf{E}_2, \ldots, \mathbf{E}_m$ are the elementary matrices corresponding to the row operations performed during Gauss-Jordan elimination, the total number of which we are calling $m$. Because multiplying by $\mathbf{M}$ produces the identity matrix, the product $\mathbf{E}_m \mathbf{E}_{m-1} \cdots \mathbf{E}_2 \mathbf{E}_1$ is actually the inverse of $\mathbf{M}$, and we can construct the inverse by applying each elementary row operation to a matrix that starts out as the identity matrix at the same time that we apply it to $\mathbf{M}'$.

An invertible matrix $\mathbf{M}$ can always be written as a product of elementary matrices by multiplying the right side of Equation (1.88) by the inverse of each $\mathbf{E}_i$.

(See Exercise 13 for proof that elementary matrices are always invertible.) If two matrices **A** and **B** are both invertible, then they can both be factored completely into elementary matrices. The product rule for determinants listed in Table 1.6 always holds for elementary matrices, so it must also hold for the product **AB**. Furthermore, the determinants of all the elementary matrices are nonzero, so the determinant of any invertible matrix cannot be zero.

A matrix that is not invertible is called *singular*, and this word is used in the sense that such matrices are exceedingly rare if you consider the entire set of $n \times n$ matrices. If Step A of the Gauss-Jordan elimination process fails to find a nonzero entry in column $k$ in some row $r \geq k$, then row $k$ ends up being all zeros after the process is continued through the remaining columns. A matrix containing a row of zeros cannot be inverted (see Exercise 15), and it always has a determinant of zero. Because it can be expressed as a product of elementary matrices and a matrix having a row of zeros, any singular matrix must have a determinant of zero. This is a test that can used to determine whether a matrix can be inverted without actually trying to calculate the inverse.

The inverse of the matrix product **AB** is equal to $\mathbf{B}^{-1}\mathbf{A}^{-1}$, the product of the inverses of **A** and **B** in reverse order. This is easily verified by multiplying **AB** by its inverse on either side as in

$$\mathbf{AB}\left(\mathbf{B}^{-1}\mathbf{A}^{-1}\right) = \mathbf{A}\left(\mathbf{BB}^{-1}\right)\mathbf{A}^{-1} = \mathbf{AA}^{-1} = \mathbf{I}. \tag{1.89}$$

If either **A** or **B** is singular, then the product **AB** must also be singular. In this case, the product rule for determinants still holds because both sides of the equation $\det(\mathbf{AB}) = \det(\mathbf{A})\det(\mathbf{B})$ are zero.

### 1.7.5 Inverses of Small Matrices

For matrices of size $4 \times 4$ and smaller, like those that appear in game engines most of the time, inverses can be calculated using an approach that is more direct than Gauss-Jordan elimination. This approach uses the minors with alternating signs that appear in the formula for the determinant given by Equation (1.76). The quantity $(-1)^{i+j}\left|\mathbf{M}_{\overline{ij}}\right|$, the minor multiplied by a positive or negative one, is called the *cofactor* of the $(i, j)$ entry of **M**. We define the function $C_{ij}(\mathbf{M})$ as

$$C_{ij}(\mathbf{M}) = (-1)^{i+j}\left|\mathbf{M}_{\overline{ij}}\right|. \tag{1.90}$$

The *cofactor matrix* $\mathbf{C}(\mathbf{M})$ of an $n \times n$ matrix **M** is the matrix in which every entry of **M** has been replaced by the corresponding cofactor. Using these definitions, a formula for the inverse of a matrix **M** can be stated very simply as

$$\mathbf{M}^{-1} = \frac{\mathbf{C}^{\mathrm{T}}(\mathbf{M})}{\det(\mathbf{M})}. \tag{1.91}$$

That is, the inverse of $\mathbf{M}$ is equal to the transpose of its cofactor matrix divided by its determinant.

The matrix $\mathbf{C}^{\mathrm{T}}(\mathbf{M})$ is called the *adjugate* of the matrix $\mathbf{M}$, and it is denoted by $\mathrm{adj}(\mathbf{M})$. The adjugate of $\mathbf{M}$ always exists, even if $\mathbf{M}$ is singular, and it's easier to calculate than the inverse of $\mathbf{M}$ because we don't need to calculate the determinant and divide by it. The adjugate will appear again in Chapter 3.

We can verify that Equation (1.91) is correct by directly carrying out its multiplication by $\mathbf{M}$ using Equation (1.26), which gives us

$$\left(\mathbf{M}^{-1}\mathbf{M}\right)_{ij} = \sum_{k=0}^{n-1} \frac{\mathbf{C}_{ik}^{\mathrm{T}}(\mathbf{M})}{\det(\mathbf{M})} M_{kj}$$

$$= \frac{1}{\det(\mathbf{M})} \sum_{k=0}^{n-1} C_{ki}(\mathbf{M}) M_{kj}. \tag{1.92}$$

When $i = j$, the summation is equal to the determinant of $\mathbf{M}$ as calculated by Equation (1.76), so division by $\det(\mathbf{M})$ produces a one in the $(i, i)$ entry of the result. When $i \neq j$, the summation is equal to the determinant of $\mathbf{M}$ if it were modified so that the entries in column $j$ were replaced by the entries in column $i$. This matrix has two identical columns and must therefore have a determinant of zero, so each $(i, j)$ entry of the result, with $i \neq j$, must be zero. This demonstrates that multiplying by $\mathbf{M}$ produces the identity matrix, and a similar argument can be applied to the product $\mathbf{M}\mathbf{M}^{-1}$.

Equation (1.91) supplies us with explicit inverse formulas that can be implemented without the use of any loops. For a $2 \times 2$ matrix $\mathbf{A}$, the formula for the inverse is

$$\mathbf{A}^{-1} = \frac{1}{A_{00}A_{11} - A_{01}A_{10}} \begin{bmatrix} A_{11} & -A_{01} \\ -A_{10} & A_{00} \end{bmatrix}. \tag{1.93}$$

This is particularly simple because the minors all involve only $1 \times 1$ matrices. The inverse formula for a $3 \times 3$ matrix $\mathbf{B}$ is given by

$$\mathbf{B}^{-1} = \frac{1}{\det(\mathbf{B})} \begin{bmatrix} B_{11}B_{22} - B_{12}B_{21} & B_{02}B_{21} - B_{01}B_{22} & B_{01}B_{12} - B_{02}B_{11} \\ B_{12}B_{20} - B_{10}B_{22} & B_{00}B_{22} - B_{02}B_{20} & B_{02}B_{10} - B_{00}B_{12} \\ B_{10}B_{21} - B_{11}B_{20} & B_{01}B_{20} - B_{00}B_{21} & B_{00}B_{11} - B_{01}B_{10} \end{bmatrix}. \tag{1.94}$$

Upon close examination, we notice that each row in this formula is actually a cross product of two columns of the matrix $\mathbf{B}$. Furthermore, the determinant of a $3 \times 3$ matrix, calculated with Equation (1.73), is equal to the scalar triple product of the three columns of the matrix. These observations allow us to write the inverse of a matrix $\mathbf{M} = \begin{bmatrix} \mathbf{a} & \mathbf{b} & \mathbf{c} \end{bmatrix}$ (whose columns are the 3D vectors $\mathbf{a}$, $\mathbf{b}$, and $\mathbf{c}$) as

$$\mathbf{M}^{-1} = \frac{1}{[\mathbf{a}, \mathbf{b}, \mathbf{c}]} \begin{bmatrix} \mathbf{b} \times \mathbf{c} \\ \mathbf{c} \times \mathbf{a} \\ \mathbf{a} \times \mathbf{b} \end{bmatrix}, \qquad (1.95)$$

where the cross products are treated as row vectors. This is how the inverse for the `Matrix3D` data structure is implemented in Listing 1.10. If we consider the fact that multiplying $\mathbf{M}^{-1}$ by $\mathbf{M}$ is a matter of calculating the dot product between the rows of $\mathbf{M}^{-1}$ and the vectors $\mathbf{a}$, $\mathbf{b}$, and $\mathbf{c}$, it becomes clear that Equation (1.95) must give the correct inverse of $\mathbf{M}$. This formula can be generalized to any number of dimensions using the wedge product, as will be discussed in Section 4.3.

It would be possible to find the inverse of a $4 \times 4$ matrix with Equation (1.91), but it would require calculating 16 cofactors that are the determinants of $3 \times 3$ submatrices. This includes a significant amount of redundant computation that can be

**Listing 1.10.** This code calculates the inverse of a $3 \times 3$ matrix for the `Matrix3D` data structure.

```
Matrix3D Inverse(const Matrix3D& M)
{
    const Vector3D& a = M[0];
    const Vector3D& b = M[1];
    const Vector3D& c = M[2];

    Vector3D r0 = Cross(b, c);
    Vector3D r1 = Cross(c, a);
    Vector3D r2 = Cross(a, b);

    float invDet = 1.0F / Dot(r2, c);

    return (Matrix3D(r0.x * invDet, r0.y * invDet, r0.z * invDet,
                     r1.x * invDet, r1.y * invDet, r1.z * invDet,
                     r2.x * invDet, r2.y * invDet, r2.z * invDet));
}
```

avoided by exploiting some algebraic structure. A complete discussion of what's actually happening will have to wait until Chapter 4, but we can present a more efficient method of calculating the inverse here.

Let **M** be a $4 \times 4$ matrix whose first three rows are filled by the four 3D column vectors **a**, **b**, **c**, and **d**, and whose fourth row contains the entries $\begin{bmatrix} x & y & z & w \end{bmatrix}$, as illustrated by

$$\mathbf{M} = \begin{bmatrix} \uparrow & \uparrow & \uparrow & \uparrow \\ \mathbf{a} & \mathbf{b} & \mathbf{c} & \mathbf{d} \\ \downarrow & \downarrow & \downarrow & \downarrow \\ \hline x & y & z & w \end{bmatrix}. \tag{1.96}$$

We then define the four vectors **s**, **t**, **u**, and **v** as

$$\mathbf{s} = \mathbf{a} \times \mathbf{b}$$
$$\mathbf{t} = \mathbf{c} \times \mathbf{d}$$
$$\mathbf{u} = y\mathbf{a} - x\mathbf{b}$$
$$\mathbf{v} = w\mathbf{c} - z\mathbf{d}. \tag{1.97}$$

Using these definitions, the determinant of **M** takes the astonishingly simple form

$$\det(\mathbf{M}) = \mathbf{s} \cdot \mathbf{v} + \mathbf{t} \cdot \mathbf{u}, \tag{1.98}$$

and the inverse of **M** is given by

$$\mathbf{M}^{-1} = \frac{1}{\mathbf{s} \cdot \mathbf{v} + \mathbf{t} \cdot \mathbf{u}} \begin{bmatrix} \mathbf{b} \times \mathbf{v} + y\mathbf{t} & -\mathbf{b} \cdot \mathbf{t} \\ \mathbf{v} \times \mathbf{a} - x\mathbf{t} & \mathbf{a} \cdot \mathbf{t} \\ \mathbf{d} \times \mathbf{u} + w\mathbf{s} & -\mathbf{d} \cdot \mathbf{s} \\ \mathbf{u} \times \mathbf{c} - z\mathbf{s} & \mathbf{c} \cdot \mathbf{s} \end{bmatrix}. \tag{1.99}$$

Here, the first three columns of $\mathbf{M}^{-1}$ are filled by four 3D row vectors, and the fourth column is the 4D vector $(-\mathbf{b} \cdot \mathbf{t}, \mathbf{a} \cdot \mathbf{t}, -\mathbf{d} \cdot \mathbf{s}, \mathbf{c} \cdot \mathbf{s})$. Verifying that this is the correct inverse is straightforward but somewhat tedious, so Exercise 19 asks that only part of the work be done.

Equation (1.99) is implemented in Listing 1.11 to calculate the inverse of a $4 \times 4$ matrix stored in a Matrix4D data structure. When $4 \times 4$ matrices appear in game engines, it is almost always the case that the fourth row is $\begin{bmatrix} 0 & 0 & 0 & 1 \end{bmatrix}$. In this case, several optimizations can be made to the inverse calculation because $x = y = z = 0$ and $w = 1$ in Equation (1.96), and consequently, $\mathbf{u} = \mathbf{0}$ and $\mathbf{v} = \mathbf{c}$ in Equation (1.97). (See Section 2.6.)

**Listing 1.11.** This code calculates the inverse of a $4 \times 4$ matrix for the `Matrix4D` data structure.

```
Matrix4D Inverse(const Matrix4D& M)
{
    const Vector3D& a = reinterpret_cast<const Vector3D&>(M[0]);
    const Vector3D& b = reinterpret_cast<const Vector3D&>(M[1]);
    const Vector3D& c = reinterpret_cast<const Vector3D&>(M[2]);
    const Vector3D& d = reinterpret_cast<const Vector3D&>(M[3]);

    const float& x = M(3,0);
    const float& y = M(3,1);
    const float& z = M(3,2);
    const float& w = M(3,3);

    Vector3D s = Cross(a, b);
    Vector3D t = Cross(c, d);
    Vector3D u = a * y - b * x;
    Vector3D v = c * w - d * z;

    float invDet = 1.0F / (Dot(s, v) + Dot(t, u));
    s *= invDet;
    t *= invDet;
    u *= invDet;
    v *= invDet;

    Vector3D r0 = Cross(b, v) + t * y;
    Vector3D r1 = Cross(v, a) - t * x;
    Vector3D r2 = Cross(d, u) + s * w;
    Vector3D r3 = Cross(u, c) - s * z;

    return (Matrix4D(r0.x, r0.y, r0.z, -Dot(b, t),
                     r1.x, r1.y, r1.z,  Dot(a, t),
                     r2.x, r2.y, r2.z, -Dot(d, s),
                     r3.x, r3.y, r3.z,  Dot(c, s)));
}
```

## Exercises for Chapter 1

1. Let $\mathbf{i}$, $\mathbf{j}$, and $\mathbf{k}$ be the unit vectors aligned to the coordinate axes defined by Equation (1.59). Calculate the following.

   (a) The dot products $\mathbf{i} \cdot \mathbf{j}$, $\mathbf{j} \cdot \mathbf{k}$, and $\mathbf{k} \cdot \mathbf{i}$.
   (b) The cross products $\mathbf{i} \times \mathbf{j}$, $\mathbf{j} \times \mathbf{i}$, $\mathbf{j} \times \mathbf{k}$, $\mathbf{k} \times \mathbf{j}$, $\mathbf{k} \times \mathbf{i}$, and $\mathbf{i} \times \mathbf{k}$,
   (c) The scalar triple product $[\mathbf{i}, \mathbf{j}, \mathbf{k}]$.

2. The magnitude of the vector sum $\mathbf{a} + \mathbf{b}$ satisfies a property known as the *triangle inequality*, and this property gets its name precisely from the fact that $\mathbf{a} + \mathbf{b}$ forms the third side of a triangle whose other two sides are $\mathbf{a}$ and $\mathbf{b}$. The third side must be no longer than the sum of the lengths of the other two sides because if it were longer, then the other two sides couldn't be made to reach the end of the third side from the same starting point even if they were laid out in a straight line. Mathematically, we can express this property as

$$\|\mathbf{a} + \mathbf{b}\| \leq \|\mathbf{a}\| + \|\mathbf{b}\|.$$

   Provide an algebraic proof of this relationship by expanding the squared magnitude of $\mathbf{a} + \mathbf{b}$.

3. Prove that for two vectors $\mathbf{a}$ and $\mathbf{b}$, the relationship

$$\left| \|\mathbf{a}\| - \|\mathbf{b}\| \right| \leq \|\mathbf{a} - \mathbf{b}\|$$

   is always true. This is called the *reverse triangle inequality*.

4. For 3D vectors $\mathbf{a}$, $\mathbf{b}$, and $\mathbf{c}$, the Jacobi identity states that

$$\mathbf{a} \times (\mathbf{b} \times \mathbf{c}) + \mathbf{b} \times (\mathbf{c} \times \mathbf{a}) + \mathbf{c} \times (\mathbf{a} \times \mathbf{b}) = \mathbf{0}.$$

   Use the vector triple product identity listed in Table 1.5 to prove this.

5. Show that $\mathbf{a}_{\perp \mathbf{b}}$, the rejection of $\mathbf{a}$ from $\mathbf{b}$, can be calculated as $\dfrac{\mathbf{b} \times \mathbf{a} \times \mathbf{b}}{b^2}$ when $\mathbf{a}$ and $\mathbf{b}$ are 3D vectors.

6. Let $\mathbf{a}$ and $\mathbf{b}$ be 3D vectors. Find a $3 \times 3$ matrix $\mathbf{R}$ such that $\mathbf{R}\mathbf{a} = \mathbf{a}_{\perp \mathbf{b}}$.

7.  Show that for 3D vectors **a**, **b**, and **v**, the projections $\mathbf{v}_{\|\mathbf{a}}$ and $\left(\mathbf{v}_{\perp(\mathbf{a}\times\mathbf{b})}\right)_{\|\mathbf{a}}$ are equal, and conclude that first projecting **v** onto a plane containing **a** does not change its projection onto **a**.

8.  Prove the associative law for matrix multiplication by applying Equation (1.26) directly to the product $(\mathbf{AB})\mathbf{C}$, where **A** is an $n \times m$ matrix, **B** is an $m \times p$ matrix, and **C** is a $p \times q$ matrix.

9.  A *lower triangular* matrix **M** is one for which all entries above the main diagonal are zero. That is, $M_{ij} = 0$ for all entries with $i < j$. Show that the determinant of a lower triangular matrix is equal to the product of the entries on the main diagonal.

10. Prove the property $\det(t\mathbf{A}) = t^n \det(\mathbf{A})$ listed in Table 1.6.

11. Find all $2 \times 2$ singular matrices having the property that each entry in the matrix is either 0 or 1.

12. Let **M**, **L**, and **R** be square matrices of the same size. Prove that if $\mathbf{LM} = \mathbf{I}$ and $\mathbf{MR} = \mathbf{I}$, then $\mathbf{L} = \mathbf{R}$.

13. Find general formulas for the inverses of the elementary matrices given by Equations (1.82), (1.83), and (1.84).

14. Show how applying the permutation $\tau$ that exchanges the indices $r$ and $s$ to each term of the Leibniz formula in Equation (1.75) demonstrates that exchanging the rows $r$ and $s$ of a matrix negates its determinant.

15. Prove that a matrix **M** containing a row of zeros is singular by showing that there is no matrix by which **M** could be multiplied to produce the identity matrix. Do not simply state that the determinant of **M** is zero.

16. Prove that a matrix $\mathbf{M}^{\mathrm{T}}$ is invertible if and only if the matrix **M** is invertible, and give a formula for $\left(\mathbf{M}^{\mathrm{T}}\right)^{-1}$ in terms of $\mathbf{M}^{-1}$.

17. Show that for any $n \times n$ matrix **M**, whether it's invertible or singular, the products $\mathbf{M}\,\mathrm{adj}(\mathbf{M})$ and $\mathrm{adj}(\mathbf{M})\,\mathbf{M}$ are both equal to $\det(\mathbf{M})\mathbf{I}_n$.

**18.** For any two $n$-dimensional vectors $\mathbf{a}$ and $\mathbf{b}$, verify the matrix identity

$$\begin{bmatrix} \mathbf{I}_n & \mathbf{0} \\ \mathbf{b}^{\mathrm{T}} & 1 \end{bmatrix} \begin{bmatrix} \mathbf{I}_n + \mathbf{a} \otimes \mathbf{b} & \mathbf{a} \\ \mathbf{0} & 1 \end{bmatrix} \begin{bmatrix} \mathbf{I}_n & \mathbf{0} \\ -\mathbf{b}^{\mathrm{T}} & 1 \end{bmatrix} = \begin{bmatrix} \mathbf{I}_n & \mathbf{a} \\ \mathbf{0} & 1 + \mathbf{a} \cdot \mathbf{b} \end{bmatrix},$$

where $\otimes$ is the outer product introduced in Section 1.6, and use it to prove that $\det(\mathbf{I}_n + \mathbf{a} \otimes \mathbf{b}) = 1 + \mathbf{a} \cdot \mathbf{b}$.

**19.** Verify that the formula for $\mathbf{M}^{-1}$ given by Equation (1.99) produces ones on the main diagonal when multiplied by $\mathbf{M}$ on the right by calculating the dot product of the $k$-th row of $\mathbf{M}^{-1}$ and the $k$-th column of $\mathbf{M}$ for $0 \leq k < 4$. Pick any off-diagonal entry of $\mathbf{M}^{-1}\mathbf{M}$ and show that it is equal to zero.

**20.** Prove the 3D vector identity

$$[\mathbf{a}, \mathbf{b}, \mathbf{c}]\mathbf{d} = (\mathbf{a} \cdot \mathbf{d})(\mathbf{b} \times \mathbf{c}) + (\mathbf{b} \cdot \mathbf{d})(\mathbf{c} \times \mathbf{a}) + (\mathbf{c} \cdot \mathbf{d})(\mathbf{a} \times \mathbf{b})$$

by showing that the $x$ component of the left side of the equation is equal to the $x$ component of the right side. (Assume that the proof for the other two components is similar.)

# Chapter 2

# Transforms

A dynamic object in a game may need to move from one point to another, and it may need to rotate itself to different orientations. A model may be composed of a collection of objects arranged in a tree structure, and each part may move in a manner that is relative to another part above it in the hierarchy. It may be necessary to express positions and orientations in many different local coordinate systems used by various components of a rendering system. All of these are examples of cases that require the application of *transforms*. This chapter describes how transforms are used to convert the coordinate representations of geometric objects from one coordinate system to another. We also discuss how transforms are an important way of placing objects in the world, modifying the appearance of objects, and establishing relationships with other objects.

## 2.1 Coordinate Spaces

It is typical for a game engine to define a number of different coordinate systems. There is usually a coordinate system called *world space* or *global space* that serves as a fixed background relative to which other coordinate systems can be established. Various objects in a game, which can include things like models, light sources, and cameras, often have their own independent coordinate systems called *object space* or *local space*. When an interaction occurs between two objects using different coordinate systems, either one object needs to be transformed into the coordinate system used by the other object or both objects need to be transformed into some other common coordinate system.

## 2.1.1 Transformation Matrices

A position in a particular coordinate system is represented by a vector that gives the direction and distance that you would have to travel from the origin of the coordinate system in order to reach that point in space. The components of such a vector correspond to the distances travelled along each of the $x$, $y$, and $z$ coordinate axes. When an object is transformed from one coordinate system to another, the components of any position vector must change to account for the new position of the origin and the new orientations of the coordinate axes. The transformation from a position $\mathbf{p}_A$ in coordinate system $A$ to the position $\mathbf{p}_B$ in coordinate system $B$ can be expressed as

$$\mathbf{p}_B = \mathbf{M}\mathbf{p}_A + \mathbf{t}, \tag{2.1}$$

where $\mathbf{M}$ is a $3 \times 3$ matrix that reorients the coordinate axes, and $\mathbf{t}$ is a 3D translation vector that moves the origin of the coordinate system. The transformation expressed in Equation (2.1) is called an *affine* transformation. Assuming that $\mathbf{M}$ is invertible, we can solve this equation for $\mathbf{p}_A$ to obtain the inverse transformation from coordinate system $B$ to coordinate system $A$ as

$$\mathbf{p}_A = \mathbf{M}^{-1}(\mathbf{p}_B - \mathbf{t}). \tag{2.2}$$

In Section 2.6, we will see how the matrix $\mathbf{M}$ and the vector $\mathbf{t}$ can be combined into a single $4 \times 4$ transformation matrix. Until then, we will assume that all coordinate systems have the same origin so that we can ignore the translation vector $\mathbf{t}$ and just concentrate on how the $3 \times 3$ matrix $\mathbf{M}$ modifies the components of a vector.

In general, the linear transformation $\mathbf{v}_B = \mathbf{M}\mathbf{v}_A$ replaces the axes in coordinate system $A$ with the columns of the matrix $\mathbf{M}$ in coordinate system $B$. The vector $\mathbf{v}_B$ is then a combination of the new axes in the same way that $\mathbf{v}_A$ was a combination of the old axes. Suppose that the columns of $\mathbf{M}$ are given by $\mathbf{a}$, $\mathbf{b}$, and $\mathbf{c}$ so that we can write $\mathbf{M} = \begin{bmatrix} \mathbf{a} & \mathbf{b} & \mathbf{c} \end{bmatrix}$. Then

$$\mathbf{M}\begin{bmatrix} 1 \\ 0 \\ 0 \end{bmatrix} = \mathbf{a}, \quad \mathbf{M}\begin{bmatrix} 0 \\ 1 \\ 0 \end{bmatrix} = \mathbf{b}, \quad \mathbf{M}\begin{bmatrix} 0 \\ 0 \\ 1 \end{bmatrix} = \mathbf{c}, \tag{2.3}$$

and for an arbitrary vector $\mathbf{v}$,

$$\mathbf{M}\mathbf{v} = v_x\mathbf{a} + v_y\mathbf{b} + v_z\mathbf{c}. \tag{2.4}$$

### 2.1.2 Orthogonal Transforms

There is no requirement that the vectors **a**, **b**, and **c** in Equation (2.4) be perpendicular to each other or that they have unit length. For the matrix **M** to be invertible, it's only necessary that its columns form a linearly independent set. However, many transformation matrices appearing in game engines do have mutually perpendicular unit-length columns, and such matrices are called *orthogonal* matrices. Orthogonal matrices have a number of interesting properties, the first of which is that the inverse of an orthogonal matrix is equal its transpose. Assuming that **a**, **b**, and **c** all have unit length and are mutually perpendicular, we can calculate the product $\mathbf{M}^{\mathrm{T}}\mathbf{M}$ as

$$\mathbf{M}^{\mathrm{T}}\mathbf{M} = \begin{bmatrix} \leftarrow & \mathbf{a}^{\mathrm{T}} & \rightarrow \\ \leftarrow & \mathbf{b}^{\mathrm{T}} & \rightarrow \\ \leftarrow & \mathbf{c}^{\mathrm{T}} & \rightarrow \end{bmatrix} \begin{bmatrix} \uparrow & \uparrow & \uparrow \\ \mathbf{a} & \mathbf{b} & \mathbf{c} \\ \downarrow & \downarrow & \downarrow \end{bmatrix} = \begin{bmatrix} a^2 & \mathbf{a}\cdot\mathbf{b} & \mathbf{a}\cdot\mathbf{c} \\ \mathbf{b}\cdot\mathbf{a} & b^2 & \mathbf{b}\cdot\mathbf{c} \\ \mathbf{c}\cdot\mathbf{a} & \mathbf{c}\cdot\mathbf{b} & c^2 \end{bmatrix}. \tag{2.5}$$

Since **a**, **b**, and **c** each have unit length, the entries along the main diagonal are all ones. Since **a**, **b**, and **c** are mutually perpendicular, all of the other entries are zero. We conclude that it must be true that $\mathbf{M}^{-1} = \mathbf{M}^{\mathrm{T}}$. Equation (2.5) also demonstrates that the reverse implication is true. If we assume that $\mathbf{M}^{-1} = \mathbf{M}^{\mathrm{T}}$, then the right side of the equation must be the identity matrix, so **a**, **b**, and **c** must be mutually perpendicular and have unit length. Additionally, if **M** is orthogonal, then $\mathbf{M}^{\mathrm{T}}$ must also be orthogonal because its inverse is equal to its transpose, which is just **M**. This implies that the columns of $\mathbf{M}^{\mathrm{T}}$ form a set of mutually perpendicular unit-length vectors, and that is equivalent to making the same statement about the rows of **M**. Thus, the following list of statements all have the same meaning, and each one implies all of the others.

- **M** is an orthogonal matrix.
- The inverse of **M** is equal to $\mathbf{M}^{\mathrm{T}}$.
- The columns of **M** are mutually perpendicular unit-length vectors.
- The rows of **M** are mutually perpendicular unit-length vectors.

When an object is transformed by an orthogonal matrix, it may be reoriented in space and/or reflected in a mirror, but it still has the exact same shape that it had before the transformation. Orthogonal matrices preserve the dot product between any two vectors **a** and **b**, and this is easily proven by considering the dot product of the two vectors after they are transformed by an orthogonal matrix **M** as in

$$(\mathbf{Ma})\cdot(\mathbf{Mb}) = (\mathbf{Ma})^{\mathrm{T}}(\mathbf{Mb}) = \mathbf{a}^{\mathrm{T}}\mathbf{M}^{\mathrm{T}}\mathbf{Mb} = \mathbf{a}^{\mathrm{T}}\mathbf{b} = \mathbf{a}\cdot\mathbf{b}. \tag{2.6}$$

Since $\mathbf{a} \cdot \mathbf{a}$ gives the squared magnitude of $\mathbf{a}$, this also proves that the length of a vector is not changed by an orthogonal matrix. It must therefore be true that the angle $\theta$ between $\mathbf{a}$ and $\mathbf{b}$ is preserved as well because the dot product would otherwise change due to its relationship to the cosine of $\theta$.

The transform performed by an orthogonal matrix is always a rotation, a reflection, or a combination of the two. The determinant of an orthogonal matrix is always $\pm 1$, positive for a pure rotation, and negative for a transform that includes a reflection. Transforms that include a reflection reverse the handedness of the coordinate system, changing a right-handed coordinate system into a left-handed one, and vice versa.

## 2.1.3 Transform Composition

It is often the case that multiple transforms need to be applied to an object to either change its shape in several steps or to express its position and orientation in a common coordinate system that might be several levels away in a hierarchical model. Whenever a vector $\mathbf{v}$ needs to be transformed first by a matrix $\mathbf{M}_1$ and then by another matrix $\mathbf{M}_2$, we calculate the result $\mathbf{v}'$ as

$$\mathbf{v}' = \mathbf{M}_2 \left( \mathbf{M}_1 \mathbf{v} \right). \tag{2.7}$$

Since matrix multiplication is associative, we can multiply the two transformation matrices together first to create a single combined matrix $\mathbf{N} = \mathbf{M}_2 \mathbf{M}_1$, and then we can calculate $\mathbf{v}'$ with the simpler equation $\mathbf{v}' = \mathbf{N}\mathbf{v}$. This can be continued indefinitely with $n$ transformation matrices, and their product $\mathbf{M}_n \mathbf{M}_{n-1} \cdots \mathbf{M}_2 \mathbf{M}_1$ can be precomputed and stored as a single transform.

There are times when a transform is expressed in one coordinate system but needs to be applied to an object using a different coordinate system. For example, it's convenient to express a scale transform in a coordinate system where the scale factors apply in directions parallel to the coordinate axes. If a particular transform $\mathbf{A}$ can be applied in coordinate system $A$, but we have an object using coordinate system $B$, then the equivalent transform $\mathbf{B}$ in coordinate system $B$ is given by

$$\boxed{\mathbf{B} = \mathbf{M}\mathbf{A}\mathbf{M}^{-1},} \tag{2.8}$$

where the matrix $\mathbf{M}$ transforms vectors from coordinate system $A$ to coordinate system $B$. When the transform $\mathbf{B}$ is applied to a vector $\mathbf{v}$ in coordinate system $B$, you can think of it as first transforming $\mathbf{v}$ from coordinate system $B$ to coordinate system $A$ with the matrix $\mathbf{M}^{-1}$, applying the transform $\mathbf{A}$ in that setting, and then transforming back into coordinate system $B$ with the matrix $\mathbf{M}$. Equation (2.8) is, in fact, how transforms themselves are transformed from one coordinate system to another.

## 2.2 Rotations

A rotation is one of the most common types of transform used by game engines. Whenever an object spins, a hinged door is opened, an elbow or knee joint is animated, or a player simply turns his character, a rotation transform is being applied, and the list of examples could be continued indefinitely. Rotations often occur in a local coordinate system in which the axis of rotation is aligned to one of the coordinate axes, but they can also be applied about an arbitrary axis specified by a direction vector. We derive matrix representations of each kind of rotation in this section.

When a vector $\mathbf{v}$ is rotated about an axis, we can consider what happens to the components of $\mathbf{v}$ that are parallel and perpendicular to the axis. The component that is parallel to the axis is unaffected while the component that is perpendicular to the axis changes. In general, a rotation always occurs among the directions parallel to an oriented plane in space, leaving every direction orthogonal to the plane alone. In three dimensions, there is only one remaining direction, and that is what we call the axis of the rotation, but this concept does not extend to other numbers of dimensions. Although we use the term axis in this chapter, it's best to start thinking of rotations as always occurring in a 2D subspace because it will give you an early start on the ways of thinking required by Chapter 4.

To follow common convention, we consider a rotation through a positive angle about an axis to be one that is a counterclockwise rotation when the axis points toward the viewer. This is a property of right-handed coordinate systems. When the right thumb points in the direction of the axis of rotation, the fingers of the right hand curl in the direction of a rotation through a positive angle. Rotations through a negative angle go in the opposite direction.

### 2.2.1 Rotation About a Coordinate Axis

A rotation about the $x$, $y$, or $z$ axis occurs in the plane formed by the other two axes. That is, a rotation about the $x$ axis occurs in the $y$-$z$ plane, a rotation about the $y$ axis occurs in the $x$-$z$ plane, and a rotation about the $z$ axis occurs in the $x$-$y$ plane. The derivation of a transformation matrix is similar in all three cases, so we focus our discussion on a rotation about the $z$ axis, where everything of interest happens in the $x$-$y$ plane, and then show how the other two cases are related.

Suppose that we would like to rotate the vector **v** through an angle $\theta$ about the $z$ axis. Using the unit vectors **i**, **j**, and **k** parallel to the coordinate axes, we can write **v** as

$$\mathbf{v} = v_x\mathbf{i} + v_y\mathbf{j} + v_z\mathbf{k}. \tag{2.9}$$

Since **k** is parallel to the $z$ axis, the component $v_z$ does not change during the rotation. It is only the component $v_x\mathbf{i} + v_y\mathbf{j}$ that changes, and it does so in such a way that the vectors **i** and **j** are both rotated through the angle $\theta$. As shown in Figure 2.1, when the vector $v_x\mathbf{i}$ is rotated through the angle $\theta$, the result is a new vector having the same length $v_x$ that can be written as a sum of vectors parallel to **i** and **j**, forming a right triangle. Basic trigonometry tells us that their lengths are $v_x\cos\theta$ and $v_x\sin\theta$, respectively, so we can write the rotated vector as

$$v_x\cos\theta\,\mathbf{i} + v_x\sin\theta\,\mathbf{j}. \tag{2.10}$$

This represents the rotation only of the vector $v_x\mathbf{i}$. We must also account for the vector $v_y\mathbf{j}$, and the result of its rotation is similar in a setting that's rotated 90 degrees counterclockwise, so it is written in terms of **j** and $-\mathbf{i}$ instead of **i** and **j**. The rotation of $v_y\mathbf{j}$ through the angle $\theta$ is

$$v_y\cos\theta\,\mathbf{j} - v_y\sin\theta\,\mathbf{i}. \tag{2.11}$$

When we combine Equations (2.10) and (2.11) and include the unaltered component $v_z\mathbf{k}$, we can express the complete formula for the rotated vector $\mathbf{v}'$ as

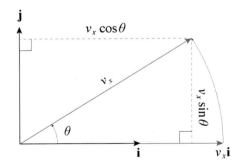

**Figure 2.1.** The vector $v_x\mathbf{i}$ is rotated through an angle $\theta$ about the $z$ axis. The rotated vector still has length $v_x$, and it can be decomposed into components parallel to the vectors **i** and **j** with lengths $v_x\cos\theta$ and $v_x\sin\theta$, respectively.

$$\mathbf{v}' = \left( v_x \cos\theta - v_y \sin\theta \right) \mathbf{i} + \left( v_x \sin\theta + v_y \cos\theta \right) \mathbf{j} + v_z \mathbf{k}. \qquad (2.12)$$

This can be written as the matrix-vector product

$$\begin{bmatrix} v_x' \\ v_y' \\ v_z' \end{bmatrix} = \begin{bmatrix} \cos\theta & -\sin\theta & 0 \\ \sin\theta & \cos\theta & 0 \\ 0 & 0 & 1 \end{bmatrix} \begin{bmatrix} v_x \\ v_y \\ v_z \end{bmatrix}. \qquad (2.13)$$

The $3 \times 3$ matrix appearing in this equation is the general transformation matrix for a rotation through the angle $\theta$ about the $z$ axis.

The same derivation can be applied to rotations about the $x$ and $y$ axes to produce similar transformation matrices. The transforms $\mathbf{M}_{\text{rot }x}(\theta)$, $\mathbf{M}_{\text{rot }y}(\theta)$, and $\mathbf{M}_{\text{rot }z}(\theta)$ that rotate a vector through an angle $\theta$ about the $x$, $y$, and $z$ axes are given by the matrices

$$\mathbf{M}_{\text{rot }x}(\theta) = \begin{bmatrix} 1 & 0 & 0 \\ 0 & \cos\theta & -\sin\theta \\ 0 & \sin\theta & \cos\theta \end{bmatrix}, \qquad (2.14)$$

$$\mathbf{M}_{\text{rot }y}(\theta) = \begin{bmatrix} \cos\theta & 0 & \sin\theta \\ 0 & 1 & 0 \\ -\sin\theta & 0 & \cos\theta \end{bmatrix}, \qquad (2.15)$$

$$\mathbf{M}_{\text{rot }z}(\theta) = \begin{bmatrix} \cos\theta & -\sin\theta & 0 \\ \sin\theta & \cos\theta & 0 \\ 0 & 0 & 1 \end{bmatrix}. \qquad (2.16)$$

Notice that the entry containing the negated sine function appears in the lower-left corner for the rotation about the $y$ axis, but it is in the upper-right position for the rotations about the $x$ and $z$ axes. The negated sine function always appears one row below and one column to the left, with wraparound, of the entry containing the one in the matrix. Functions that construct these transformation matrices are shown in Listing 2.1, and each one returns a `Matrix3D` data structure that can be multiplied by a vector to perform the rotation.

**Listing 2.1.** These functions create $3 \times 3$ matrices that represent rotations through the angle t about the $x$, $y$, and $z$ axes and return them in `Matrix3D` data structures.

```
Matrix3D MakeRotationX(float t)
{
    float c = cos(t);
    float s = sin(t);

    return (Matrix3D(1.0F, 0.0F, 0.0F,
                     0.0F, c,    -s,
                     0.0F, s,     c ));
}


Matrix3D MakeRotationY(float t)
{
    float c = cos(t);
    float s = sin(t);

    return (Matrix3D( c,   0.0F, s,
                     0.0F, 1.0F, 0.0F,
                     -s,   0.0F, c ));
}

Matrix3D MakeRotationZ(float t)
{
    float c = cos(t);
    float s = sin(t);

    return (Matrix3D( c,   -s,   0.0F,
                      s,    c,   0.0F,
                     0.0F, 0.0F, 1.0F));
}
```

## 2.2.2 Rotation About an Arbitrary Axis

Suppose that we wanted to construct a transform that rotates a vector **v** about an arbitrary axis represented by the unit vector **a**. When the vector **v** is rotated into its new orientation **v**′, the component of **v** parallel to the axis **a** remains the same, and only the component of **v** perpendicular to the axis **a** actually gets modified. Thus, it makes sense for us to consider the separate components of **v** with respect to the axis **a**.

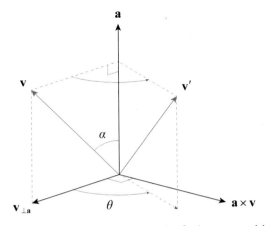

**Figure 2.2.** A vector **v** is rotated through an angle $\theta$ about an arbitrary axis **a**. This is achieved by decomposing **v** into components that are parallel and perpendicular to **a** and rotating only the perpendicular component $\mathbf{v}_{\perp\mathbf{a}}$.

Let $\alpha$ be the angle between the vectors **a** and **v** as shown in Figure 2.2. The vector $\mathbf{v}_{\perp\mathbf{a}}$ (the rejection of **v** from **a**) is perpendicular to **a**, and it has a length equal to $\|\mathbf{v}\|\sin\alpha$ because it forms the side opposite the angle $\alpha$ in the right triangle shown in the figure. It's this component that we need to rotate in the plane perpendicular to the axis **a**. As before, we can perform this rotation by expressing the result as a linear combination of the original vector and another vector in the plane that is the 90-degree counterclockwise rotation of the original vector. Fortunately, this second vector is easily obtained as $\mathbf{a}\times\mathbf{v}$, and it just happens to have the same length, $\|\mathbf{v}\|\sin\alpha$, as $\mathbf{v}_{\perp\mathbf{a}}$ does. This means that we can express the rotated vector $\mathbf{v}'$ as

$$\mathbf{v}' = \mathbf{v}_{\|\mathbf{a}} + \mathbf{v}_{\perp\mathbf{a}}\cos\theta + (\mathbf{a}\times\mathbf{v})\sin\theta, \qquad (2.17)$$

where $\theta$ is the angle of rotation about the axis **a**. The component $\mathbf{v}_{\|\mathbf{a}}$ parallel to the axis of rotation does not change, and the component $\mathbf{v}_{\perp\mathbf{a}}$ is replaced by a linear combination of $\mathbf{v}_{\perp\mathbf{a}}$ and $\mathbf{a}\times\mathbf{v}$.

When we expand the definitions of the projection and rejection, Equation (2.17) takes the form

$$\mathbf{v}' = (\mathbf{v}\cdot\mathbf{a})\mathbf{a} + [\mathbf{v} - (\mathbf{v}\cdot\mathbf{a})\mathbf{a}]\cos\theta + (\mathbf{a}\times\mathbf{v})\sin\theta, \qquad (2.18)$$

where we have omitted the divisions by $a^2$ because **a** is a unit vector. This can be simplified a little bit to obtain

$$\mathbf{v}' = \mathbf{v}\cos\theta + (\mathbf{v}\cdot\mathbf{a})\mathbf{a}(1-\cos\theta) + (\mathbf{a}\times\mathbf{v})\sin\theta. \qquad (2.19)$$

The projection $(\mathbf{v}\cdot\mathbf{a})\mathbf{a}$ and the cross product $\mathbf{a}\times\mathbf{v}$ can each be expressed as a $3\times 3$ matrix multiplying the vector $\mathbf{v}$. Making these replacements gives us

$$\mathbf{v}' = \begin{bmatrix} 1 & 0 & 0 \\ 0 & 1 & 0 \\ 0 & 0 & 1 \end{bmatrix} \mathbf{v}\cos\theta + \begin{bmatrix} a_x^2 & a_x a_y & a_x a_z \\ a_x a_y & a_y^2 & a_y a_z \\ a_x a_z & a_y a_z & a_z^2 \end{bmatrix} \mathbf{v}(1-\cos\theta)$$

$$+ \begin{bmatrix} 0 & -a_z & a_y \\ a_z & 0 & -a_x \\ -a_y & a_x & 0 \end{bmatrix} \mathbf{v}\sin\theta, \qquad (2.20)$$

where we have also inserted an identity matrix in front of the first term so that all three terms contain a $3\times 3$ matrix. When we combine everything into a single matrix, we get the formula

$$\mathbf{M}_{\mathrm{rot}}(\theta,\mathbf{a}) = \begin{bmatrix} c+(1-c)a_x^2 & (1-c)a_x a_y - sa_z & (1-c)a_x a_z + sa_y \\ (1-c)a_x a_y + sa_z & c+(1-c)a_y^2 & (1-c)a_y a_z - sa_x \\ (1-c)a_x a_z - sa_y & (1-c)a_y a_z + sa_x & c+(1-c)a_z^2 \end{bmatrix} \qquad (2.21)$$

for the transform $\mathbf{M}_{\mathrm{rot}}(\theta,\mathbf{a})$ that rotates a vector through an angle $\theta$ about the axis $\mathbf{a}$, where we have used the abbreviations $c=\cos\theta$ and $s=\sin\theta$. A function that constructs this transformation matrix and returns a `Matrix3D` data structure is shown in Listing 2.2.

**Listing 2.2.** This code creates a $3\times 3$ matrix that represents a rotation through the angle `t` about an arbitrary axis `a` and returns it in a `Matrix3D` data structure. The vector `a` is assumed to have unit length.

```
Matrix3D MakeRotation(float t, const Vector3D& a)
{
    float c = cos(t);
    float s = sin(t);
    float d = 1.0F - c;

    float x = a.x * d;
    float y = a.y * d;
```

```
    float z = a.z * d;
    float axay = x * a.y;
    float axaz = x * a.z;
    float ayaz = y * a.z;

    return (Matrix3D(c + x * a.x, axay - s * a.z, axaz + s * a.y,
                     axay + s * a.z, c + y * a.y, ayaz - s * a.x,
                     axaz - s * a.y, ayaz + s * a.x, c + z * a.z));
}
```

## 2.3 Reflections

Reflection through a plane is a common transform in game engines because it applies to things like mirrors and water surfaces. For now, we consider only planes containing the origin that are perpendicular to a given vector. In Section 3.4, we will extend the transform derived here to handle planes at arbitrary locations.

As shown in Figure 2.3, a vector $\mathbf{v}$ can be reflected through a plane perpendicular to vector $\mathbf{a}$ by decomposing $\mathbf{v}$ into its components perpendicular to $\mathbf{a}$ and parallel to $\mathbf{a}$ and then simply negating the parallel component. The original vector can be written as $\mathbf{v} = \mathbf{v}_{\perp\mathbf{a}} + \mathbf{v}_{\parallel\mathbf{a}}$, and the reflected vector $\mathbf{v}'$ is then given by

$$\mathbf{v}' = \mathbf{v}_{\perp\mathbf{a}} - \mathbf{v}_{\parallel\mathbf{a}}. \tag{2.22}$$

When we replace each component by its matrix representation, we get

$$\mathbf{v}' = \begin{bmatrix} 1-a_x^2 & -a_x a_y & -a_x a_z \\ -a_x a_y & 1-a_y^2 & -a_y a_z \\ -a_x a_z & -a_y a_z & 1-a_z^2 \end{bmatrix} \mathbf{v} - \begin{bmatrix} a_x^2 & a_x a_y & a_x a_z \\ a_x a_y & a_y^2 & a_y a_z \\ a_x a_z & a_y a_z & a_z^2 \end{bmatrix} \mathbf{v}, \tag{2.23}$$

where we have assumed that $\mathbf{a}$ has unit length. By combining these terms into a single matrix, we arrive at the formula

$$\mathbf{M}_{\text{reflect}}(\mathbf{a}) = \begin{bmatrix} 1-2a_x^2 & -2a_x a_y & -2a_x a_z \\ -2a_x a_y & 1-2a_y^2 & -2a_y a_z \\ -2a_x a_z & -2a_y a_z & 1-2a_z^2 \end{bmatrix} \tag{2.24}$$

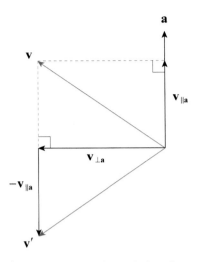

**Figure 2.3.** The reflection $\mathbf{v}'$ of the vector $\mathbf{v}$ through the plane perpendicular to the vector $\mathbf{a}$ is obtained by decomposing $\mathbf{v}$ into the components $\mathbf{v}_{\|\mathbf{a}}$ and $\mathbf{v}_{\perp\mathbf{a}}$ and negating the parallel component so that $\mathbf{v}' = \mathbf{v}_{\perp\mathbf{a}} - \mathbf{v}_{\|\mathbf{a}}$.

for the transform $\mathbf{M}_{\text{reflect}}(\mathbf{a})$ that reflects a vector through the plane perpendicular to the unit vector $\mathbf{a}$. A function that constructs this transformation matrix and returns a `Matrix3D` data structure is shown in Listing 2.3.

The transform $\mathbf{M}_{\text{reflect}}(\mathbf{a})$ always has a determinant of $-1$. This can be understood intuitively if you consider the fact that there exists some coordinate system in which the unit vector $\mathbf{a}$ is aligned to the $x$ axis. In this case, the transform is simply an identity matrix with the $(0,0)$ entry replaced by $-1$. A concrete proof can be obtained by using the identity $\det(\mathbf{I} + \mathbf{a} \otimes \mathbf{b}) = 1 + \mathbf{a} \cdot \mathbf{b}$ (see Exercise 18 in Chapter 1), with $\mathbf{b} = -2\mathbf{a}$ because $\mathbf{M}_{\text{reflect}}(\mathbf{a}) = \mathbf{I} - 2\mathbf{a} \otimes \mathbf{a}$.

The matrix $\mathbf{M}_{\text{reflect}}(\mathbf{a})$ reflects through a plane by negating the component of a vector parallel to a one-dimensional subspace represented by the direction $\mathbf{a}$. We can also construct a transform that instead negates the perpendicular component and leaves the parallel component unchanged as shown in Figure 2.4. Constructing this transform is a simple matter of negating Equation (2.22) to get

$$\mathbf{v}' = \mathbf{v}_{\|\mathbf{a}} - \mathbf{v}_{\perp\mathbf{a}}. \tag{2.25}$$

Since the component $\mathbf{v}_{\perp\mathbf{a}}$ represents everything that is perpendicular to $\mathbf{a}$, we are actually negating a two-dimensional subspace by performing two reflections aligned to vectors that are both orthogonal to $\mathbf{a}$ and each other. The composition

**Listing 2.3.** This code creates a $3 \times 3$ matrix that represents a reflection through the plane perpendicular to an arbitrary vector `a` and returns it in a `Matrix3D` data structure. The vector `a` is assumed to have unit length.

```
Matrix3D MakeReflection(const Vector3D& a)
{
    float x = a.x * -2.0F;
    float y = a.y * -2.0F;
    float z = a.z * -2.0F;
    float axay = x * a.y;
    float axaz = x * a.z;
    float ayaz = y * a.z;

    return (Matrix3D(x * a.x + 1.0F, axay, axaz,
                     axay, y * a.y + 1.0F, ayaz,
                     axaz, ayaz, z * a.z + 1.0F));
}
```

of two reflections is a rotation, so Equation (2.25) really represents a transform belonging to a larger set of transforms called involutions. An *involution* is a matrix that, when multiplied by itself, produces the identity matrix. Examples include reflections and rotations by 180 degrees. Calling it $\mathbf{M}_{invol}(\mathbf{a})$, the matrix form of Equation (2.25) is given by

$$\mathbf{M}_{invol}(\mathbf{a}) = \begin{bmatrix} 2a_x^2 - 1 & 2a_x a_y & 2a_x a_z \\ 2a_x a_y & 2a_y^2 - 1 & 2a_y a_z \\ 2a_x a_z & 2a_y a_z & 2a_z^2 - 1 \end{bmatrix}, \qquad (2.26)$$

which is, of course, just the negation of the matrix $\mathbf{M}_{reflect}(\mathbf{a})$ given by Equation (2.24). A function that constructs this transformation matrix and returns a `Matrix3D` data structure is shown in Listing 2.4.

Generalizing to $n$ dimensions, the matrix $\mathbf{M}_{invol}(\mathbf{a})$ represents a composition of $n-1$ reflections through a set of $n-1$ orthogonal planes containing the vector $\mathbf{a}$, whereas the matrix $\mathbf{M}_{reflect}(\mathbf{a})$ represents a single reflection through one plane perpendicular to the vector $\mathbf{a}$. Since $\mathbf{M}_{invol} = -\mathbf{M}_{reflect}$, the determinant can be calculated as

$$\det(\mathbf{M}_{invol}) = (-1)^n \det(\mathbf{M}_{reflect}). \qquad (2.27)$$

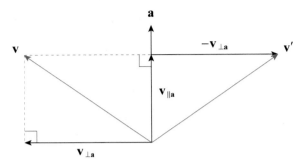

**Figure 2.4.** The involution $\mathbf{v}'$ of the vector $\mathbf{v}$ through the vector $\mathbf{a}$ is obtained by decomposing $\mathbf{v}$ into the components $\mathbf{v}_{\parallel \mathbf{a}}$ and $\mathbf{v}_{\perp \mathbf{a}}$ and negating the perpendicular component so that $\mathbf{v}' = \mathbf{v}_{\parallel \mathbf{a}} - \mathbf{v}_{\perp \mathbf{a}}$.

The determinant of $\mathbf{M}_{\text{reflect}}$ is always $-1$, so the determinant of $\mathbf{M}_{\text{invol}}$ is $-1$ when $n$ is even and $+1$ when $n$ is odd. It's straightforward to verify that in the three-dimensional case, the matrix in Equation (2.26) has a determinant of $+1$.

The involution matrix is not typically used by game engines to transform among coordinate systems or to modify the shape of an object. We introduce it here for completeness and because familiarity with it will be useful in the discussion of rotors in Section 4.4.

**Listing 2.4.** This code creates a $3 \times 3$ matrix that represents an involution through an arbitrary vector a and returns it in a `Matrix3D` data structure. The vector a is assumed to have unit length.

```
Matrix3D MakeInvolution(const Vector3D& a)
{
    float x = a.x * 2.0F;
    float y = a.y * 2.0F;
    float z = a.z * 2.0F;
    float axay = x * a.y;
    float axaz = x * a.z;
    float ayaz = y * a.z;

    return (Matrix3D(x * a.x - 1.0F, axay, axaz,
                     axay, y * a.y - 1.0F, ayaz,
                     axaz, ayaz, z * a.z - 1.0F));
}
```

## 2.4 Scales

A *scale* transform is used to enlarge or shrink an object to a new overall size. If the scale changes the size equally in every direction, then it is called a *uniform scale*. If the scale expands or compresses an object more in some directions than it does in other directions, then it is called a *nonuniform scale*.

A uniform scale simply multiplies all vectors $\mathbf{v}$ by a scale factor $s$ so that the transformed vector $\mathbf{v}'$ is given by

$$\mathbf{v}' = s\mathbf{v} = \begin{bmatrix} s & 0 & 0 \\ 0 & s & 0 \\ 0 & 0 & s \end{bmatrix} \mathbf{v}. \tag{2.28}$$

A nonuniform scale aligned to the coordinate axes is similar, but the scale factors appearing on the main diagonal of the transformation matrix are not all equal to the same value. An example of a nonuniform scale is shown in Figure 2.5. The transform that scales by different amounts along the $x$, $y$, and $z$ axes is given by

$$\mathbf{M}_{\text{scale}}\left(s_x, s_y, s_z\right) = \begin{bmatrix} s_x & 0 & 0 \\ 0 & s_y & 0 \\ 0 & 0 & s_z \end{bmatrix}. \tag{2.29}$$

A function that returns this matrix in a `Matrix3D` data structure is implemented in Listing 2.5.

We can scale an object along a single arbitrary direction $\mathbf{a}$ while preserving the object's size in every direction orthogonal to $\mathbf{a}$ by decomposing a vector $\mathbf{v}$ into its components $\mathbf{v}_{\parallel \mathbf{a}}$ and $\mathbf{v}_{\perp \mathbf{a}}$ and scaling only the parallel component, as shown in Figure 2.6. The scaled vector $\mathbf{v}'$ is then given by

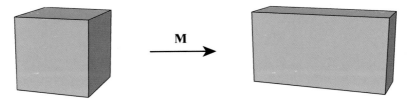

**Figure 2.5.** In this example of a nonuniform scale by a matrix $\mathbf{M}$, a cube has been stretched in one direction and compressed in another.

$$\mathbf{v}' = s\mathbf{v}_{\parallel \mathbf{a}} + \mathbf{v}_{\perp \mathbf{a}} \tag{2.30}$$

for a scale factor $s$. When we combine the matrix representations of the components, we obtain

$$\mathbf{M}_{\text{scale}}(s, \mathbf{a}) = \begin{bmatrix} (s-1)a_x^2 + 1 & (s-1)a_x a_y & (s-1)a_x a_z \\ (s-1)a_x a_y & (s-1)a_y^2 + 1 & (s-1)a_y a_z \\ (s-1)a_x a_z & (s-1)a_y a_z & (s-1)a_z^2 + 1 \end{bmatrix} \tag{2.31}$$

as the transform $\mathbf{M}_{\text{scale}}(s, \mathbf{a})$ that scales by a factor of $s$ along the direction $\mathbf{a}$. A function that calculates this transform and returns a `Matrix3D` data structure is implemented in Listing 2.6.

**Listing 2.5.** This code creates a $3 \times 3$ matrix that represents a scale by factors of `sx`, `sy`, and `sz` along the $x$, $y$, and $z$ axes and returns it in a `Matrix3D` data structure.

```
Matrix3D MakeScale(float sx, float sy, float sz)
{
    return (Matrix3D(sx, 0.0F, 0.0F, 0.0F, sy, 0.0F, 0.0F, 0.0F, sz));
}
```

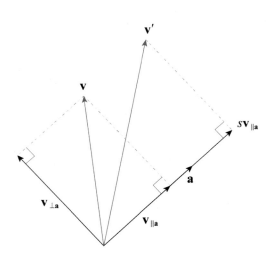

**Figure 2.6.** The vector $\mathbf{v}$ is scaled by a factor of $s$ in the direction $\mathbf{a}$ to produce a new vector $\mathbf{v}'$ by decomposing $\mathbf{v}$ into the components $\mathbf{v}_{\parallel \mathbf{a}}$ and $\mathbf{v}_{\perp \mathbf{a}}$ and scaling only the parallel component so that $\mathbf{v}' = s\mathbf{v}_{\parallel \mathbf{a}} + \mathbf{v}_{\perp \mathbf{a}}$.

**Listing 2.6.** This code creates a $3 \times 3$ matrix that represents a scale by a factor of s along an arbitrary direction a and returns it in a `Matrix3D` data structure. The vector a is assumed to have unit length.

```
Matrix3D MakeScale(float s, const Vector3D& a)
{
    s -= 1.0F;
    float x = a.x * s;
    float y = a.y * s;
    float z = a.z * s;
    float axay = x * a.y;
    float axaz = x * a.z;
    float ayaz = y * a.z;

    return (Matrix3D(x * a.x + 1.0F, axay, axaz,
                     axay, y * a.y + 1.0F, ayaz,
                     axaz, ayaz, z * a.z + 1.0F));
}
```

## 2.5 Skews

A *skew* transform is used to shear an object along one direction by an angle made with a perpendicular direction. An example of a skew along the $x$ axis by an angle $\theta$ made with the $y$ axis is shown in Figure 2.7.

Let the unit vector **a** represent the direction in which we want to skew, and let the unit vector **b** represent the direction perpendicular to **a** along which vectors are measured to determine how far to skew. As shown in Figure 2.8, a vector **v** is skewed by adding a vector parallel to **a** of length $(\mathbf{b} \cdot \mathbf{v}) \tan \theta$ to it, where the factor $\mathbf{b} \cdot \mathbf{v}$ represents the length of the projection of **v** onto **b**. The skewed vector **v**′ is given by

$$\mathbf{v}' = \mathbf{v} + \mathbf{a}(\mathbf{b} \cdot \mathbf{v}) \tan \theta, \tag{2.32}$$

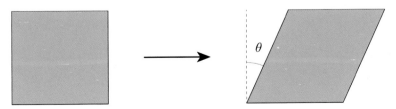

**Figure 2.7.** This box is skewed by an angle $\theta$ in the direction to the right.

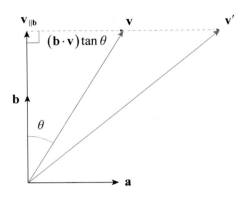

**Figure 2.8.** The vector $\mathbf{v}$ is skewed by an angle $\theta$ along the direction $\mathbf{a}$ based on the projected length of $\mathbf{v}$ along the direction $\mathbf{b}$ orthogonal to $\mathbf{a}$. Assuming that $\mathbf{b}$ has unit length, the size of the skew in the direction $\mathbf{a}$ is given by $(\mathbf{b} \cdot \mathbf{v}) \tan \theta$.

where the factor $\tan \theta$ is the ratio of the skew distance along $\mathbf{a}$ to the projected length of $\mathbf{v}$ along $\mathbf{b}$, which can be interpreted as the amount by which $\mathbf{b} \cdot \mathbf{v}$ needs to be multiplied to obtain a skew by the angle $\theta$. In the figure, we are actually projecting $\mathbf{v}$ onto the plane spanned by $\mathbf{a}$ and $\mathbf{b}$ first, but this has no effect on the magnitude of the projection onto $\mathbf{b}$ (see Exercise 7 in Chapter 1).

Equation (2.32) can be written as the transform $\mathbf{v}' = \mathbf{M}\mathbf{v}$ using the matrix

$$\mathbf{M}_{\text{skew}}(\theta, \mathbf{a}, \mathbf{b}) = \begin{bmatrix} a_x b_x \tan \theta + 1 & a_x b_y \tan \theta & a_x b_z \tan \theta \\ a_y b_x \tan \theta & a_y b_y \tan \theta + 1 & a_y b_z \tan \theta \\ a_z b_x \tan \theta & a_z b_y \tan \theta & a_z b_z \tan \theta + 1 \end{bmatrix}. \quad (2.33)$$

This is the transform that skews by the angle $\theta$ in the direction $\mathbf{a}$ based on the length of the projection onto $\mathbf{b}$. A function that calculates this transform and returns a `Matrix3D` data structure is implemented in Listing 2.7. When $\mathbf{a}$ and $\mathbf{b}$ are aligned to the coordinate axes, this matrix becomes considerably simpler. For example, for $\mathbf{a} = (1, 0, 0)$ and $\mathbf{b} = (0, 1, 0)$, the transform is

$$\mathbf{M}_{\text{skew}}(\theta, \mathbf{i}, \mathbf{j}) = \begin{bmatrix} 1 & \tan \theta & 0 \\ 0 & 1 & 0 \\ 0 & 0 & 1 \end{bmatrix}. \quad (2.34)$$

An interesting property of skews is that they preserve volumes. That is, after an object is modified by a skew transform, it has the same volume as it did before

**Listing 2.7.** This function creates a $3 \times 3$ matrix that represents a skew by the angle `t` along the direction `a` based on the projected length along the direction `b` and returns it in a `Matrix3D` data structure. The vectors `a` and `b` are assumed to be orthogonal and to have unit length.

```
Matrix3D MakeSkew(float t, const Vector3D& a, const Vector3D& b)
{
    t = tan(t);
    float x = a.x * t;
    float y = a.y * t;
    float z = a.z * t;

    return (Matrix3D(x * b.x + 1.0F, x * b.y, x * b.z,
                     y * b.x, y * b.y + 1.0F, y * b.z,
                     z * b.x, z * b.y, z * b.z + 1.0F));
}
```

the transform was applied. One way to think about this is to imagine that an object is composed of a large number of thin slices parallel to the plane spanned by the vectors $\mathbf{a}$ and $\mathbf{a} \times \mathbf{b}$. The skew transform causes all of the slices to slide in the direction of $\mathbf{a}$, but the sum of the volumes of the slices does not change. Taking this approximation to the limit in which the thickness of the slices is infinitesimally small shows that the volume of any arbitrary shape is preserved by a skew.

Algebraically, we can recognize that the transform matrix given by Equation (2.33) is equivalent to

$$\mathbf{M}_{\text{skew}}(\theta, \mathbf{a}, \mathbf{b}) = \mathbf{I} + \tan \theta (\mathbf{a} \otimes \mathbf{b}). \tag{2.35}$$

Thus, the determinant of $\mathbf{M}_{\text{skew}}$ is equal to $1 + \tan \theta (\mathbf{a} \cdot \mathbf{b})$. But $\mathbf{a}$ and $\mathbf{b}$ are perpendicular, so $\mathbf{a} \cdot \mathbf{b} = 0$ and $\det(\mathbf{M}_{\text{skew}}) = 1$. Now suppose that the vectors $\mathbf{u}$, $\mathbf{v}$, and $\mathbf{w}$ form the edges of a parallelepiped. If we construct the matrix whose columns are $\mathbf{u}$, $\mathbf{v}$, and $\mathbf{w}$, then the volume $V$ of the parallelepiped is given by

$$V = \left| \det \left( \begin{bmatrix} \mathbf{u} & \mathbf{v} & \mathbf{w} \end{bmatrix} \right) \right|. \tag{2.36}$$

When the vectors are transformed by $\mathbf{M}_{\text{skew}}$, the new volume $V'$ of the parallelepiped is given by

$$V' = \left| \det \left( \mathbf{M}_{\text{skew}} \begin{bmatrix} \mathbf{u} & \mathbf{v} & \mathbf{w} \end{bmatrix} \right) \right| = \left| \det(\mathbf{M}_{\text{skew}}) \det \left( \begin{bmatrix} \mathbf{u} & \mathbf{v} & \mathbf{w} \end{bmatrix} \right) \right|. \tag{2.37}$$

Since $\det(\mathbf{M}_{\text{skew}}) = 1$, this is the same as the original volume $V$.

## 2.6 Homogeneous Coordinates

Our discussion of vectors in Chapter 1 highlighted the fact that they each represent nothing more than a magnitude and direction. The matrices discussed so far in this chapter have all performed some kind of transformation that is centered at the origin. What we have lacked until now is a concrete way of handling different *locations* in space, whether it be for moving objects to new positions or transforming among coordinate systems that have different origins. Game engines and other types of computer graphics applications integrate location into their transforms by using a four-dimensional projective space called *homogeneous coordinates*. In this section, we will use homogeneous coordinates to add translations to our transform matrices and to make a distinction between direction vectors and position vectors. In Chapter 3, the utility of the 4D projective space will be expanded to include lines and planes, and everything will be naturally unified within a single algebraic system in Chapter 4.

In homogeneous coordinates, we append a fourth number called the $w$ coordinate to every vector so that an arbitrary vector $\mathbf{v}$ is written as $(v_x, v_y, v_z, v_w)$. A point in 3D space is associated with each 4D vector $\mathbf{v}$ by considering a line of infinite extent that passes through the origin in 4D space and is parallel to $\mathbf{v}$. The 3D point corresponding to $\mathbf{v}$ is given by the $x$, $y$, and $z$ coordinates at the unique location where a point on the associated line has a $w$ coordinate equal to one. Because all scalar multiples of $\mathbf{v}$ correspond to offsets from the origin to points on the line parallel to $\mathbf{v}$, we can simply divide all of the components of $\mathbf{v}$ by the coordinate $v_w$ to find the location where the line intersects the subspace for which $w = 1$, as shown in Figure 2.9. Homogeneous coordinates are so named because any nonzero scalar multiple of a 4D vector $\mathbf{v}$ produces the same 3D point after dividing by the $w$ coordinate. This is a projection of an intrinsically one-dimensional object, a line, to an intrinsically zero-dimensional object, a point, accomplished by viewing only one 3D slice of 4D space.

If $v_w = 0$, we clearly cannot divide by the $w$ coordinate of $\mathbf{v}$ to produce a 3D point. A line running in the direction of the vector $(x, y, z, 0)$ is parallel to the subspace where $w = 1$, so there is no intersection at any finite location. Thus, the vector $(x, y, z, 0)$, having a $w$ coordinate of zero, is considered to be the point at infinity in the direction $(x, y, z)$ when projected into 3D space. Such a point is often used in a game engine to describe the location of an object like the sun that, within all practical limits, is infinitely far away. In these cases, we are describing the location of the object not by providing its absolute position, but by providing the direction that points toward the object.

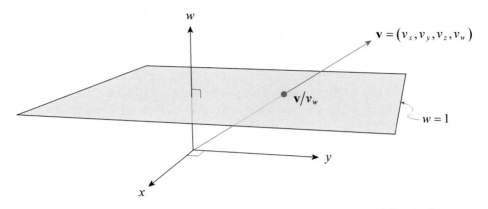

**Figure 2.9.** A homogeneous vector $\mathbf{v}$ is projected into 3D space by dividing by its $w$ coordinate to determine the point where it intersects the subspace for which $w = 1$. The $z$ axis is omitted from the figure due to the difficulties inherent in drawing a four-dimensional diagram on a two-dimensional page, but it should be understood that the subspace for which $w = 1$ is three-dimensional and extends in the $z$ direction as well as the $x$ and $y$ directions.

Generally, 4D homogeneous vectors fall into two classes determined by whether the $w$ coordinate is zero or nonzero. This lets us make an important distinction between 3D vectors that are intended to represent directions and 3D vectors that are intended to represent positions. It is often unnecessary to carry around a fourth coordinate in memory when computing with either type of vector because we can design our data structures in such a way that the value of the $w$ coordinate is implied. We will continue using 3D vectors for both directions and positions, but we will establish a rule for converting each type to a 4D homogeneous vector wherever it's necessary. A 3D vector $\mathbf{v}$ is converted to a 4D vector by appending a $w$ coordinate equal to zero, and a 3D point $\boldsymbol{p}$ is converted to a 4D homogeneous vector by appending a $w$ coordinate equal to one, as in the example

$$\mathbf{v} = (v_x, v_y, v_z, 0)$$
$$\boldsymbol{p} = (p_x, p_y, p_z, 1). \tag{2.38}$$

We have written the position vector $\boldsymbol{p}$ in a bold script style to differentiate it from a direction vector, which we continue to write in a bold plain style. This is not a standard convention, but it provides a helpful clarification when the two types of vectors are mixed in the same context.

One of the main advantages to using homogeneous coordinates is the ability to incorporate translations into our transforms by using $4 \times 4$ matrices. Recall that a general affine transformation from coordinate system $A$ to coordinate system $B$ is given by

$$\mathbf{p}_B = \mathbf{M}\mathbf{p}_A + \mathbf{t}, \tag{2.39}$$

where $\mathbf{M}$ is a $3 \times 3$ transformation matrix and $\mathbf{t}$ is a 3D translation vector. These can be combined into a single $4 \times 4$ transformation matrix $\mathbf{H}$ having the form

$$\mathbf{H} = \begin{bmatrix} \mathbf{M} & \mathbf{t} \\ \mathbf{0} & 1 \end{bmatrix} = \begin{bmatrix} M_{00} & M_{01} & M_{02} & t_x \\ M_{10} & M_{11} & M_{12} & t_y \\ M_{20} & M_{21} & M_{22} & t_z \\ \hline 0 & 0 & 0 & 1 \end{bmatrix}. \tag{2.40}$$

When we multiply the matrix $\mathbf{H}$ by the 3D point $\boldsymbol{p}_A$, where we are using the script style now to indicate that the point has an implicit $w$ coordinate of one, the product is a 3D point $\boldsymbol{p}_B$ that has been transformed in exactly the same way as in Equation (2.39). The result still has a $w$ coordinate of one because the fourth row of the matrix $\mathbf{H}$ is $\begin{bmatrix} 0 & 0 & 0 & 1 \end{bmatrix}$, which preserves the $w$ coordinate of any 4D vector that it multiplies.

When the matrix $\mathbf{H}$ is used to transform a direction vector $\mathbf{v}$ having an implicit $w$ coordinate of zero, the translation in the fourth column of $\mathbf{H}$ has no effect because those entries are always multiplied by the fourth coordinate of $\mathbf{v}$. A direction vector carries no position information and is not altered by a translation of the coordinate system. Only the upper-left $3 \times 3$ portion of $\mathbf{H}$ containing the matrix $\mathbf{M}$ participates in the transformation of a direction vector.

We can accumulate transforms by multiplying as many matrices like $\mathbf{H}$ together as we want, and we will still have a matrix that has a fourth row equal to $\begin{bmatrix} 0 & 0 & 0 & 1 \end{bmatrix}$ (see Exercise 7). Matrices of the form shown in Equation (2.40) belong to a multiplicatively closed subset of the entire set of $4 \times 4$ matrices. It is this type of matrix that is used by game engines to represent a general transform from one coordinate space to another. Each object in the world typically has such a transform associated with it that describes how the object's local coordinate system is embedded within some higher space in a model hierarchy or within the global coordinate system. The first three columns of the $4 \times 4$ transform correspond to the directions in which the object's local $x$, $y$, and $z$ axes point in the global coordinate system, and the fourth column of the $4 \times 4$ transform corresponds to the position of the object's local origin in the global coordinate system.

We would expect that the matrix $\mathbf{H}$ could be inverted as long as the matrix $\mathbf{M}$ occupying the upper-left $3 \times 3$ portion of $\mathbf{H}$ represented some kind of invertible transform because the translation in the fourth column of **H** is something that can always be reversed. If we calculate the determinant of **H** in Equation (2.40) by expanding minors along the fourth row (using Equation (1.76) with $k = 3$), then it becomes apparent that it's the same as the determinant of the matrix **M**. This makes sense because solving Equation (2.39) for $\mathbf{p}_A$ give us

$$\mathbf{p}_A = \mathbf{M}^{-1}(\mathbf{p}_B - \mathbf{t}), \tag{2.41}$$

which requires only that we can invert **M**. Using this equation for transforming in the reverse direction from coordinate system $B$ back into coordinate system $A$, the inverse of **H** should be given by

$$\mathbf{H}^{-1} = \begin{bmatrix} \mathbf{M}^{-1} & -\mathbf{M}^{-1}\mathbf{t} \\ \mathbf{0} & 1 \end{bmatrix}, \tag{2.42}$$

and this is easily verified to be correct.

In order to support two types of three-component vectors with different transformation properties, we need to introduce a second data structure to complement the `Vector3D` data structure introduced in Chapter 1. The `Vector3D` structure continues to represent a direction vector, and it possesses an implicit $w$ coordinate of zero when necessary. A new data structure called `Point3D` is used to represent a position vector, and it possesses an implicit $w$ coordinate of one. As shown in Listing 2.8, we choose to make the `Point3D` structure a subclass of the `Vector3D` structure so that it inherits the same data members and so that a `Point3D` structure is accepted anywhere that a `Vector3D` structure is expected.

The code in Listing 2.8 includes overloaded addition and subtraction operators that highlight a particular relationship between direction vectors and position vectors. When a direction vector **v** is added to a position vector $p$, it yields a new point in space that you would arrive at if you started at the point $p$ and travelled along the direction and length of **v**. If we consider the result of adding $p$ and **v** as 4D vectors with $w$ coordinates of one and zero, respectively, then the sum has a $w$ coordinate of one, indicating that it is a position vector. Conversely, if we subtract a position vector $b$ from a position vector $a$, then the difference has a $w$ coordinate of zero. This indicates that the result is a direction vector, and this can be understood as the direction and distance that you would need to travel to go from the point $a$ to the point $b$.

We also define a data structure called `Transform4D` that represents a $4 \times 4$ matrix having the form shown in Equation (2.40). We choose to make this structure a subclass of the `Matrix4D` data structure so that it can be used wherever a general

**Listing 2.8.** This is the definition of the `Point3D` data structure that represents a 3D position vector. It is a subclass of the `Vector3D` data structure so that it inherits the same data members and has the same properties except in cases that are explicitly overridden.

```
struct Point3D : Vector3D
{
    Point3D() = default;

    Point3D(float a, float b, float c) : Vector3D(a, b, c) {}
};

inline Point3D operator +(const Point3D& a, const Vector3D& b)
{
    return (Point3D(a.x + b.x, a.y + b.y, a.z + b.z));
}

inline Vector3D operator -(const Point3D& a, const Point3D& b)
{
    return (Vector3D(a.x - b.x, a.y - b.y, a.z - b.z));
}
```

$4 \times 4$ matrix is expected, but we assume that its fourth row is always equal to $[0 \ 0 \ 0 \ 1]$ whenever we perform calculations with it. As shown in Listing 2.9, the constructors for the `Transform4D` structure take data only for the first three rows and set the fourth row to $[0 \ 0 \ 0 \ 1]$. The first three columns are treated as 3D direction vectors due to the fact that each column has a zero in its fourth entry. Likewise, the fourth column is treated as a 3D position vector due to the fact that it has a one in its fourth entry. This behavior is implemented by the overridden bracket operators and the `GetTranslation()` and `SetTranslation()` functions.

The `Inverse()` function in Listing 2.9 is a simplified version of the full $4 \times 4$ inverse given in Listing 1.11 that accounts for the constant values in the fourth row of the matrix represented by the `Transform4D` data structure. The matrix-matrix multiplication operator for `Transform4D` data structures also takes advantage of the known values in the fourth row. Finally, functions that multiply a `Transform4D` data structure by `Vector3D` and `Point3D` data structures account for the $w$ coordinates implied by each type of vector.

**Listing 2.9.** This is the definition of the `Transform4D` data structure that holds the entries of a $4 \times 4$ matrix for which the fourth row is always $[0 \quad 0 \quad 0 \quad 1]$. It is a subclass of the general `Matrix4D` data structure so that it inherits the same data members and has the same properties except in cases that are explicitly overridden. Functions are provided for calculating the inverse, multiplying two transforms, multiplying by a direction vector, and multiplying by a position vector.

```cpp
struct Transform4D : Matrix4D
{
    Transform4D() = default;

    Transform4D(float n00, float n01, float n02, float n03,
                float n10, float n11, float n12, float n13,
                float n20, float n21, float n22, float n23)
    {
        n[0][0] = n00; n[0][1] = n10; n[0][2] = n20;
        n[1][0] = n01; n[1][1] = n11; n[1][2] = n21;
        n[2][0] = n02; n[2][1] = n12; n[2][2] = n22;
        n[3][0] = n03; n[3][1] = n13; n[3][2] = n23;

        n[0][3] = n[1][3] = n[2][3] = 0.0F;
        n[3][3] = 1.0F;
    }

    Transform4D(const Vector3D& a, const Vector3D& b,
                const Vector3D& c, const Point3D& p)
    {
        n[0][0] = a.x; n[0][1] = a.y; n[0][2] = a.z;
        n[1][0] = b.x; n[1][1] = b.y; n[1][2] = b.z;
        n[2][0] = c.x; n[2][1] = c.y; n[2][2] = c.z;
        n[3][0] = p.x; n[3][1] = p.y; n[3][2] = p.z;

        n[0][3] = n[1][3] = n[2][3] = 0.0F;
        n[3][3] = 1.0F;
    }

    Vector3D& operator [](int j)
    {
        return (*reinterpret_cast<Vector3D *>(n[j]));
    }
```

```cpp
    const Vector3D& operator [](int j) const
    {
        return (*reinterpret_cast<const Vector3D *>(n[j]));
    }

    const Point3D& GetTranslation(void) const
    {
        return (*reinterpret_cast<const Point3D *>(n[3]));
    }

    void SetTranslation(const Point3D& p)
    {
        n[3][0] = p.x;
        n[3][1] = p.y;
        n[3][2] = p.z;
    }
};

Transform4D Inverse(const Transform4D& H)
{
    const Vector3D& a = H[0];
    const Vector3D& b = H[1];
    const Vector3D& c = H[2];
    const Vector3D& d = H[3];

    Vector3D s = Cross(a, b);
    Vector3D t = Cross(c, d);

    float invDet = 1.0F / Dot(s, c);

    s *= invDet;
    t *= invDet;
    Vector3D v = c * invDet;

    Vector3D r0 = Cross(b, v);
    Vector3D r1 = Cross(v, a);

    return (Transform4D(r0.x, r0.y, r0.z, -Dot(b, t),
                        r1.x, r1.y, r1.z,  Dot(a, t),
                         s.x,  s.y,  s.z, -Dot(d, s)));
}
```

```
Transform4D operator *(const Transform4D& A, const Transform4D& B)
{
    return (Transform4D(
        A(0,0) * B(0,0) + A(0,1) * B(1,0) + A(0,2) * B(2,0),
        A(0,0) * B(0,1) + A(0,1) * B(1,1) + A(0,2) * B(2,1),
        A(0,0) * B(0,2) + A(0,1) * B(1,2) + A(0,2) * B(2,2),
        A(0,0) * B(0,3) + A(0,1) * B(1,3) + A(0,2) * B(2,3) + A(0,3),
        A(1,0) * B(0,0) + A(1,1) * B(1,0) + A(1,2) * B(2,0),
        A(1,0) * B(0,1) + A(1,1) * B(1,1) + A(1,2) * B(2,1),
        A(1,0) * B(0,2) + A(1,1) * B(1,2) + A(1,2) * B(2,2),
        A(1,0) * B(0,3) + A(1,1) * B(1,3) + A(1,2) * B(2,3) + A(1,3),
        A(2,0) * B(0,0) + A(2,1) * B(1,0) + A(2,2) * B(2,0),
        A(2,0) * B(0,1) + A(2,1) * B(1,1) + A(2,2) * B(2,1),
        A(2,0) * B(0,2) + A(2,1) * B(1,2) + A(2,2) * B(2,2),
        A(2,0) * B(0,3) + A(2,1) * B(1,3) + A(2,2) * B(2,3) + A(2,3)));
}


Vector3D operator *(const Transform4D& H, const Vector3D& v)
{
    return (Vector3D(H(0,0) * v.x + H(0,1) * v.y + H(0,2) * v.z,
                     H(1,0) * v.x + H(1,1) * v.y + H(1,2) * v.z,
                     H(2,0) * v.x + H(2,1) * v.y + H(2,2) * v.z));
}


Point3D operator *(const Transform4D& H, const Point3D& p)
{
    return (Point3D(H(0,0) * p.x + H(0,1) * p.y + H(0,2) * p.z + H(0,3),
                    H(1,0) * p.x + H(1,1) * p.y + H(1,2) * p.z + H(1,3),
                    H(2,0) * p.x + H(2,1) * p.y + H(2,2) * p.z + H(2,3)));
}
```

# 2.7 Quaternions

In the mid-nineteenth century, the Irish scientist William Rowan Hamilton (1805–1865) was studying the nature of the complex numbers. He thought of the complex numbers as the set of pairs $(a, b)$ of real numbers following a specific rule for multiplication. Hamilton attempted to extend the same principles to a three-dimensional set whose members are triplets of real numbers, but failed to find a logically sound rule for multiplication after exerting considerable effort. So he turned his attention to four-dimensional numbers, and upon having an epiphany one morning in 1843, Hamilton excitedly etched the multiplication rule

$$i^2 = j^2 = k^2 = ijk = -1 \tag{2.43}$$

into the stones of a nearby bridge. Today, Hamilton's original carving is no longer visible, but a stone plaque adorns the Broome bridge in Dublin to mark the location where his "flash of genius" took place.

## 2.7.1 Quaternion Fundamentals

The set of *quaternions*, denoted by the letter $\mathbb{H}$ in honor of Hamilton's discovery, is formed by adjoining the three imaginary units $i, j$, and $k$, to the set of real numbers. A typical quaternion $\mathbf{q}$ has four components that can be written as

$$\mathbf{q} = xi + yj + zk + w, \tag{2.44}$$

where $x$, $y$, $z$, and $w$ are real numbers. It doesn't matter what order these components are written in because multiplication by $i, j$, and $k$ provide all the necessary identification for the imaginary terms. Many textbooks write the real $w$ component first, but we choose to write it last to be consistent with the general convention used throughout the field of computer graphics that places the $w$ coordinate last in a 4D vector $(x, y, z, w)$. This is particularly useful for avoiding confusion in shader programs when a quaternion is stored in a variable having a vector type.

Although quaternions are sometimes treated as if they were 4D vectors, and they are even written in bold to reflect their multicomponent nature, it is important to realize that they are *not* actually 4D vectors. A quaternion is more properly understood as the sum of a scalar and a 3D vector, and Hamilton himself is credited with coining the terms *scalar* and *vector* to identify these different parts. It is often convenient to write a quaternion in the form $\mathbf{q} = \mathbf{v} + s$, where $\mathbf{v}$, called the *vector part*, corresponds to the imaginary triplet $(x, y, z)$ in Equation (2.44), and $s$, called the *scalar part*, corresponds to the real component $w$. Note, however, that calling

**v** a vector still isn't quite correct, but this terminology will suffice until we reach the more precise discussion of quaternions in Section 4.4.

As with ordinary vectors and complex numbers, quaternion addition is performed componentwise. Multiplication, however, follows the rule given by Hamilton in Equation (2.43), which can also be expressed in the more explicit form

$$
\begin{aligned}
i^2 &= j^2 = k^2 = -1 \\
ij &= -ji = k \\
jk &= -kj = i \\
ki &= -ik = j.
\end{aligned}
\tag{2.45}
$$

This summarization of the multiplication rule is less succinct than Hamilton's, but it provides a more immediate guide for multiplication between any two of the imaginary units. Equation (2.45) also illustrates the fact that quaternions do not possess the commutative property. Reversing the order in which any two imaginary units are multiplied negates their product.

By following the rules given above, we can calculate the general product of two quaternions $\mathbf{q}_1 = x_1 i + y_1 j + z_1 k + w_1$ and $\mathbf{q}_2 = x_2 i + y_2 j + z_2 k + w_2$ to obtain

$$
\begin{aligned}
\mathbf{q}_1 \mathbf{q}_2 = &\left( x_1 w_2 + y_1 z_2 - z_1 y_2 + w_1 x_2 \right) i \\
&+ \left( y_1 w_2 + z_1 x_2 + w_1 y_2 - x_1 z_2 \right) j \\
&+ \left( z_1 w_2 + w_1 z_2 + x_1 y_2 - y_1 x_2 \right) k \\
&+ \left( w_1 w_2 - x_1 x_2 - y_1 y_2 - z_1 z_2 \right).
\end{aligned}
\tag{2.46}
$$

If we represent the quaternions by $\mathbf{q}_1 = \mathbf{v}_1 + s_1$ and $\mathbf{q}_2 = \mathbf{v}_2 + s_2$ instead, then the product can be written as

$$
\mathbf{q}_1 \mathbf{q}_2 = \mathbf{v}_1 \times \mathbf{v}_2 + s_1 \mathbf{v}_2 + s_2 \mathbf{v}_1 + s_1 s_2 - \mathbf{v}_1 \cdot \mathbf{v}_2.
\tag{2.47}
$$

The first three terms form the vector part of the product, and the last two terms form the scalar part. The only noncommutative piece appearing in Equation (2.47) is the cross product, a fact from which we can quickly deduce that reversing the order of the factors in quaternion multiplication changes the product by twice the cross product between the vector parts, as stated by

$$
\mathbf{q}_2 \mathbf{q}_1 = \mathbf{q}_1 \mathbf{q}_2 - 2 \left( \mathbf{v}_1 \times \mathbf{v}_2 \right).
\tag{2.48}
$$

This exposes the fact that two quaternions commute only if their vector parts are parallel because when that is the case, the cross product $\mathbf{v}_1 \times \mathbf{v}_2$ is zero.

A quaternion $\mathbf{q}$ has a *conjugate* denoted by $\mathbf{q}^*$ that is similar to the complex conjugate except that we are now negating three imaginary components instead of just one. That is, the conjugate of a quaternion $\mathbf{q} = \mathbf{v} + s$ is given by

$$\mathbf{q}^* = -\mathbf{v} + s. \tag{2.49}$$

The product of a quaternion and its conjugate gives us

$$\mathbf{q}\mathbf{q}^* = \mathbf{q}^*\mathbf{q} = v^2 + s^2, \tag{2.50}$$

which is a real number that we equate to the squared magnitude of the quaternion. We denote the magnitude of a quaternion using two vertical bars, as with ordinary vectors, and define it as

$$\|\mathbf{q}\| = \sqrt{\mathbf{q}\mathbf{q}^*} = \sqrt{v^2 + s^2}. \tag{2.51}$$

As with vectors, multiplying a quaternion $\mathbf{q}$ by a scalar value $t$ has the effect of multiplying the magnitude of $\mathbf{q}$ by $|t|$. Quaternions also have the property that the magnitude of the product of two quaternions $\mathbf{q}_1$ and $\mathbf{q}_2$ is equal to the product of their individual magnitudes (see Exercise 9), which we can state as

$$\|\mathbf{q}_1\mathbf{q}_2\| = \|\mathbf{q}_1\|\|\mathbf{q}_2\|. \tag{2.52}$$

The real numbers $\mathbb{R}$ form a subset of the entire set of quaternions $\mathbb{H}$, and it consists of all the quaternions having the vector part $(0, 0, 0)$. In particular, the number one is a quaternion, and it continues to fill the role of the multiplicative identity element as it does in the sets of real numbers and complex numbers. For any quaternion $\mathbf{q} = \mathbf{v} + s$ that has a nonzero magnitude, we can divide the product shown in Equation (2.50) by the squared magnitude of $\mathbf{q}$ to obtain the identity element, and this means that $\mathbf{q}$ has a multiplicative inverse given by

$$\mathbf{q}^{-1} = \frac{\mathbf{q}^*}{\mathbf{q}\mathbf{q}^*} = \frac{-\mathbf{v} + s}{v^2 + s^2}. \tag{2.53}$$

The basic properties of quaternion addition and multiplication are listed in Table 2.1. They are all easy to verify, and none of them should come as any surprise. Due to the noncommutativity of quaternion multiplication, the last two properties listed in the table show that the conjugate or inverse of a product of quaternions is equal to the conjugate or inverse of each factor multiplied in reverse order. This is similar to how the transpose and inverse of matrix products work.

| Property | Description |
|---|---|
| $(\mathbf{q}_1 + \mathbf{q}_2) + \mathbf{q}_3 = \mathbf{q}_1 + (\mathbf{q}_2 + \mathbf{q}_3)$ | Associative law for quaternion addition. |
| $\mathbf{q}_1 + \mathbf{q}_2 = \mathbf{q}_2 + \mathbf{q}_1$ | Commutative law for quaternion addition. |
| $(st)\mathbf{q} = s(t\mathbf{q})$ | Associative law for scalar-quaternion multiplication. |
| $t\mathbf{q} = \mathbf{q}t$ | Commutative law for scalar-quaternion multiplication. |
| $t(\mathbf{q}_1 + \mathbf{q}_2) = t\mathbf{q}_1 + t\mathbf{q}_2$ <br> $(s+t)\mathbf{q} = s\mathbf{q} + t\mathbf{q}$ | Distributive laws for scalar-quaternion multiplication. |
| $\mathbf{q}_1(\mathbf{q}_2\mathbf{q}_3) = (\mathbf{q}_1\mathbf{q}_2)\mathbf{q}_3$ | Associative law for quaternion multiplication. |
| $\mathbf{q}_1(\mathbf{q}_2 + \mathbf{q}_3) = \mathbf{q}_1\mathbf{q}_2 + \mathbf{q}_1\mathbf{q}_3$ <br> $(\mathbf{q}_1 + \mathbf{q}_2)\mathbf{q}_3 = \mathbf{q}_1\mathbf{q}_3 + \mathbf{q}_2\mathbf{q}_3$ | Distributive laws for quaternion multiplication. |
| $(t\mathbf{q}_1)\mathbf{q}_2 = \mathbf{q}_1(t\mathbf{q}_2) = t(\mathbf{q}_1\mathbf{q}_2)$ | Scalar factorization for quaternions. |
| $(\mathbf{q}_1\mathbf{q}_2)^* = \mathbf{q}_2^*\mathbf{q}_1^*$ | Product rule for quaternion conjugate. |
| $(\mathbf{q}_1\mathbf{q}_2)^{-1} = \mathbf{q}_2^{-1}\mathbf{q}_1^{-1}$ | Product rule for quaternion inverse. |

**Table 2.1.** These are the basic properties of quaternion addition and multiplication. Each letter $\mathbf{q}$, with or without a subscript, represents a quaternion, and the letters $s$ and $t$ represent scalar values.

The definition of a simple data structure called Quaternion is shown in Listing 2.10. It holds four floating-point components x, y, z, and w representing the vector and scalar parts of a quaternion, and they can be accessed directly. The data structure has a default constructor that performs no initialization and two additional constructors that take either all four components separately or a Vector3D data structure and a scalar. The code includes an overloaded operator that calculates the product between two quaternions. Overloaded operators for other types of quaternion calculations are omitted, but it is a simple matter to implement addition, subtraction, multiplication by scalar values, etc.

**Listing 2.10.** This is the definition of a simple data structure holding the four components of a quaternion. Many of the basic arithmetic operations are omitted because their implementations are trivial. The `GetRotationMatrix()` and `SetRotationMatrix()` functions are implemented later in this section.

```
struct Quaternion
{
    float       x, y, z, w;

    Quaternion() = default;

    Quaternion(float a, float b, float c, float s)
    {
        x = a; y = b; z = c;
        w = s;
    }

    Quaternion(const Vector3D& v, float s)
    {
        x = v.x; y = v.y; z = v.z;
        w = s;
    }

    const Vector3D& GetVectorPart(void) const
    {
        return (reinterpret_cast<const Vector3D&>(x));
    }

    Matrix3D GetRotationMatrix(void);
    void SetRotationMatrix(const Matrix3D& m);
};

Quaternion operator *(const Quaternion& q1, const Quaternion& q2)
{
    return (Quaternion(
        q1.w * q2.x + q1.x * q2.w + q1.y * q2.z - q1.z * q2.y,
        q1.w * q2.y - q1.x * q2.z + q1.y * q2.w + q1.z * q2.x,
        q1.w * q2.z + q1.x * q2.y - q1.y * q2.x + q1.z * q2.w,
        q1.w * q2.w - q1.x * q2.x - q1.y * q2.y - q1.z * q2.z));
}
```

### 2.7.2 Rotations With Quaternions

Quaternions appear in game engine development because they can be used to represent rotations in a way that has several advantages over $3 \times 3$ matrices. In this section, we present a conventional description of how a quaternion corresponding to a particular rotation through any angle about any axis is constructed and how such a quaternion transforms an ordinary vector. We'll be able to provide greater insight into the reasons why quaternions work the way they do in Section 4.4. The advantages to interpolating quaternions compared to $3 \times 3$ matrices will be a topic covered in Volume 3.

Given a quaternion $\mathbf{q} = xi + yj + zk + w$ and a vector $\mathbf{v} = (v_x, v_y, v_z)$, a rotation is performed by considering the vector to be the quaternion $v_x i + v_y j + v_z k$ and calculating a new vector $\mathbf{v}'$ with the product

$$\mathbf{v}' = \mathbf{q}\mathbf{v}\mathbf{q}^{-1}. \tag{2.54}$$

To be clear, each of the products in this equation is a quaternion multiplied by a quaternion. This is sometimes called the *sandwich product* because the quaternion $\mathbf{v}$ is sandwiched between the quaternion $\mathbf{q}$ and its inverse. The quaternion $\mathbf{v}$ is known as a *pure* quaternion, which is any quaternion that has a zero scalar component and is thus made up of only imaginary terms. When $\mathbf{v}$ is a pure quaternion, the sandwich product $\mathbf{q}\mathbf{v}\mathbf{q}^{-1}$ always yields another pure quaternion. Since we have established an equivalence between vectors and pure quaternions, we can say that the sandwich product transforms a vector $\mathbf{v}$ into another vector $\mathbf{v}'$.

The magnitude of $\mathbf{q}$ in Equation (2.54) doesn't matter, as long as it's nonzero, because if $\|\mathbf{q}\| = m$, then $m$ can be factored out of $\mathbf{q}$, and $1/m$ can be factored out of $\mathbf{q}^{-1}$. These cancel each other out and leave quaternions with magnitudes of one behind. A quaternion $\mathbf{q}$ having a magnitude of one is called a *unit quaternion*, and it has the special property that its inverse is simply equal to its conjugate because $\mathbf{q}\mathbf{q}^* = 1$. In the case that $\mathbf{q}$ is a unit quaternion, Equation (2.54) simplifies to

$$\boxed{\mathbf{v}' = \mathbf{q}\mathbf{v}\mathbf{q}^*.} \tag{2.55}$$

The set of unit quaternions form a multiplicatively closed subset of $\mathbb{H}$ because the product of any two unit quaternions is another unit quaternion. For this reason and the fact that vector transforms become simpler, only unit quaternions are typically used to represent rotations in practice.

To see how the sandwich product shown in Equation (2.55) performs a rotation, we can write $\mathbf{q} = \mathbf{b} + c$ and expand the quaternion products using Equation (2.47), keeping in mind that the scalar part of $\mathbf{v}$ is zero. The product $\mathbf{q}\mathbf{v}$ is given by

$$qv = (\mathbf{b} + c)\mathbf{v} = \mathbf{b} \times \mathbf{v} + c\mathbf{v} - \mathbf{b} \cdot \mathbf{v}. \tag{2.56}$$

When we multiply this by $\mathbf{q}^* = -\mathbf{b} + c$, we get

$$\begin{aligned} \mathbf{qvq}^* &= (\mathbf{b} \times \mathbf{v} + c\mathbf{v} - \mathbf{b} \cdot \mathbf{v})(-\mathbf{b} + c) \\ &= (c^2 - b^2)\mathbf{v} + 2(\mathbf{v} \cdot \mathbf{b})\mathbf{b} + 2c(\mathbf{b} \times \mathbf{v}) \end{aligned} \tag{2.57}$$

after some simplification that includes an application of the vector triple product identity $-\mathbf{b} \times \mathbf{v} \times \mathbf{b} = (\mathbf{b} \cdot \mathbf{v})\mathbf{b} - b^2\mathbf{v}$. If we set $\mathbf{b} = s\mathbf{a}$, where $s = \|\mathbf{b}\|$ and $\mathbf{a}$ is a unit vector, then we can write $\mathbf{qvq}^*$ as

$$\mathbf{qvq}^* = (c^2 - s^2)\mathbf{v} + 2s^2(\mathbf{v} \cdot \mathbf{a})\mathbf{a} + 2cs(\mathbf{a} \times \mathbf{v}). \tag{2.58}$$

The right side of this equation has the same three terms that appear in the formula for rotation about an arbitrary axis $\mathbf{a}$ given by Equation (2.19) except that the scalar coefficients are written in a different way. In order for Equation (2.58) to perform a rotation through an angle $\theta$, the values of $c$ and $s$ must satisfy the equalities

$$\begin{aligned} c^2 - s^2 &= \cos\theta \\ 2s^2 &= 1 - \cos\theta \\ 2cs &= \sin\theta. \end{aligned} \tag{2.59}$$

All three of these requirements are satisfied when we choose

$$\begin{aligned} c &= \cos\frac{\theta}{2} \\ s &= \sin\frac{\theta}{2} \end{aligned} \tag{2.60}$$

because these values produce valid trigonometric identities. (This reveals why the letters $c$ and $s$ were selected for this derivation.) We conclude that the quaternion

$$\boxed{\mathbf{q} = \left(\sin\frac{\theta}{2}\right)\mathbf{a} + \cos\frac{\theta}{2}} \tag{2.61}$$

represents a rotation through the angle $\theta$ about the unit-length axis $\mathbf{a}$ that can be applied to a vector $\mathbf{v}$ using the sandwich product $\mathbf{qvq}^*$. As with all the rotations previously described in this chapter, a quaternion rotation through a positive angle is counterclockwise when the axis points toward the viewer.

Quaternion rotation is implemented in Listing 2.11 using the formula given by Equation (2.57). In terms of computational cost, this method of performing a rotation on a vector $\mathbf{v}$ is more expensive than multiplying $\mathbf{v}$ by a $3 \times 3$ rotation matrix. The advantages to using quaternions exist elsewhere, and some of them are discussed at various points in the remainder of this section.

One advantage to using quaternions is that multiple rotations can easily be composed. To first rotate a vector $\mathbf{v}$ using a quaternion $\mathbf{q}_1$ and then rotate the result using another quaternion $\mathbf{q}_2$, we calculate the sandwich product of a sandwich product as in

$$\mathbf{v}' = \mathbf{q}_2 \left( \mathbf{q}_1 \mathbf{v} \mathbf{q}_1^* \right) \mathbf{q}_2^*. \tag{2.62}$$

By reassociating the factors, this can be written as

$$\mathbf{v}' = \left( \mathbf{q}_2 \mathbf{q}_1 \right) \mathbf{v} \left( \mathbf{q}_2 \mathbf{q}_1 \right)^*, \tag{2.63}$$

showing that the two successive rotations are equivalent to a single rotation using the quaternion given by $\mathbf{q}_2 \mathbf{q}_1$. The product of two quaternions can be calculated with 16 multiplies and 12 adds using Equation (2.46), and that has a significantly lower cost than the 27 multiplies and 18 adds required to calculate the product of two $3 \times 3$ matrices.

A quaternion also has the advantage that it has much lower storage requirements because it comprises only four floating-point components compared to the nine floating-point entries needed by an equivalent $3 \times 3$ rotation matrix. It is often the case, however, that a quaternion needs to be converted to a matrix at some point in order to carry out calculations that involve transformations other than rotations. To make this conversion, we can examine each of the terms of the sandwich product $\mathbf{q}\mathbf{v}\mathbf{q}^*$ shown in Equation (2.57), where $\mathbf{q} = \mathbf{b} + c$, and express their effects on $\mathbf{v}$ as $3 \times 3$ matrices to obtain

**Listing 2.11.** This code rotates the vector $v$ using the quaternion $q$ by calculating the sandwich product shown in Equation (2.57). It is assumed that $q$ is a unit quaternion.

```
Vector3D Transform(const Vector3D& v, const Quaternion& q)
{
    const Vector3D& b = q.GetVectorPart();
    float b2 = b.x * b.x + b.y * b.y + b.z * b.z;
    return (v * (q.w * q.w - b2) + b * (Dot(v, b) * 2.0F)
        + Cross(b, v) * (q.w * 2.0F));
}
```

$$\mathbf{qvq}^{*} = \begin{bmatrix} c^2 - b^2 & 0 & 0 \\ 0 & c^2 - b^2 & 0 \\ 0 & 0 & c^2 - b^2 \end{bmatrix} \mathbf{v} + \begin{bmatrix} 2b_x^2 & 2b_xb_y & 2b_xb_z \\ 2b_xb_y & 2b_y^2 & 2b_yb_z \\ 2b_xb_z & 2b_yb_z & 2b_z^2 \end{bmatrix} \mathbf{v}$$

$$+ \begin{bmatrix} 0 & -2cb_z & 2cb_y \\ 2cb_z & 0 & -2cb_x \\ -2cb_y & 2cb_x & 0 \end{bmatrix} \mathbf{v}. \qquad (2.64)$$

Since $\mathbf{q}$ is a unit quaternion, we know that $c^2 + b^2 = 1$, so we can rewrite $c^2 - b^2$ as $1 - 2b^2$. This allows us to simplify the diagonal entries a little when we combine the three matrices because, as exemplified by the $(0,0)$ entry, we can make the replacement

$$c^2 - b^2 + 2b_x^2 = 1 - 2b_y^2 - 2b_z^2. \qquad (2.65)$$

For a general unit quaternion $\mathbf{q} = xi + yj + zk + w$, where we equate $\mathbf{b} = (x, y, z)$ and $c = w$, a single $3 \times 3$ matrix $\mathbf{M}_{\mathrm{rot}}(\mathbf{q})$ corresponding to the sandwich product $\mathbf{qvq}^{*}$ is thus given by

$$\mathbf{M}_{\mathrm{rot}}(\mathbf{q}) = \begin{bmatrix} 1 - 2y^2 - 2z^2 & 2(xy - wz) & 2(xz + wy) \\ 2(xy + wz) & 1 - 2x^2 - 2z^2 & 2(yz - wx) \\ 2(xz - wy) & 2(yz + wx) & 1 - 2x^2 - 2y^2 \end{bmatrix}. \qquad (2.66)$$

A function that constructs this transformation matrix for a given Quaternion data structure and returns a Matrix3D data structure is shown in Listing 2.12.

If we take a close look at Equation (2.57), we notice that negating both $\mathbf{b}$ and $c$ has no effect on the transformation of $\mathbf{v}$. There are two negations in each term that cancel each other out. The same property is also apparent in the formula for $\mathbf{M}_{\mathrm{rot}}(\mathbf{q})$ if we were to negate all four components $x, y, z,$ and $w$. This demonstrates that for any unit quaternion $\mathbf{q}$, the quaternion $-\mathbf{q}$ represents exactly the same rotation. Further insight can be gained by considering the number $-1$ itself as a quaternion and matching it to Equation (2.61). In this case, we must have $\cos(\theta/2) = -1$ and $\sin(\theta/2) = 0$, which are conditions satisfied when $\theta = 2\pi$, so the quaternion $\mathbf{q} = -1$ corresponds to a full revolution about any axis.

The fact the $\mathbf{q}$ and $-\mathbf{q}$ represent the same rotation can be used to reduce the amount of storage space needed by a unit quaternion to just three floating-point values. Once the components of a quaternion $\mathbf{q} = \mathbf{b} + c$ have been calculated for a particular angle and axis, we can choose whether to keep $\mathbf{q}$ or change it to $-\mathbf{q}$ based

**Listing 2.12.** This function creates a $3 \times 3$ matrix that corresponds to the `Quaternion` data structure for which it's called. It is assumed that the quaternion has a magnitude of one.

```
Matrix3D Quaternion::GetRotationMatrix(void)
{
    float x2 = x * x;
    float y2 = y * y;
    float z2 = z * z;
    float xy = x * y;
    float xz = x * z;
    float yz = y * z;
    float wx = w * x;
    float wy = w * y;
    float wz = w * z;

    return (Matrix3D(
        1.0F - 2.0F * (y2 + z2), 2.0F * (xy - wz), 2.0F * (xz + wy),
        2.0F * (xy + wz), 1.0F - 2.0F * (x2 + z2), 2.0F * (yz - wx),
        2.0F * (xz - wy), 2.0F * (yz + wx), 1.0F - 2.0F * (x2 + y2)));
}
```

on whether the scalar part $c$ is nonnegative. If we know that $c \geq 0$, then it can be calculated from the vector part **b** as

$$c = \sqrt{1 - b_x^2 - b_y^2 - b_z^2} \tag{2.67}$$

because the magnitude of **q** must be one. Thus, if storage space is important, then a quaternion can be negated if necessary so that the scalar part is not negative and stored as only the three components of the vector part. A short calculation is able to reconstitute the scalar part when it is needed.

Given a $3 \times 3$ matrix **M** that represents a rotation, we can convert to a quaternion $q = xi + yj + zk + w$ by assuming that the entries of the matrix have the form shown in Equation (2.66) and solving for the individual components. We start by making an observation about the sum of the diagonal entries of **M**, which is

$$M_{00} + M_{11} + M_{22} = 3 - 4(x^2 + y^2 + z^2). \tag{2.68}$$

By requiring **q** to be a unit quaternion, we can replace $x^2 + y^2 + z^2$ with $1 - w^2$ and solve for $w$ to get

$$w = \pm \frac{1}{2}\sqrt{M_{00} + M_{11} + M_{22} + 1}, \tag{2.69}$$

where we are free to choose whether $w$ is positive or negative. (The value under the radical is never negative because $x^2 + y^2 + z^2 \leq 1$.) Once we have calculated the value of $w$, we can use it to find the values of $x$, $y$, and $z$ using the relationships

$$M_{21} - M_{12} = 4wx$$
$$M_{02} - M_{20} = 4wy$$
$$M_{10} - M_{01} = 4wz, \tag{2.70}$$

each of which simply requires a division by $4w$.

Unfortunately, in cases when $w$ is very small, dividing by it can cause floating-point precision problems, so we need alternative methods that calculate the largest of $x$, $y$, or $z$ first and then solve for the other components. If $M_{00} + M_{11} + M_{22} > 0$, then $|w|$ is guaranteed to be larger than $1/2$, and we can safely use Equations (2.69) and (2.70) to calculate $\mathbf{q}$. Otherwise, we make use of three more relationships involving the diagonal entries of $\mathbf{M}$, given by

$$M_{00} - M_{11} - M_{22} + 1 = 4x^2$$
$$-M_{00} + M_{11} - M_{22} + 1 = 4y^2$$
$$-M_{00} - M_{11} + M_{22} + 1 = 4z^2. \tag{2.71}$$

At first, it might seem like we can use these in conjunction with Equation (2.69) to calculate all four components of $\mathbf{q}$, but we do not have enough information to select the correct signs. We are able to arbitrarily choose the sign of one component, but making that choice determines the signs of the other components when they are subsequently calculated using off-diagonal entries of $\mathbf{M}$. To determine which of $x$, $y$, and $z$ is largest, we can manipulate Equation (2.70) by replacing the negated entries of $\mathbf{M}$ with the values shown in Equation (2.66) to obtain

$$2x^2 = M_{00} - 2w^2 + 1$$
$$2y^2 = M_{11} - 2w^2 + 1$$
$$2z^2 = M_{22} - 2w^2 + 1, \tag{2.72}$$

where we have used the fact that $w^2 = 1 - x^2 - y^2 - z^2$. These equations show that the sizes of $x$, $y$, and $z$ are directly related to the sizes of $M_{00}$, $M_{11}$, and $M_{22}$. Once the largest diagonal entry has been identified, we calculate the corresponding component of $\mathbf{q}$ using one of the relationships in Equation (2.71) and then calculate the remaining two imaginary components of $\mathbf{q}$ using the relationships

$$M_{10} + M_{01} = 4xy$$
$$M_{02} + M_{20} = 4xz$$
$$M_{21} + M_{12} = 4yz. \tag{2.73}$$

The $w$ component is always calculated using one of the relationships shown in Equation (2.70). Making an example of the case in which $M_{00}$ is the largest diagonal entry, we calculate $x$ with the formula

$$x = \pm\frac{1}{2}\sqrt{M_{00} - M_{11} - M_{22} + 1}. \tag{2.74}$$

The $y$, $z$, and $w$ components are then given by

$$y = \frac{M_{10} + M_{01}}{4x}$$
$$z = \frac{M_{02} + M_{20}}{4x}$$
$$w = \frac{M_{21} - M_{12}}{4x}. \tag{2.75}$$

The function shown in Listing 2.13 implements the complete conversion of a $3 \times 3$ matrix to a quaternion. The code assumes that the input is a true rotation matrix, meaning that it is orthogonal and has a determinant of $+1$.

**Listing 2.13.** This function sets the members of the Quaternion data structure for which it's called to the values corresponding to a quaternion equivalent to the $3 \times 3$ rotation matrix m.

```
void Quaternion::SetRotationMatrix(const Matrix3D& m)
{
    float m00 = m(0,0);
    float m11 = m(1,1);
    float m22 = m(2,2);
    float sum = m00 + m11 + m22;

    if (sum > 0.0F)
    {
        w = sqrt(sum + 1.0F) * 0.5F;
        float f = 0.25F / w;
```

```
        x = (m(2,1) - m(1,2)) * f;
        y = (m(0,2) - m(2,0)) * f;
        z = (m(1,0) - m(0,1)) * f;
    }
    else if ((m00 > m11) && (m00 > m22))
    {
        x = sqrt(m00 - m11 - m22 + 1.0F) * 0.5F;
        float f = 0.25F / x;

        y = (m(1,0) + m(0,1)) * f;
        z = (m(0,2) + m(2,0)) * f;
        w = (m(2,1) - m(1,2)) * f;
    }
    else if (m11 > m22)
    {
        y = sqrt(m11 - m00 - m22 + 1.0F) * 0.5F;
        float f = 0.25F / y;

        x = (m(1,0) + m(0,1)) * f;
        z = (m(2,1) + m(1,2)) * f;
        w = (m(0,2) - m(2,0)) * f;
    }
    else
    {
        z = sqrt(m22 - m00 - m11 + 1.0F) * 0.5F;
        float f = 0.25F / z;

        x = (m(0,2) + m(2,0)) * f;
        y = (m(2,1) + m(1,2)) * f;
        w = (m(1,0) - m(0,1)) * f;
    }
}
```

# Exercises for Chapter 2

1. Show that every involution must have a determinant of either $+1$ or $-1$.

2. Suppose that $\mathbf{A}$ and $\mathbf{B}$ are orthogonal matrices. Prove that $\mathbf{AB}$ is also an orthogonal matrix.

3. Prove that a symmetric matrix that is also an involution must be orthogonal, and prove that an orthogonal matrix that is also an involution must be symmetric.

4. Let $\mathbf{M} = [\mathbf{a} \quad \mathbf{b} \quad \mathbf{c}]$, where the column vectors $\mathbf{a}$, $\mathbf{b}$, and $\mathbf{c}$ are mutually perpendicular but don't necessarily have unit length. Find a diagonal matrix $\mathbf{N}$ such that $\mathbf{M}^{-1} = \mathbf{N}\mathbf{M}^{\mathrm{T}}$.

5. Derive a transformation matrix that scales a vector $\mathbf{v}$ by a factor $s$ in every direction perpendicular to a direction $\mathbf{a}$ but does not scale in the direction $\mathbf{a}$ so that a transformed vector $\mathbf{v}'$ is given by $\mathbf{v}' = \mathbf{v}_{\parallel\mathbf{a}} + s\mathbf{v}_{\perp\mathbf{a}}$.

6. Find simplified transformation matrices for skews in the following cases:

   (a) $\mathbf{a} = (1, 0, 0)$ and $\mathbf{b} = (0, 0, 1)$
   (b) $\mathbf{a} = (0, 1, 0)$ and $\mathbf{b} = (0, 0, 1)$
   (c) $\mathbf{a} = (0, 1, 0)$ and $\mathbf{b} = (1, 0, 0)$

7. Let $\mathbf{H}$ and $\mathbf{G}$ be $4 \times 4$ transformation matrices that each have a fourth row equal to $[0 \quad 0 \quad 0 \quad 1]$. Prove that the product $\mathbf{HG}$ also has a fourth row equal to $[0 \quad 0 \quad 0 \quad 1]$.

8. Derive a single $4 \times 4$ matrix that transforms an arbitrary point with a $3 \times 3$ matrix $\mathbf{M}$, but does so about a given center position $c$. First, apply a translation so that the point $c$ is moved to the origin, then apply the matrix $\mathbf{M}$, and finally apply the reverse translation that moves the origin back to the point $c$.

9. For any two quaternions $\mathbf{q}_1$ and $\mathbf{q}_2$, prove that $\|\mathbf{q}_1\mathbf{q}_2\|^2 = \|\mathbf{q}_1\|^2\|\mathbf{q}_2\|^2$, and conclude that the magnitude of the product of two quaternions is equal to the product of their magnitudes.

10. Let $\mathbf{q}$ be a quaternion with $\mathbf{q} = \mathbf{v} + s$. Find functions $f(\mathbf{q})$ and $g(\mathbf{q})$ such that $f(\mathbf{q}) = s$ and $g(\mathbf{q}) = \mathbf{v}$, which extract the scalar and vector parts of $\mathbf{q}$, using only $\mathbf{q}$ and $\mathbf{q}^*$ without referring to any components of $\mathbf{q}$ directly.

11. Show that the quaternion $\mathbf{q}$ given by Equation (2.61) must be a unit quaternion for any angle $\theta$ as long as $\|\mathbf{a}\| = 1$.

12. Describe the rotations performed by the quaternions $\mathbf{q} = i$, $\mathbf{q} = j$, and $\mathbf{q} = k$ when applied to a vector $\mathbf{v}$ with the sandwich product $\mathbf{q}\mathbf{v}\mathbf{q}^*$.

13. Find quaternions corresponding to counterclockwise rotations through $90°$ about each of the $x$, $y$, and $z$ axes.

14. Let $\mathbf{v}_1$ and $\mathbf{v}_2$ be nonparallel 3D unit vectors, and let $\theta$ be the angle between them. Find the unit quaternion $\mathbf{q} = s\mathbf{a} + c$ with $\mathbf{a} = (\mathbf{v}_1 \times \mathbf{v}_2)/\sin\theta$ that rotates the vector $\mathbf{v}_1$ to the vector $\mathbf{v}_2$ (that is, $\mathbf{v}_2 = \mathbf{q}\mathbf{v}_1\mathbf{q}^*$). Use trigonometric identities to eliminate all sine and cosine functions.

# Chapter **3**

# Geometry

Most of the computation performed by a game engine involves some kind of geometry. Geometry defines the world in which a game takes place, geometry describes the characters in a game and their movements, geometry tells the graphics hardware how to render a scene, geometry allows an engine to determine what's visible to the camera, and geometry is necessary for detecting collisions between various objects. The list of areas in which geometry plays an essential role in game engine mechanics continues without end. After a short introduction to triangle meshes, this chapter discusses the details of several basic geometric topics that are fundamentally important in the development of more complex systems.

## 3.1 Triangle Meshes

With the exception of cases involving exotic rendering methods, objects drawn by a game engine are composed of triangles. A *triangle mesh* is a collection of triangles that fit together to model the surface of a solid volume. At a minimum, the data associated with a triangle mesh includes a list of vertex positions stored as 3D points with floating-point coordinates. In most cases, the data also includes an *index list* that contains a triplet of integer indices for each triangle in the mesh specifying which three vertices define the triangle's boundary. There is typically more data stored with each vertex, but aside from the mention of normal vectors in the next section, a discussion of the details about this additional information will have to wait until Volume 2.

As an example, consider the box shown in Figure 3.1. Its triangle mesh is made up of 8 vertices and 12 triangles. Each of the box's six rectangular faces is divided into two coplanar triangles, and this is typical because the graphics hardware can-

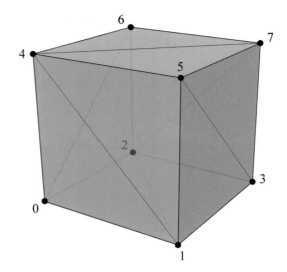

**Figure 3.1.** This simple box is composed of 8 vertices and 12 triangles.

not directly process polygons having more than three sides. There are always multiple ways to break a polygon having at least four vertices into triangles. The particular choice of triangles composing an entire mesh is called its *triangulation*.

The fact that there are fewer vertices than there are triangles demonstrates how each vertex is shared by multiple triangles. In the box shown in Figure 3.1, every vertex is used by either four triangles or five triangles, but it is possible to arrange the triangles in a different way so that some vertices are used by as few as three triangles and other vertices are used by as many as six. Sometimes, an application will store a list of triangle numbers with each vertex so that it's easy to determine which triangles make use of any particular vertex. This information would ordinarily be used only for editing purposes, however, and not in the course of actually rendering a model.

A triangle mesh is called *closed* if it is the case that every edge is used by exactly two triangles. That is, for any pair of vertices used by one triangle, there must be one more triangle, and no others, that also uses the same pair of vertices for one of its edges but does not share the third vertex with the first triangle. A closed triangle mesh satisfies the *Euler formula*, which states

$$V - E + F = 2,$$
(3.1)

where $V$ is the number of vertices, $E$ is the number of edges, and $F$ is the number of faces. When we talk about the number of faces here, we mean the number of triangles in the mesh, and not the number of faces belonging to an ideal solid. Likewise, the number of edges is the number of boundaries existing between all pairs of adjacent triangles, even if the triangles are coplanar. Whereas an ideal box has 8 vertices, 12 edges, and 6 faces, the triangulated box in Figure 3.1 has 8 vertices, 18 edges, and 12 faces. Both sets of numbers satisfy Equation (3.1).

An important property of a triangle mesh is the *winding direction* used by its triangles. When a triangle is viewed from its front side, which is the side facing the mesh's exterior, we have a choice as to whether the vertices referenced by the triangle occur in clockwise order or counterclockwise order. Either convention works equally well because the graphics hardware lets us specify which convention we are using, but we have to be consistent over an entire triangle mesh for a variety of reasons that include normal vector calculation. In this book, we choose the counterclockwise winding direction so that triangles satisfy a right-hand rule. When the fingers of the right hand are curled in the counterclockwise direction, the right thumb points outward from the front side of a triangle. In Figure 3.1, the lower-left triangle is wound in the counterclockwise direction when its vertices are referenced in the order $(0, 1, 4)$, $(1, 4, 0)$, or $(4, 0, 1)$.

# 3.2 Normal Vectors

A *normal vector*, or just *normal* for short, is a vector that is perpendicular to a surface, and the direction in which it points is said to be *normal* to the surface. A flat plane has only one normal direction, but most surfaces aren't so simple and thus have normal vectors that vary from point to point. Normal vectors are used for a wide variety of reasons in game engine development that include surface shading, collision detection, and physical interaction.

## 3.2.1 Calculating Normal Vectors

There are a few ways in which normal vectors can be calculated, and the best method in any particular case really depends on how a surface is described from a mathematical standpoint. In the case that a surface is defined implicitly by a scalar function $f(p)$, the normal vector at $p = (x, y, z)$ is given by the gradient $\nabla f(p)$ because it is perpendicular to every direction tangent to the level surface of $f$ at $p$.

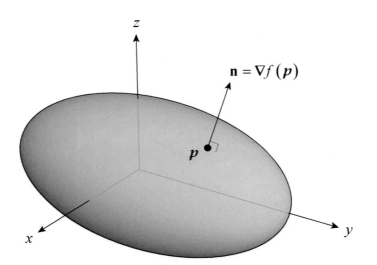

**Figure 3.2.** The normal vector **n** at a particular point $p$ on a surface implicitly defined by the equation $f(p) = 0$ is given by the gradient $\nabla f(p)$.

For example, suppose we have the ellipsoid shown in Figure 3.2, defined by the equation

$$f(p) = x^2 + \frac{y^2}{4} + z^2 - 1 = 0. \tag{3.2}$$

The point $p = \left(\frac{\sqrt{6}}{4}, 1, \frac{\sqrt{6}}{4}\right)$ lies on the surface of this ellipsoid, and the normal vector **n** at that point is given by

$$\mathbf{n} = \nabla f(p) = \left(\frac{\partial f}{\partial x}, \frac{\partial f}{\partial y}, \frac{\partial f}{\partial z}\right)\bigg|_p = \left(2x, \frac{y}{2}, 2z\right) = \left(\frac{\sqrt{6}}{2}, \frac{1}{2}, \frac{\sqrt{6}}{2}\right). \tag{3.3}$$

Calculating normal vectors with the gradient is something that's usually done only in the process of constructing a triangle mesh to approximate an ideal surface described by some mathematical formula. The normal vectors are typically scaled to unit length and stored with the vertex coordinates that they're associated with. Most of the time, a game engine is working with a triangle mesh having an arbitrary shape that was created in a modeling program, and the only information available is the set of vertex coordinates and the list of indices that tell how vertices are grouped into triangles.

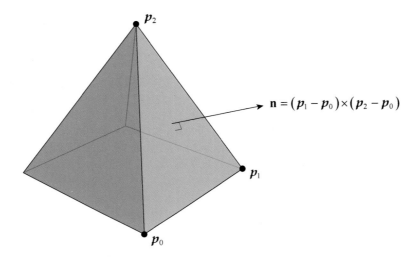

**Figure 3.3.** The normal vector **n** for a triangular face having vertices $p_0$, $p_1$, and $p_2$ is given by the cross product between vectors corresponding to two edges of the triangle.

As illustrated in Figure 3.3, the normal vector **n** for a single triangular face can be calculated by taking the cross product between vectors aligned with two of the triangle's edges. Let $p_0$, $p_1$, and $p_2$ be the vertices of a triangle wound in the counterclockwise direction. An outward-facing normal vector is then given by

$$\mathbf{n} = ( p_1 - p_0 ) \times ( p_2 - p_0 ).$$
(3.4)

Any permutation of the subscripts that keeps them in the same cyclic order produces the same normal vector. It doesn't matter which vertex is chosen to be subtracted from the other two as long as the first factor in the cross product involves the next vertex in the counterclockwise order. If the order is reversed, then the calculated normal vector still lies along the same line, but it points in the opposite direction.

To calculate per-vertex normal vectors for a triangle mesh, it is typical for a game engine's model processing pipeline to calculate all of the per-face normal vectors and then take an average at each vertex over all of the faces that use that vertex. The average may be weighted based on triangle area or other factors to create a smooth field of normal vectors over a curved surface. In cases in which a hard edge is desired, such as for a cube or the pyramid in Figure 3.3, vertex positions are typically duplicated, and different normal vectors corresponding to different faces are associated with the various copies of the vertex coordinates.

### 3.2.2 Transforming Normal Vectors

When a model is transformed by a matrix $\mathbf{M}$ in order to alter its geometry, every point $p$ belonging to the original model becomes a point $\mathbf{M}p$ in the transformed model. Since a tangent vector $\mathbf{t}$ can be approximated by the difference of points $p$ and $q$ on a surface, or is often exactly equal to such a difference, it is transformed in the same way as a point to become $\mathbf{M}\mathbf{t}$ because the difference between the new points $\mathbf{M}p$ and $\mathbf{M}q$ is tangent to the new surface. Problems arise, however, if we try to apply the same transformation to normal vectors.

Consider the shape shown in Figure 3.4 that has a normal vector $\mathbf{n}$ on its slanted side. Let $\mathbf{M}$ be a transformation matrix that scales by a factor of two in the horizontal direction but does not scale in the vertical direction. If the matrix $\mathbf{M}$ is multiplied by $\mathbf{n}$, then the resulting vector $\mathbf{M}\mathbf{n}$ is stretched horizontally and, as clearly visible in the figure, is no longer perpendicular to the surface. This indicates that something is inherently different about normal vectors, and if we want to preserve perpendicularity, then we must find another way to transform them that produces the correct results. Taking a closer look at how a matrix transforms a vector provides some insight. We restrict our discussion to $3\times 3$ matrices here since normal vectors are not affected by translation, but the same conclusions will apply to $4\times 4$ matrices in the discussion of planes later in this chapter.

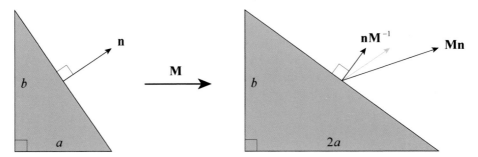

**Figure 3.4.** A shape is transformed by a matrix $\mathbf{M}$ that scales by a factor of two only in the horizontal direction. The normal vector $\mathbf{n}$ is perpendicular to the original surface, but if it is treated as a column vector and transformed by the matrix $\mathbf{M}$, then it is not perpendicular to the transformed surface. The normal vector is correctly transformed by treating it as a row vector and multiplying by $\mathbf{M}^{-1}$. (The original normal vector is shown in light gray on the transformed surface.)

Let $\mathbf{v}^A$ be a vector whose coordinates are expressed in coordinate system $A$ as indicated by its superscript, and consider the fact that the components of $\mathbf{v}^A$ measure distances along the coordinate axes. A distance $\Delta x^A$ along the $x$ direction in coordinate system $A$ is equivalent to the sum of distances $\Delta x^B$, $\Delta y^B$, and $\Delta z^B$ along the axis-aligned directions in another coordinate system $B$. The $x$ component of $\mathbf{v}^A$ can therefore be expressed as the vector

$$\left( \frac{\Delta x^B}{\Delta x^A} v_x^A, \frac{\Delta y^B}{\Delta x^A} v_x^A, \frac{\Delta z^B}{\Delta x^A} v_x^A \right) \tag{3.5}$$

in coordinate system $B$. Similar expressions with $\Delta y^A$ and $\Delta z^A$ in the denominators can be used to express the $y$ and $z$ components of $\mathbf{v}$ in coordinate system $B$. Adding them up gives us a transformed vector $\mathbf{v}^B$ in coordinate system $B$ that corresponds to the original vector $\mathbf{v}^A$ in its entirety, and this can be written as the matrix transformation

$$\mathbf{v}^B = \begin{bmatrix} \dfrac{\Delta x^B}{\Delta x^A} & \dfrac{\Delta x^B}{\Delta y^A} & \dfrac{\Delta x^B}{\Delta z^A} \\[2mm] \dfrac{\Delta y^B}{\Delta x^A} & \dfrac{\Delta y^B}{\Delta y^A} & \dfrac{\Delta y^B}{\Delta z^A} \\[2mm] \dfrac{\Delta z^B}{\Delta x^A} & \dfrac{\Delta z^B}{\Delta y^A} & \dfrac{\Delta z^B}{\Delta z^A} \end{bmatrix} \mathbf{v}^A. \tag{3.6}$$

Each entry of this matrix multiplies a component of $\mathbf{v}^A$ by a ratio of axis-aligned distances, and the axis appearing in the denominator of each ratio corresponds to the component of $\mathbf{v}^A$ by which the ratio is multiplied. This has the effect of cancelling the distances in coordinate system $A$ and replacing them with distances in coordinate system $B$.

Now let us consider a normal vector that was calculated as a gradient. The key to understanding how such normal vectors transform is realizing that the components of a gradient do not measure distances along the coordinate axes, but instead measure *reciprocal* distances. In the partial derivatives that compose a vector $(\partial f/\partial x, \partial f/\partial y, \partial f/\partial z)$, distances along the $x$, $y$, and $z$ axes appear in the denominators. This is fundamentally different from the measurements made by the components of an ordinary vector, and it's the source of the problem exemplified by the nonuniform scale shown in Figure 3.4. Whereas an ordinary vector $\mathbf{v}$ is treated as a *column* matrix with components $(v_x, v_y, v_z)$, we write a normal vector $\mathbf{n}$ as the *row* matrix

$$\mathbf{n} = \begin{bmatrix} \dfrac{1}{n_x} & \dfrac{1}{n_y} & \dfrac{1}{n_z} \end{bmatrix}. \tag{3.7}$$

It then becomes apparent that multiplying this vector on the right by the matrix in Equation (3.6) has the effect of cancelling reciprocal distances in coordinate system $B$ and replacing them with reciprocal distances in coordinate system $A$. Calling the matrix $\mathbf{M}$, we can state that it is *simultaneously* the transform that takes ordinary vectors from $A$ to $B$ through the product $\mathbf{v}^B = \mathbf{M}\mathbf{v}^A$ *and* the transform that takes normal vectors, in the opposite sense, from $B$ to $A$ through the product $\mathbf{n}^A = \mathbf{n}^B\mathbf{M}$. Inverting the matrix reverses both of these transformations, so we conclude that the correct transformation from $A$ to $B$ for a normal vector, at least one calculated with a gradient, is given by

$$\boxed{\mathbf{n}^B = \mathbf{n}^A\mathbf{M}^{-1}.} \tag{3.8}$$

The correctness of Equation (3.8) can be verified by demonstrating that a transformed normal vector remains perpendicular to any transformed tangent vector. Suppose that $\mathbf{n}^A$ and $\mathbf{t}^A$ are normal and tangent to a surface at some point in coordinate system $A$. By definition, they are perpendicular, and we must have $\mathbf{n}^A \cdot \mathbf{t}^A = 0$. (Since $\mathbf{n}^A$ is a row vector and $\mathbf{t}^A$ is a column vector, the matrix product $\mathbf{n}^A\mathbf{t}^A$ is actually what we're calculating here, but the dot is still included by convention, even though the notation is not technically correct, to make it clear that we are producing a scalar quantity.) Let $\mathbf{M}$ be a matrix that transforms ordinary vectors from coordinate system $A$ to coordinate system $B$. Then the transformed normal $\mathbf{n}^B$ is given by $\mathbf{n}^A\mathbf{M}^{-1}$, and the transformed tangent $\mathbf{t}^B$ is given by $\mathbf{M}\mathbf{t}^A$. Their product is

$$\mathbf{n}^B \cdot \mathbf{t}^B = \mathbf{n}^A\mathbf{M}^{-1}\mathbf{M}\mathbf{t}^A = \mathbf{n}^A \cdot \mathbf{t}^A = 0, \tag{3.9}$$

and this establishes the fact that they are still perpendicular in coordinate system $B$ after the transformation by $\mathbf{M}$.

Getting back to the example in Figure 3.4, the transformation matrix $\mathbf{M}$ is

$$\mathbf{M} = \begin{bmatrix} 2 & 0 & 0 \\ 0 & 1 & 0 \\ 0 & 0 & 1 \end{bmatrix} \tag{3.10}$$

when we align the $x$ axis with the horizontal direction and the $y$ axis with the vertical direction. We can take the normal vector before the transformation to be $\mathbf{n} = \begin{bmatrix} b & a & 0 \end{bmatrix}$. Transforming this with Equation (3.8) gives us a new normal vector equal to $\begin{bmatrix} b/2 & a & 0 \end{bmatrix}$, which is perpendicular to the transformed surface. The important observation to make is that the matrix $\mathbf{M}$ scales $x$ values by a factor of two, but because normal vectors use reciprocal coordinates as shown in Equation (3.7), multiplying $n_x$ by two is equivalent to multiplying the $x$ component of $\mathbf{n}$ by a factor of one half, which is exactly what $\mathbf{M}^{-1}$ does.

In the case that a normal vector $\mathbf{n}^A$ is calculated as the cross product $\mathbf{s} \times \mathbf{t}$ between two tangent vectors $\mathbf{s}$ and $\mathbf{t}$, the transformed normal vector $\mathbf{n}^B$ should be equal to the cross product between the transformed tangent vectors. Again, let $\mathbf{M}$ be a matrix that transforms ordinary vectors from coordinate system $A$ to coordinate system $B$. Then $\mathbf{n}^B = \mathbf{Ms} \times \mathbf{Mt}$, but we need to be able to calculate $\mathbf{n}^B$ without any knowledge of the vectors $\mathbf{s}$ and $\mathbf{t}$. Expanding the matrix-vector products by columns with Equation (1.28), we can write

$$\mathbf{n}^B = \left( s_x \mathbf{M}_{[0]} + s_y \mathbf{M}_{[1]} + s_z \mathbf{M}_{[2]} \right) \times \left( t_x \mathbf{M}_{[0]} + t_y \mathbf{M}_{[1]} + t_z \mathbf{M}_{[2]} \right), \quad (3.11)$$

where we are using the notation $\mathbf{M}_{[i]}$ to mean column $i$ of the matrix $\mathbf{M}$ (matching the meaning of the [ ] operator in our matrix data structures). After distributing the cross product to all of these terms and simplifying, we arrive at

$$\begin{aligned} \mathbf{n}^B = \ & \left( s_y t_z - s_z t_y \right) \left( \mathbf{M}_{[1]} \times \mathbf{M}_{[2]} \right) \\ & + \left( s_z t_x - s_x t_z \right) \left( \mathbf{M}_{[2]} \times \mathbf{M}_{[0]} \right) \\ & + \left( s_x t_y - s_y t_x \right) \left( \mathbf{M}_{[0]} \times \mathbf{M}_{[1]} \right). \end{aligned} \quad (3.12)$$

The cross product $\mathbf{n}^A = \mathbf{s} \times \mathbf{t}$ is clearly visible here, but it may be a little less obvious that the cross products of the matrix columns form the rows of $\det(\mathbf{M})\, \mathbf{M}^{-1}$, which follows from Equation (1.95). We conclude that a normal vector calculated with a cross product is correctly transformed according to

$$\boxed{\mathbf{n}^B = \mathbf{n}^A \det(\mathbf{M})\, \mathbf{M}^{-1}.} \quad (3.13)$$

Using the adjugate of $\mathbf{M}$, defined in Section 1.7.5, we can also write this as

$$\boxed{\mathbf{n}^B = \mathbf{n}^A \operatorname{adj}(\mathbf{M}).} \quad (3.14)$$

This is not only how normal vectors transform, but it's how *any* vector resulting from a cross product between ordinary vectors transforms.

Equation (3.13) differs from Equation (3.8) only by the additional factor of $\det(\mathbf{M})$, showing that the two types of normal vectors are closely related. Since normal vectors are almost always rescaled to unit length after they're calculated, in practice, the size of $\det(\mathbf{M})$ is inconsequential and often ignored, making the two normal vector transformation equations identical. However, there is one situation in which $\det(\mathbf{M})$ may have an impact, and that is the case when the transform performed by $\mathbf{M}$ contains a reflection. When the vertices of a triangle are reflected in a mirror, their winding orientation is reversed, and this causes a normal vector calculated with the cross product of the triangle's edges to reverse direction as well. This is exactly the effect that a negative determinant of $\mathbf{M}$ would have on a normal vector that is transformed by Equation (3.13).

The code in Listing 3.1 multiplies a normal vector, stored in a Vector3D data structure and treated as a row matrix, by a Transform4D data structure on the right, but it ignores the fourth column of the transformation matrix. When positions and normals are being transformed by a $4 \times 4$ matrix $\mathbf{H}$, a point $p$ is transformed as $\mathbf{H}p$, but a normal $\mathbf{n}$ has to be transformed as $\mathbf{n}\mathbf{M}^{-1}$, where $\mathbf{M}$ is the upper-left $3 \times 3$ portion of $\mathbf{H}$. Being able to multiply by a Transform4D data structure is convenient when both $\mathbf{H}$ and $\mathbf{H}^{-1}$ are already available so that the matrix $\mathbf{M}^{-1}$ doesn't need to be extracted.

In the general case, both $\mathbf{H}$ and $\mathbf{M}^{-1}$ are needed to transform both positions and normals. If $\mathbf{M}$ happens to be orthogonal, which is often the case, then its inverse is simply equal to its transpose, so the transformed normal is just $\mathbf{n}\mathbf{M}^{\mathrm{T}}$, but this is equivalent to $\mathbf{M}\mathbf{n}$ if we treat $\mathbf{n}$ as a column matrix. Thus, it is common to see game engines treat ordinary vectors and normal vectors as the same kind of mathematical element and use multiplication by the same matrix $\mathbf{H}$ on the left to transform both kinds among different coordinate systems.

**Listing 3.1.** This multiplication operator multiplies a Vector3D data structure representing a normal vector as a row matrix on the right by a Transform4D data structure to transform a normal vector from coordinate system $A$ to coordinate system $A$. The transformation matrix is treated as a $3 \times 3$ matrix, ignoring the fourth column. Note that this transforms a normal vector in the opposite sense in relation to how the same matrix would transform an ordinary vector from coordinate system $A$ to coordinate system $B$.

```
Vector3D operator *(const Vector3D& n, const Transform4D& H)
{
    return (Vector3D(n.x * H(0,0) + n.y * H(1,0) + n.z * H(2,0),
                     n.x * H(0,1) + n.y * H(1,1) + n.z * H(2,1),
                     n.x * H(0,2) + n.y * H(1,2) + n.z * H(2,2)));
}
```

# 3.3 Lines and Rays

Lines and rays show up in numerous places throughout game engine development and are used for many purposes that include rendering, collision detection, and user interaction. Lines and rays are basically the same thing mathematically, with the only distinction being that a line extends to infinity in both directions while a ray starts at a point and goes to infinity in one direction. This section introduces the parametric form of a line and discusses some of the calculations that can be done with it. Later in this chapter, we will encounter a different mathematical formulation for lines that will also appear in a different context in Section 4.2.

## 3.3.1 Parametric Lines

Given two points $p_1$ and $p_2$, we can define the function

$$\mathcal{L}(t) = (1-t)\,p_1 + t\,p_2 \tag{3.15}$$

that produces points on the line passing through $p_1$ and $p_2$ in terms of a single parameter $t$ that ranges over all real numbers. When $0 \le t \le 1$, the points fall inside the segment connecting $p_1$ and $p_2$. Otherwise, the points fall elsewhere on the line extending to infinity in both directions.

The function $\mathcal{L}(t)$ can be rewritten as

$$\mathcal{L}(t) = p_1 + t\,(p_2 - p_1), \tag{3.16}$$

which is equivalent to Equation (3.15) but makes it clear that a line can be expressed in terms of a point and a direction. We can express both lines and rays with the parametric function

$$\boxed{\mathcal{L}(t) = p + t\mathbf{v},} \tag{3.17}$$

where $p$ is a point on the line, and $\mathbf{v}$ is a direction parallel to the line, as shown in Figure 3.5. The only difference between a line and a ray is that for a line, $t$ can have any value, but for a ray, $t$ can't be negative. It is often the case that $\mathbf{v}$ is normalized to unit length so that the parameter $t$ corresponds to the actual distance from the starting point $p$.

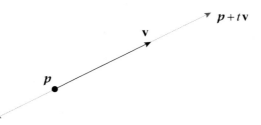

**Figure 3.5.** A parametric line is defined by a point $p$ on the line and a direction vector $\mathbf{v}$ parallel to the line.

### 3.3.2 Distance Between a Point and a Line

Suppose that we want to find the shortest distance $d$ between a point $q$ and any point on a line given by $\mathcal{L}(t) = p + t\mathbf{v}$. For convenience, we define $\mathbf{u} = q - p$. As shown in Figure 3.6, $d$ is equal to the magnitude of the rejection of $\mathbf{u}$ from $\mathbf{v}$, which corresponds to one side of a right triangle having a hypotenuse of length $\|\mathbf{u}\|$. The length of the remaining side is the magnitude of the projection of $\mathbf{u}$ onto $\mathbf{v}$, so we can express $d^2$ as

$$d^2 = u^2 - \left(\mathbf{u}_{\|\mathbf{v}}\right)^2 = u^2 - \left(\frac{\mathbf{u} \cdot \mathbf{v}}{v^2}\mathbf{v}\right)^2. \tag{3.18}$$

Simplifying the term corresponding to the projection and taking a square root gives us the formula

$$d = \sqrt{u^2 - \frac{(\mathbf{u} \cdot \mathbf{v})^2}{v^2}}. \tag{3.19}$$

If $\mathbf{v}$ is known to have unit length, then the division by $v^2$ can be omitted because it is equal to one.

   If the points $p$ and $q$ are far apart, which doesn't necessarily mean that $q$ is far from the line, then the sizes of $\|\mathbf{u}\|$ and $\mathbf{u} \cdot \mathbf{v}$ can become very large. Squaring these quantities makes them even larger, and subtracting two large floating-point numbers, as done inside the radical in Equation (3.19), results in a loss of precision that can be severe. Fortunately, this problem can be mitigated to a degree by using an alternative method to calculate the distance. The magnitude of $\mathbf{u} \times \mathbf{v}$ is equal to the area of the shaded parallelogram in Figure 3.6. Dividing by the magnitude of $\mathbf{v}$, which corresponds to the base of the parallelogram, gives us the value of $d$, which

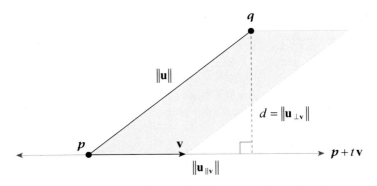

**Figure 3.6.** The distance $d$ from a point $q$ to the line $p + t\mathbf{v}$ is equal to the magnitude of the rejection of $\mathbf{u}$ from $\mathbf{v}$, where $\mathbf{u} = q - p$. The shaded parallelogram has an area equal to $\|\mathbf{u} \times \mathbf{v}\|$, so $d$ is also given by this area divided by the length of $\mathbf{v}$.

corresponds to the height of the parallelogram. Thus, we can also express the distance from a point to a line as

$$d = \sqrt{\frac{(\mathbf{u} \times \mathbf{v})^2}{v^2}}, \tag{3.20}$$

and as before, the division by $v^2$ can be avoided if we know that $\|\mathbf{v}\| = 1$. In the case that $\mathbf{u}$ has a large magnitude, there is still a subtraction of two large numbers happening inside the cross product, but we are not squaring them first, so they are much smaller in size than the numbers arising in Equation (3.19). The formula given by Equation (3.20) is implemented in Listing 3.2.

**Listing 3.2.** This function calculates the distance between the point q and the line determined by the point p and the direction v.

```
float DistPointLine(const Point3D& q, const Point3D& p, const Vector3D& v)
{
    Vector3D a = Cross(q - p, v);
    return (sqrt(Dot(a, a) / Dot(v, v)));
}
```

### 3.3.3 Distance Between Two Lines

In three-dimensional space, two lines that don't lie in the same plane are called *skew lines*. Skew lines are not parallel, and they do not intersect, but they do possess unique points at which they come closest to each other. As shown in Figure 3.7, the shortest distance $d$ between two lines is the length of the segment that is simultaneously perpendicular to both lines. Let the lines be described by the functions

$$\mathcal{L}_1(t_1) = \boldsymbol{p}_1 + t_1 \boldsymbol{v}_1$$
$$\mathcal{L}_2(t_2) = \boldsymbol{p}_2 + t_2 \boldsymbol{v}_2. \tag{3.21}$$

We need to find the values of $t_1$ and $t_2$ such that the difference $\mathcal{L}_2(t_2) - \mathcal{L}_1(t_1)$ is orthogonal to both $\boldsymbol{v}_1$ and $\boldsymbol{v}_2$. We can express this condition as the pair of dot products

$$(\boldsymbol{p}_2 + t_2 \boldsymbol{v}_2 - \boldsymbol{p}_1 - t_1 \boldsymbol{v}_1) \cdot \boldsymbol{v}_1 = 0$$
$$(\boldsymbol{p}_2 + t_2 \boldsymbol{v}_2 - \boldsymbol{p}_1 - t_1 \boldsymbol{v}_1) \cdot \boldsymbol{v}_2 = 0. \tag{3.22}$$

This is a linear system that can be rewritten in matrix form as

$$\begin{bmatrix} v_1^2 & -\boldsymbol{v}_1 \cdot \boldsymbol{v}_2 \\ \boldsymbol{v}_1 \cdot \boldsymbol{v}_2 & -v_2^2 \end{bmatrix} \begin{bmatrix} t_1 \\ t_2 \end{bmatrix} = \begin{bmatrix} (\boldsymbol{p}_2 - \boldsymbol{p}_1) \cdot \boldsymbol{v}_1 \\ (\boldsymbol{p}_2 - \boldsymbol{p}_1) \cdot \boldsymbol{v}_2 \end{bmatrix}. \tag{3.23}$$

We solve for $t_1$ and $t_2$ by inverting the $2 \times 2$ matrix to obtain

$$\begin{bmatrix} t_1 \\ t_2 \end{bmatrix} = \begin{bmatrix} v_1^2 & -\boldsymbol{v}_1 \cdot \boldsymbol{v}_2 \\ \boldsymbol{v}_1 \cdot \boldsymbol{v}_2 & -v_2^2 \end{bmatrix}^{-1} \begin{bmatrix} (\boldsymbol{p}_2 - \boldsymbol{p}_1) \cdot \boldsymbol{v}_1 \\ (\boldsymbol{p}_2 - \boldsymbol{p}_1) \cdot \boldsymbol{v}_2 \end{bmatrix}$$
$$= \frac{1}{(\boldsymbol{v}_1 \cdot \boldsymbol{v}_2)^2 - v_1^2 v_2^2} \begin{bmatrix} -v_2^2 & \boldsymbol{v}_1 \cdot \boldsymbol{v}_2 \\ -\boldsymbol{v}_1 \cdot \boldsymbol{v}_2 & v_1^2 \end{bmatrix} \begin{bmatrix} (\boldsymbol{p}_2 - \boldsymbol{p}_1) \cdot \boldsymbol{v}_1 \\ (\boldsymbol{p}_2 - \boldsymbol{p}_1) \cdot \boldsymbol{v}_2 \end{bmatrix}. \tag{3.24}$$

When these values of $t_1$ and $t_2$ are plugged back into the line functions given by Equation (3.21), they produce the points at which the lines are closest to each other. The shortest distance $d$ between the two lines is equal to

$$d = \|\mathcal{L}_2(t_2) - \mathcal{L}_1(t_1)\|, \tag{3.25}$$

which is the magnitude of the difference between the closest points.

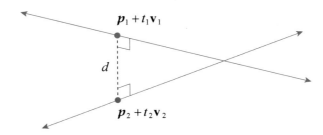

**Figure 3.7.** The distance $d$ between skew lines is equal to the length of the segment connecting points on the two lines that is simultaneously perpendicular to both lines.

If the determinant $(\mathbf{v}_1 \cdot \mathbf{v}_2)^2 - v_1^2 v_2^2$ in Equation (3.24) is zero, then the lines are actually parallel and not skew as presumed. In this case, we can measure the distance $d$ between the two lines by simply calculating the distance between the point $\boldsymbol{p}_2$ and the line $\mathcal{L}_1(t_1)$ using Equation (3.20), which gives us

$$d = \sqrt{\frac{\left[(\boldsymbol{p}_2 - \boldsymbol{p}_1) \times \mathbf{v}_1\right]^2}{v_1^2}}. \tag{3.26}$$

The formula used to calculate $t_1$ and $t_2$ in Equation (3.24) is implemented in Listing 3.3, which uses the parameters to calculate the distance between two lines. If the determinant is found to be very small, then the code assumes that the lines are parallel and calculates the distance between them with Equation (3.26).

**Listing 3.3.** This function calculates the distance between two lines determined by the points p1 and p2 and the directions v1 and v2.

```
float DistLineLine(const Point3D& p1, const Vector3D& v1,
                   const Point3D& p2, const Vector3D& v2)
{
    Vector3D dp = p2 - p1;

    float v12 = Dot(v1, v1);
    float v22 = Dot(v2, v2);
    float v1v2 = Dot(v1, v2);

    float det = v1v2 * v1v2 - v12 * v22;
```

```
if (fabs(det) > FLT_MIN)
{
    det = 1.0F / det;

    float dpv1 = Dot(dp, v1);
    float dpv2 = Dot(dp, v2);
    float t1 = (v1v2 * dpv2 - v22 * dpv1) * det;
    float t2 = (v12 * dpv2 - v1v2 * dpv1) * det;

    return (Magnitude(dp + v2 * t2 - v1 * t1));
}

// The lines are nearly parallel.

Vector3D a = Cross(dp, v1);
return (sqrt(Dot(a, a) / v12));
}
```

## 3.4 Planes

Because a function of one parameter can describe the intrinsically one-dimensional geometry of a line, it is logical to expect that a function of two parameters can describe the intrinsically two-dimensional geometry of a plane. Indeed, given three points $p_1$, $p_2$, and $p_3$ that lie in a plane and are not collinear, the function

$$Q(s,t) = p_1 + s(p_2 - p_1) + t(p_3 - p_1) \qquad (3.27)$$

produces all of the points in the entire plane as the parameters $s$ and $t$ range over all real numbers. As with lines, we can replace the differences between points with two direction vectors $\mathbf{u}$ and $\mathbf{v}$, and that gives us the parametric form of a plane

$$Q(s,t) = p + s\mathbf{u} + t\mathbf{v}. \qquad (3.28)$$

However, a function of this type is not typically used by game engines to represent planes. The implicit form described next provides a superior alternative and is the preferred representation in virtually all applications.

### 3.4.1 Implicit Planes

Since the vectors **u** and **v** in Equation (3.28) both lie in the plane, we can calculate the cross product between them to obtain a normal vector **n**, as shown in Figure 3.8. The normal vector is perpendicular to the difference between any two points in the plane, so if we know a point $q$ lying in the plane, and we know the plane's normal vector **n**, we can write the equation

$$\mathbf{n} \cdot (p - q) = 0 \tag{3.29}$$

to describe the entire set of points $p$ that lie in the plane. For any particular plane, the quantity $-\mathbf{n} \cdot q$ is a constant value that we call $d$. It is the same for all points $q$ lying in the plane and is thus an implicit property of the plane that allows us to throw away knowledge of any particular point and write

$$\mathbf{n} \cdot p + d = 0. \tag{3.30}$$

A plane is implicitly described by the four numbers $n_x$, $n_y$, $n_z$, and $d$ that constitute the components of a four-dimensional row vector $\mathbf{f} = \begin{bmatrix} n_x & n_y & n_z & d \end{bmatrix}$, which we write using the shorthand notation $[\mathbf{n} \,|\, d]$. With this, Equation (3.30) becomes the more compact

$$\boxed{\mathbf{f} \cdot p = 0,} \tag{3.31}$$

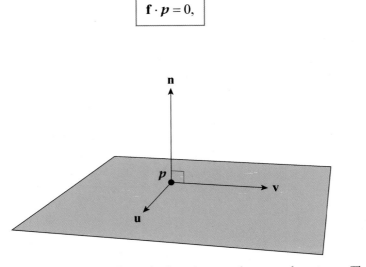

**Figure 3.8.** A plane is determined by a single point $p$ and a normal vector **n**. The normal vector is perpendicular to any directions lying in the plane, such as the vectors **u** and **v** that could be used to describe the plane parametrically.

where we extend the point $p$ to four dimensions by using its implicit $w$ coordinate of one. All points $p$ satisfying this equation lie in the plane $\mathbf{f} = [\mathbf{n} \mid d]$.

As with normal vectors earlier in this chapter, we defined $\mathbf{f}$ as a row vector. Since $p$ is a column vector, the matrix product $\mathbf{f}p$ actually gives us the left side of Equation (3.30), but the dot is still included by convention to make it clear that we are calculating $f_x p_x + f_y p_y + f_z p_z + f_w$. In Section 4.2, we will replace the dot with a different symbol when the algebraic nature of planes is discussed more thoroughly.

The definition of a simple data structure named `Plane` holding the four components of a plane is shown in Listing 3.4. It has floating-point members named x, y, z, and w that can be accessed directly, and they reflect the fact that a plane can be treated as a generic 4D row vector. The first three components correspond to the normal vector $\mathbf{n}$, and the $w$ component corresponds to the value of $d$. The normal vector can be retrieved as a `Vector3D` data structure by calling the `GetNormal()` member function. Two nonmember functions named `Dot()` are included, and they calculate the dot product between a plane and a `Vector3D` or `Point3D` data structure, accounting for the fact that a direction has an implicit $w$ coordinate of zero, and a point has an implicit $w$ coordinate of one.

**Listing 3.4.** This is the definition of a simple data structure holding the four components of an implicit plane.

```
struct Plane
{
    float       x, y, z, w;

    Plane() = default;

    Plane(float nx, float ny, float nz, float d)
    {
        x = nx;
        y = ny;
        z = nz;
        w = d;
    }

    Plane(const Vector3D& n, float d)
    {
        x = n.x;
```

```
        y = n.y;
        z = n.z;
        w = d;
    }

    const Vector3D& GetNormal(void) const
    {
        return (reinterpret_cast<const Vector3D&>(x));
    }
};

float Dot(const Plane& f, const Vector3D& v)
{
    return (f.x * v.x + f.y * v.y + f.z * v.z);
}

float Dot(const Plane& f, const Point3D& p)
{
    return (f.x * p.x + f.y * p.y + f.z * p.z + f.w);
}
```

### 3.4.2 Distance Between a Point and a Plane

Multiplying both sides of Equation (3.31) by a nonzero scalar quantity $s$ has no effect on the set of points that satisfy the equation. This implies that $\mathbf{f} = [\,\mathbf{n}\,|\,d\,]$ and $s\mathbf{f} = [\,s\mathbf{n}\,|\,sd\,]$ both represent the same geometric plane in space, and it motivates us ask whether there is a value of $s$ that gives the plane $s\mathbf{f}$ any appealing qualities. The answer is yes, and it is the value $s = 1/\|\mathbf{n}\|$. In this case, the plane $s\mathbf{f}$ is said to be *normalized* because its normal vector has unit length. However, it's important to realize that this is not the same meaning of the word "normalized" as it would apply to a generic 4D vector or a quaternion because the value of $d$ for the plane can still be any size. To normalize a plane, we multiply all four components by $1/\|\mathbf{n}\|$, but it's only the three-component normal vector that ends up having unit length.

The advantage to having a normalized plane $\mathbf{f}$ is that the dot product $\mathbf{f} \cdot \boldsymbol{p}$ is equal to the signed perpendicular distance between the plane and the point $\boldsymbol{p}$. When $\mathbf{n}$ has unit length, the dot product $\mathbf{n} \cdot \boldsymbol{p}$ is equal to the length of the projection of $\boldsymbol{p}$ onto $\mathbf{n}$. The value of $-d = \mathbf{n} \cdot \boldsymbol{q}$ is equal to the length of the projection of any point $\boldsymbol{q}$ in the plane onto $\mathbf{n}$. As illustrated in Figure 3.9, the value of $\mathbf{f} \cdot \boldsymbol{p}$ is the difference between these lengths, equal to $\mathbf{n} \cdot \boldsymbol{p} + d$, corresponding to the number of times the normal vector can be stacked on the plane before reaching the point $\boldsymbol{p}$. The value of $d$ is sometimes called the distance to the origin because it's what you get when you evaluate the dot product $\mathbf{f} \cdot \boldsymbol{o}$ for the origin $o$.

The sign of the distance given by $\mathbf{f} \cdot \boldsymbol{p}$ depends on which side of the plane $\boldsymbol{p}$ lies. If the normal vector $\mathbf{n}$ were to be drawn so that its arrow starts on the plane, then it points away from the *front side* of the plane. This is also called the *positive side* of the plane because for any points lying on this side, $\mathbf{f} \cdot \boldsymbol{p}$ is a positive value. Naturally, the other side of the plane is called the *back side* or *negative side* of the plane, and for points lying on that side, $\mathbf{f} \cdot \boldsymbol{p}$ is a negative value. The meaning of front and back can be reversed by simply negating the plane $\mathbf{f}$ because $-\mathbf{f}$ represents the same set of points, but with a reversed normal vector.

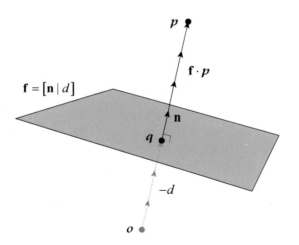

**Figure 3.9.** The signed perpendicular distance between a point $\boldsymbol{p}$ and a normalized plane $\mathbf{f} = [\mathbf{n} \mid d]$ is given by the dot product $\mathbf{f} \cdot \boldsymbol{p}$. This can be understood as the difference between the distance, perpendicular to the plane, from $\boldsymbol{p}$ to the origin $o$ and the distance, perpendicular to the plane, from a point $\boldsymbol{q}$ in the plane to the origin. The perpendicular distances are calculated by projecting onto the normal vector so that the difference becomes $\mathbf{n} \cdot \boldsymbol{p} - \mathbf{n} \cdot \boldsymbol{q} = \mathbf{n} \cdot \boldsymbol{p} + d$. As illustrated, the value of $\mathbf{f} \cdot \boldsymbol{p}$ corresponds to the number of normal vectors that fit between the plane and the point $\boldsymbol{p}$, and the value of $-d$ corresponds to the number of normal vectors needed to reach the plane itself.

### 3.4.3 Reflection Through a Plane

When a point $p$ is reflected through a plane, the new point $p'$ lies at the same distance from the plane but on the opposite side, and the line segment connecting the original point and the new point is parallel to the plane's normal vector. Let $\mathbf{f} = [\mathbf{n} \mid d]$ be a plane such that $\mathbf{n}$ has unit length, and let $q$ be the point closest to $p$ lying in the plane. As shown in Figure 3.10, the difference between $p$ and $q$ is equal to $(\mathbf{f} \cdot p)\mathbf{n}$ because the scalar quantity $\mathbf{f} \cdot p$ is the perpendicular distance between the plane $\mathbf{f}$ and the point $p$. When this vector is subtracted from $p$, the result is the point $q$. A second subtraction of this vector produces the reflected point $p'$ that's just as far away from the plane as the original point $p$ but on the opposite side. Thus, a formula for calculating $p'$ is given by

$$p' = p - 2(\mathbf{f} \cdot p)\mathbf{n}. \tag{3.32}$$

A $4 \times 4$ transformation matrix corresponding to the reflection through a plane can be determined by regarding $\mathbf{n}$ as a 4D column vector with a $w$ coordinate of zero (because we're using it as a direction), and rewriting Equation (3.32) as the matrix product

$$p' = p - 2\mathbf{n}\mathbf{f}p = (\mathbf{I}_4 - 2\mathbf{n} \otimes \mathbf{f})\,p. \tag{3.33}$$

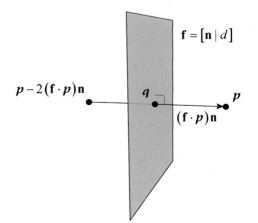

**Figure 3.10.** A point $p$ is reflected through a normalized plane $\mathbf{f} = [\mathbf{n} \mid d]$ by subtracting the vector $(\mathbf{f} \cdot p)\mathbf{n}$ twice. The first subtraction yields the point $q$ closest to $p$ in the plane.

When we expand each entry in the matrix multiplying $p$, we find that the matrix $\mathbf{H}_{\text{reflect}}(\mathbf{f})$ representing the reflection through a plane $\mathbf{f}$ is given by

$$\mathbf{H}_{\text{reflect}}(\mathbf{f}) = \begin{bmatrix} 1-2n_x^2 & -2n_x n_y & -2n_x n_z & -2n_x d \\ -2n_x n_y & 1-2n_y^2 & -2n_y n_z & -2n_y d \\ -2n_x n_z & -2n_y n_z & 1-2n_z^2 & -2n_z d \\ 0 & 0 & 0 & 1 \end{bmatrix}. \tag{3.34}$$

When $d = 0$, the translation in the fourth column disappears, and the matrix reduces to the 4D equivalent of the transform given by Equation (2.24) for the reflection through a plane that contains the origin. A function that constructs the transformation matrix in Equation (3.34) and returns a `Transform4D` data structure is shown in Listing 3.5.

**Listing 3.5.** This code creates a $4 \times 4$ matrix that represents a reflection through the plane `f` and returns it in a `Transform4D` data structure. The plane `f` is assumed to be normalized.

```
Transform4D MakeReflection(const Plane& f)
{
    float x = f.x * -2.0F;
    float y = f.y * -2.0F;
    float z = f.z * -2.0F;
    float nxny = x * f.y;
    float nxnz = x * f.z;
    float nynz = y * f.z;

    return (Transform4D(x * f.x + 1.0F, nxny, nxnz, x * f.w,
                        nxny, y * f.y + 1.0F, nynz, y * f.w,
                        nxnz, nynz, z * f.z + 1.0F, z * f.w));
}
```

### 3.4.4 Intersection of a Line and a Plane

Let $\mathbf{f} = [\mathbf{n} \mid d]$ be the plane shown in Figure 3.11, and let $\mathcal{L}(t) = \boldsymbol{p} + t\mathbf{v}$ be a line such that $\mathbf{n} \cdot \mathbf{v} \neq 0$, meaning that the line is not parallel to the plane. We can find the point $\boldsymbol{q}$ at which the line intersects the plane by solving for the value of $t$ that satisfies $\mathbf{f} \cdot \mathcal{L}(t) = 0$. A little algebra brings us to

$$t = -\frac{\mathbf{f} \cdot \boldsymbol{p}}{\mathbf{f} \cdot \mathbf{v}}, \tag{3.35}$$

where it should be carefully noted that the numerator is calculated using a 4D dot product in which $p_w$ is implicitly one, but the denominator is calculated using the equivalent of a 3D dot product because $v_w$ is implicitly zero. (The Dot() functions in Listing 3.4 handle these different cases automatically when the correct data types are used.) Plugging this value of $t$ back into $\mathcal{L}(t)$ gives us

$$\boxed{\boldsymbol{q} = \boldsymbol{p} - \frac{\mathbf{f} \cdot \boldsymbol{p}}{\mathbf{f} \cdot \mathbf{v}} \mathbf{v}} \tag{3.36}$$

as the point of intersection $\boldsymbol{q}$. This formula is implemented in Listing 3.6.

In the case that $\mathcal{L}(t)$ is regarded as a ray, you could impose the condition that an intersection with the plane $\mathbf{f}$ occurs only if $t \geq 0$. Otherwise, the intersection happens behind the ray's starting point. Furthermore, you may want to consider only intersections for which the ray starts on the front side of the plane. A quick

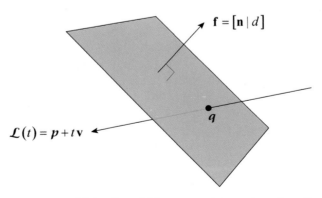

**Figure 3.11.** The point $\boldsymbol{q}$ at which a line $\mathcal{L}(t) = \boldsymbol{p} + t\mathbf{v}$ intersects a plane $\mathbf{f} = [\mathbf{n} \mid d]$ is found by solving for the value of $t$ such that $\mathbf{f} \cdot (\boldsymbol{p} + t\mathbf{v}) = 0$.

**Listing 3.6.** This function calculates the point q at which the line determined by p and v intersects the plane f and returns true if such a point exists and false if v is parallel to the plane.

```
float IntersectLinePlane(const Point3D& p, const Vector3D& v,
                         const Plane& f, Point3D *q)
{
    float fv = Dot(f, v);
    if (fabs(fv) > FLT_MIN)
    {
        *q = p - v * (Dot(f, p) / fv);
        return (true);
    }

    return (false);
}
```

test of $\mathbf{f} \cdot \boldsymbol{p} > 0$ determines whether this condition is satisfied. For a ray intersection to occur at a positive value of $t$, we must also have $\mathbf{f} \cdot \mathbf{v} < 0$ so that the ray is pointing toward the front side of the plane.

### 3.4.5 Intersection of Three Planes

Let $[\mathbf{n}_1 \mid d_1], [\mathbf{n}_2 \mid d_2]$, and $[\mathbf{n}_3 \mid d_3]$ be planes. As long as the normal vectors $\mathbf{n}_1, \mathbf{n}_2$, and $\mathbf{n}_3$ are linearly independent, the planes intersect at a single point $\boldsymbol{p}$ in space, as illustrated in Figure 3.12. Since this point lies in all three planes, we know that $[\mathbf{n}_i \mid d_i] \cdot \boldsymbol{p} = 0$ for $i = 1, 2, 3$, and this can be expressed as the linear system

$$\begin{bmatrix} \leftarrow & \mathbf{n}_1 & \rightarrow \\ \leftarrow & \mathbf{n}_2 & \rightarrow \\ \leftarrow & \mathbf{n}_3 & \rightarrow \end{bmatrix} \boldsymbol{p} = \begin{bmatrix} -d_1 \\ -d_2 \\ -d_3 \end{bmatrix} \tag{3.37}$$

in which the normal vectors compose the rows of a $3 \times 3$ matrix. Solving for $\boldsymbol{p}$ is a simple matter of multiplying both sides by the inverse of the matrix. Equation (1.95) gives a formula for the inverse of a $3 \times 3$ matrix whose columns are expressed as three vectors, and the same formula applies if we swap the meaning of rows and columns. Thus, the inverse of the matrix in Equation (3.37) is

$$\begin{bmatrix} \leftarrow & \mathbf{n}_1 & \rightarrow \\ \leftarrow & \mathbf{n}_2 & \rightarrow \\ \leftarrow & \mathbf{n}_3 & \rightarrow \end{bmatrix}^{-1} = \frac{1}{[\mathbf{n}_1, \mathbf{n}_2, \mathbf{n}_3]} \begin{bmatrix} \uparrow & \uparrow & \uparrow \\ \mathbf{n}_2 \times \mathbf{n}_3 & \mathbf{n}_3 \times \mathbf{n}_1 & \mathbf{n}_1 \times \mathbf{n}_2 \\ \downarrow & \downarrow & \downarrow \end{bmatrix}. \tag{3.38}$$

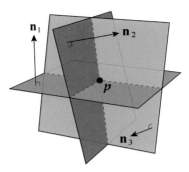

**Figure 3.12.** Three planes with linearly independent normal vectors $\mathbf{n}_1$, $\mathbf{n}_2$, and $\mathbf{n}_3$ intersect at a single point $p$.

Multiplying by the constant vector $(-d_1, -d_2, -d_3)$ yields the intersection point

$$p = \frac{d_1(\mathbf{n}_3 \times \mathbf{n}_2) + d_2(\mathbf{n}_1 \times \mathbf{n}_3) + d_3(\mathbf{n}_2 \times \mathbf{n}_1)}{[\mathbf{n}_1, \mathbf{n}_2, \mathbf{n}_3]}, \tag{3.39}$$

where the order of the factors in each cross product has been reversed to cancel the minus signs. This formula is implemented in Listing 3.7.

In the case that the three normal vectors $\mathbf{n}_1$, $\mathbf{n}_2$, and $\mathbf{n}_3$ are not linearly independent, the determinant $[\mathbf{n}_1, \mathbf{n}_2, \mathbf{n}_3]$ in Equation (3.39) is zero, and the planes do not intersect at a single point. As shown in Figure 3.13(a), this could mean that at least two of the planes are parallel to each other. There is also the possibility that no two planes are parallel to each other, but the intersections of each pair of planes occur along parallel lines, as shown in Figure 3.13(b).

**Listing 3.7.** This function calculates the point p at which three planes f1, f2, and f3 intersect and returns true if such a point exists. If the normal vectors are not linearly independent, then the function returns false.

```
bool IntersectThreePlanes(const Plane& f1, const Plane& f2,
                          const Plane& f3, Point3D *p)
{
    const Vector3D& n1 = f1.GetNormal();
    const Vector3D& n2 = f2.GetNormal();
    const Vector3D& n3 = f3.GetNormal();
```

```
Vector3D n1xn2 = Cross(n1, n2);
float det = Dot(n1xn2, n3);
if (fabs(det) > FLT_MIN)
{
    *p = (Cross(n3, n2) * f1.w + Cross(n1, n3) * f2.w
            - n1xn2 * f3.w) / det;
    return (true);
}

return (false);
}
```

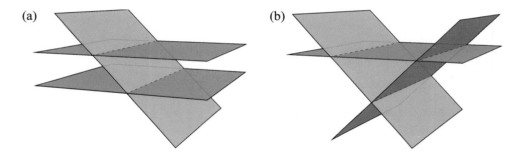

**Figure 3.13.** When the normal vectors for three planes are not linearly independent, either (a) at least two of the planes are parallel, or (b) there is no pair of parallel planes, but they all intersect at parallel lines.

### 3.4.6 Intersection of Two Planes

Two nonparallel planes $[\mathbf{n}_1 \mid d_1]$ and $[\mathbf{n}_2 \mid d_2]$ intersect at a line that is contained in both planes. To express this line in the parametric form $\mathcal{L}(t) = \boldsymbol{p} + t\mathbf{v}$, we need to find any starting point $\boldsymbol{p}$ on the line and the direction $\mathbf{v}$ to which the line runs parallel. Fortunately, the direction $\mathbf{v}$ is easily calculated as

$$\mathbf{v} = \mathbf{n}_1 \times \mathbf{n}_2 \tag{3.40}$$

because it must be perpendicular to both normal vectors. The point $\boldsymbol{p}$ can be calculated by introducing a third plane $[\mathbf{v} \mid 0]$ containing the origin $o$, as shown in Figure 3.14, and then solving the problem of a three-plane intersection. In this case, Equation (3.37) becomes

$$\begin{bmatrix} \leftarrow & \mathbf{n}_1 & \rightarrow \\ \leftarrow & \mathbf{n}_2 & \rightarrow \\ \leftarrow & \mathbf{v} & \rightarrow \end{bmatrix} \boldsymbol{p} = \begin{bmatrix} -d_1 \\ -d_2 \\ 0 \end{bmatrix}, \tag{3.41}$$

and the solution for $\boldsymbol{p}$ is

$$\boldsymbol{p} = \frac{d_1 (\mathbf{v} \times \mathbf{n}_2) + d_2 (\mathbf{n}_1 \times \mathbf{v})}{v^2}. \tag{3.42}$$

This formula is implemented in Listing 3.8, which returns both the point $\boldsymbol{p}$ and the direction $\mathbf{v}$.

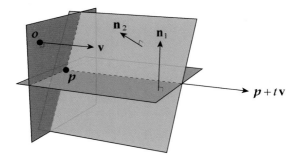

**Figure 3.14.** Two planes with nonparallel normal vectors $\mathbf{n}_1$ and $\mathbf{n}_2$ intersect at a line $\boldsymbol{p} + t\mathbf{v}$ for which $\mathbf{v} = \mathbf{n}_1 \times \mathbf{n}_2$. The point $\boldsymbol{p}$ is found by calculating the point where the two planes intersect the third plane $[\mathbf{v} \,|\, 0]$.

**Listing 3.8.** This function calculates the line determined by the point p and direction v at which two planes f1 and f2 intersect and returns true if it exists. If the normal vectors are parallel, then the function returns false.

```
bool IntersectTwoPlanes(const Plane& f1, const Plane& f2,
                        Point3D *p, Vector3D *v)
{
    const Vector3D& n1 = f1.GetNormal();
    const Vector3D& n2 = f2.GetNormal();

    *v = Cross(n1, n2);
    float det = Dot(*v, *v);
```

```
if (fabs(det) > FLT_MIN)
{
    *p = (Cross(*v, n2) * f1.w + Cross(n1, *v) * f2.w) / det;
    return (true);
}

return (false);
}
```

### 3.4.7 Transforming Planes

Let $\mathbf{f}^A = \begin{bmatrix} \mathbf{n}^A \mid d^A \end{bmatrix}$ be a plane that contains the point $q^A$ in coordinate system $A$, and let $\mathbf{H}$ be a $4 \times 4$ matrix having the form

$$\mathbf{H} = \begin{bmatrix} \mathbf{M} & \mathbf{t} \\ \mathbf{0} & 1 \end{bmatrix}, \tag{3.43}$$

where $\mathbf{M}$ is a $3 \times 3$ matrix and $\mathbf{t}$ is a 3D translation, that performs an affine transformation from coordinate system $A$ to coordinate system $B$. Our goal is to find the correct method for transforming $\mathbf{f}^A$ into $\mathbf{f}^B$ using the matrix $\mathbf{H}$. We know that the normal vector must transform as $\mathbf{n}^B = \mathbf{n}^A \operatorname{adj}(\mathbf{M})$ according to Equation (3.14), so the only question is what to do with $d^A$ to transform it into $d^B$.

Because the original plane contains $q^A$, we know that $d^A = -\mathbf{n}^A \cdot q^A$. For the transformed plane, we must have $d^B = -\mathbf{n}^B \cdot q^B$. We can transform each part of this product independently to get

$$\begin{aligned} d^B &= -\mathbf{n}^A \operatorname{adj}(\mathbf{M}) \mathbf{H} q^A \\ &= -\mathbf{n}^A \operatorname{adj}(\mathbf{M})(\mathbf{M} q^A + \mathbf{t}) \\ &= -\mathbf{n}^A \det(\mathbf{M}) q^A - \mathbf{n}^A \operatorname{adj}(\mathbf{M}) \mathbf{t} \\ &= \det(\mathbf{M})(d^A - \mathbf{n}^A \mathbf{M}^{-1} \mathbf{t}). \end{aligned} \tag{3.44}$$

Except for the extra factor of $\det(\mathbf{M})$, this is exactly the value produced by multiplying the plane $\mathbf{f}^A$ by the fourth column of $\mathbf{H}^{-1}$, which is given by Equation (2.42). Using the fact that $\det(\mathbf{H}) = \det(\mathbf{M})$ due to the specific form of $\mathbf{H}$, we come to the conclusion that a plane is transformed as

$$\boxed{\mathbf{f}^B = \mathbf{f}^A \det(\mathbf{H}) \mathbf{H}^{-1} = \mathbf{f}^A \operatorname{adj}(\mathbf{H}),} \tag{3.45}$$

and this is the four-dimensional analog of Equations (3.13) and (3.14). As with normal vectors, the determinant is usually ignored because planes are typically normalized so that $(f_x, f_y, f_z)$ is a unit vector. Normal vectors in three dimensions and planes in four dimensions both transform in the above manner because they are each examples of a mathematical element called an *antivector*, which is a central topic in Chapter 4.

Code that implements a plane transformation by calculating the product of a `Plane` data structure and a `Transform4D` data structure is provided in Listing 3.9. As with the transformation of a normal vector in Listing 3.1, the input matrix would need to be inverted before being passed to this function in order to calculate the correct transformation. Unlike the case of normal vectors, we cannot avoid the inversion if **M** is an orthogonal matrix because the translation **t** plays a part in the transformation of the plane.

**Listing 3.9.** This multiplication operator multiplies a `Plane` data structure, which corresponds to a 4D row vector, on the right by a `Transform4D` data structure to transform a plane from coordinate system $B$ to coordinate system $A$. Note that this transforms a plane in the opposite sense in relation to how the same matrix would transform a point from coordinate system $A$ to coordinate system $B$.

```
Plane operator *(const Plane& f, const Transform4D& H)
{
    return (Plane(f.x * H(0,0) + f.y * H(1,0) + f.z * H(2,0),
                  f.x * H(0,1) + f.y * H(1,1) + f.z * H(2,1),
                  f.x * H(0,2) + f.y * H(1,2) + f.z * H(2,2),
                  f.x * H(0,3) + f.y * H(1,3) + f.z * H(2,3) + f.w));
}
```

## 3.5 Plücker Coordinates

Earlier in this chapter, we discussed lines in a parametric form that required knowledge of a particular point on any given line. We were able to do away with a similar requirement for planes by finding a property that implicitly applied to all points in a given plane, and it turns out that we can do the same for lines. An implicit form for lines in three dimensions was discovered by Julius Plücker (1801–1868), and the components that make up these lines are hence called *Plücker coordinates*. Our discussion of Plücker coordinates in this section is somewhat abbreviated because the topic is wholly subsumed by the algebraic system presented in Chapter 4, where formulas that may presently appear to have been plucked out of thin air will be shown to arise naturally.

### 3.5.1 Implicit Lines

The Plücker coordinates for a line are composed of six components that can be grouped as two 3D vectors. Given a line that passes through the distinct points $p_1$ and $p_2$, one of those 3D vectors is the difference $\mathbf{v} = p_2 - p_1$, which is simply the direction parallel to the line. Once $\mathbf{v}$ has been calculated, it no longer contains any information about specific points on the line. The difference between any two points on the line separated by the same distance produces the same value of $\mathbf{v}$. The second 3D vector is the cross product $\mathbf{m} = p_1 \times p_2$, and we use the letter $\mathbf{m}$ because this is called the *moment* of the line. Although it may not be immediately obvious, the moment of a line is also the same value for any pair of points on the line separated by the same distance. To demonstrate this, suppose that the points $q_1$ and $q_2$ also lie on the line and satisfy $q_2 - q_1 = p_2 - p_1$, as shown in Figure 3.15. Let $\mathbf{r} = q_1 - p_1$, and then we can write

$$\begin{aligned} q_1 \times q_2 &= (p_1 + \mathbf{r}) \times (p_2 + \mathbf{r}) \\ &= p_1 \times p_2 + \mathbf{r} \times (p_2 - p_1) + \mathbf{r} \times \mathbf{r} \\ &= p_1 \times p_2. \end{aligned} \tag{3.46}$$

The cross product $\mathbf{r} \times (p_2 - p_1)$ is zero because $\mathbf{r}$ is parallel to the line direction $p_2 - p_1$. The moment $\mathbf{m}$ is thus an implicit property of the line that does not depend on the particular points that were used to calculate it.

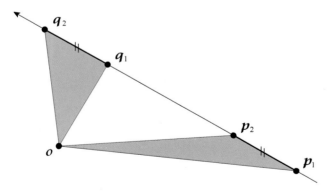

**Figure 3.15.** The moment $\mathbf{m}$ of a line, which points out of the page in this figure, is equal to $p_1 \times p_2$ for any two points $p_1$ and $p_2$ on the line. If another pair of points $q_1$ and $q_2$ on the line are separated by the same distance (in the same direction), then their cross product has the same value $\mathbf{m}$. The areas of the blue triangles are equal to each other because they are each half of the magnitude of the moment $\mathbf{m}$.

The direction $\mathbf{v}$ and moment $\mathbf{m}$, calculated with the same pair of points $\boldsymbol{p}_1$ and $\boldsymbol{p}_2$, constitute the six Plücker coordinates for a line, and we write this using the notation $\{\mathbf{v}\,|\,\mathbf{m}\}$. A line specified with Plücker coordinates is *homogeneous*, meaning that any nonzero scalar multiple of the components, applied to both $\mathbf{v}$ and $\mathbf{m}$, represents the same line. Multiplying by a scalar is equivalent to moving the points $\boldsymbol{p}_1$ and $\boldsymbol{p}_2$ on the line closer together or farther apart. A line is considered normalized when its direction $\mathbf{v}$ has unit length, accomplished by dividing all six components of the line by $\|\mathbf{v}\|$.

The moment vector $\mathbf{m}$ of a line is always perpendicular to its direction vector $\mathbf{v}$, and it's trivial to verify that $\mathbf{v} \cdot \mathbf{m} = 0$. As illustrated in Figure 3.16, the direction in which the moment vector points is determined by the right-hand rule. When the fingers of the right hand point in the direction vector $\mathbf{v}$, and the palm faces the origin, the right thumb points in the direction of the moment vector $\mathbf{m}$. For a normalized line, the magnitude of $\mathbf{m}$ is equal to the distance between the origin and the closest point on the line. This means that for any line $\{\mathbf{v}\,|\,\mathbf{m}\}$, normalized or not, the perpendicular distance to the origin is $\|\mathbf{m}\|/\|\mathbf{v}\|$.

The definition of a simple data structure named `Line` holding the six components of a line using Plücker coordinates is shown in Listing 3.10. The direction vector and moment vector are stored as `Vector3D` structure members that can be accessed directly. We do not provide any overloaded operators for performing operations with the `Line` data structure here because they wouldn't really make

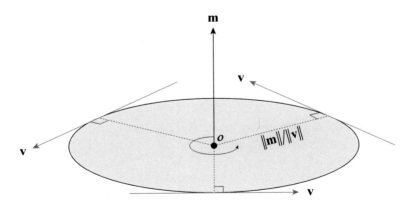

**Figure 3.16.** The moment vector $\mathbf{m}$ of a line $\{\mathbf{v}\,|\,\mathbf{m}\}$ is perpendicular to the direction vector $\mathbf{v}$, and the direction in which it points is determined by the right-hand rule. When the fingers of the right hand point in the direction vector $\mathbf{v}$, and the palm faces the origin, the right thumb points in the direction of the moment vector $\mathbf{m}$. The perpendicular distance between the origin $o$ and the line is equal to $\|\mathbf{m}\|/\|\mathbf{v}\|$.

sense for something that we're basically interpreting as a pair of vectors at this point. In Section 4.2, this will change, and we will be able to define a mathematically coherent set of operations among lines, points, and planes that does not require lines to be separated into these parts.

**Listing 3.10.** This is the definition of a simple data structure holding the six components of an implicit line using Plücker coordinates.

```
struct Line
{
    Vector3D    direction;
    Vector3D    moment;

    Line() = default;

    Line(float vx, float vy, float vz, float mx, float my, float mz) :
        direction(vx, vy, vz), moment(mx, my, mz)
    {
    }

    Line(const Vector3D& v, const Vector3D& m)
    {
        direction = v;
        moment = m;
    }
};
```

### 3.5.2 Homogeneous Formulas

Table 3.1 contains many formulas that can be used to calculate interesting quantities involving points, lines, and planes. In addition to the notation $\{\mathbf{v}\,|\,\mathbf{m}\}$ for a line, we continue using the notation $[\mathbf{n}\,|\,d]$ for a plane, and we introduce the similar notation $(\mathbf{p}\,|\,w)$ for a 4D vector composed of a 3D vector $\mathbf{p}$ and a scalar $w$. It's important to realize that all three of these representations of geometric entities are homogeneous. Multiplying any of them by a nonzero scalar, and in particular negating any of them, has no effect on their geometric meaning. As they appear in the table, the signs of the formulas have been chosen to be consistent whenever there is a relationship among multiple formulas. For example, the planes given by rows M and N are oriented so that the origin is on the positive side.

| | Formula | Description |
|---|---|---|
| **A** | $\{\mathbf{v} \mid \boldsymbol{p} \times \mathbf{v}\}$ | Line through point $\boldsymbol{p}$ with direction $\mathbf{v}$. |
| **B** | $\{\boldsymbol{p}_2 - \boldsymbol{p}_1 \mid \boldsymbol{p}_1 \times \boldsymbol{p}_2\}$ | Line through two points $\boldsymbol{p}_1$ and $\boldsymbol{p}_2$. |
| **C** | $\{\boldsymbol{p} \mid \mathbf{0}\}$ | Line through point $\boldsymbol{p}$ and origin. |
| **D** | $\{w_1\mathbf{p}_2 - w_2\mathbf{p}_1 \mid \mathbf{p}_1 \times \mathbf{p}_2\}$ | Line through two homogeneous points $(\mathbf{p}_1 \mid w_1)$ and $(\mathbf{p}_2 \mid w_2)$. |
| **E** | $\{\mathbf{n}_1 \times \mathbf{n}_2 \mid d_1\mathbf{n}_2 - d_2\mathbf{n}_1\}$ | Line where two planes $[\mathbf{n}_1 \mid d_1]$ and $[\mathbf{n}_2 \mid d_2]$ intersect. |
| **F** | $(\mathbf{m} \times \mathbf{n} + d\mathbf{v} \mid -\mathbf{n} \cdot \mathbf{v})$ | Homogeneous point where line $\{\mathbf{v} \mid \mathbf{m}\}$ intersects plane $[\mathbf{n} \mid d]$. |
| **G** | $(\mathbf{v} \times \mathbf{m} \mid v^2)$ | Homogeneous point closest to origin on line $\{\mathbf{v} \mid \mathbf{m}\}$. |
| **H** | $(-d\mathbf{n} \mid n^2)$ | Homogeneous point closest to origin on plane $[\mathbf{n} \mid d]$. |
| **I** | $[\mathbf{v} \times \mathbf{u} \mid -\mathbf{u} \cdot \mathbf{m}]$ | Plane containing line $\{\mathbf{v} \mid \mathbf{m}\}$ and parallel to direction $\mathbf{u}$. |
| **J** | $[\mathbf{v} \times \boldsymbol{p} + \mathbf{m} \mid -\boldsymbol{p} \cdot \mathbf{m}]$ | Plane containing line $\{\mathbf{v} \mid \mathbf{m}\}$ and point $\boldsymbol{p}$. |
| **K** | $[\mathbf{m} \mid 0]$ | Plane containing line $\{\mathbf{v} \mid \mathbf{m}\}$ and origin. |
| **L** | $[\mathbf{v} \times \mathbf{p} + w\mathbf{m} \mid -\mathbf{p} \cdot \mathbf{m}]$ | Plane containing line $\{\mathbf{v} \mid \mathbf{m}\}$ and homogeneous point $(\mathbf{p} \mid w)$. |
| **M** | $[\mathbf{m} \times \mathbf{v} \mid m^2]$ | Plane farthest from origin containing line $\{\mathbf{v} \mid \mathbf{m}\}$. |
| **N** | $[-w\mathbf{p} \mid p^2]$ | Plane farthest from origin containing point $(\mathbf{p} \mid w)$. |
| **O** | $\dfrac{\lvert \mathbf{v}_1 \cdot \mathbf{m}_2 + \mathbf{v}_2 \cdot \mathbf{m}_1 \rvert}{\lVert \mathbf{v}_1 \times \mathbf{v}_2 \rVert}$ | Distance between two lines $\{\mathbf{v}_1 \mid \mathbf{m}_1\}$ and $\{\mathbf{v}_2 \mid \mathbf{m}_2\}$. |
| **P** | $\dfrac{\lVert \mathbf{v} \times \boldsymbol{p} + \mathbf{m} \rVert}{\lVert \mathbf{v} \rVert}$ | Distance from line $\{\mathbf{v} \mid \mathbf{m}\}$ to point $\boldsymbol{p}$. |
| **Q** | $\dfrac{\lVert \mathbf{m} \rVert}{\lVert \mathbf{v} \rVert}$ | Distance from line $\{\mathbf{v} \mid \mathbf{m}\}$ to origin. |
| **R** | $\dfrac{\lvert \mathbf{n} \cdot \boldsymbol{p} + d \rvert}{\lVert \mathbf{n} \rVert}$ | Distance from plane $[\mathbf{n} \mid d]$ to point $\boldsymbol{p}$. |
| **S** | $\dfrac{\lvert d \rvert}{\lVert \mathbf{n} \rVert}$ | Distance from plane $[\mathbf{n} \mid d]$ to origin. |

**Table 3.1.** This table contains various formulas involving homogeneous points, planes, and lines described by Plücker coordinates. The notation $(\mathbf{p} \mid w)$ represents a homogeneous point with $\mathbf{p} = (x, y, z)$, the notation $[\mathbf{n} \mid d]$ represents a plane with normal direction $\mathbf{n}$ and distance to origin $d$, and the notation $\{\mathbf{v} \mid \mathbf{m}\}$ represents a line with direction $\mathbf{v}$ and moment $\mathbf{m}$. Rows with matching background colors contain formulas that are dual to each other.

Several of the formulas in Table 3.1 state instances in which specific values are plugged into more general expressions in order to explicitly highlight some common cases. Rows A and B give special formulas for a line when $w = 0$ and $w = 1$ are plugged into the general formula given by row D, and row C states the precise case in which $(\mathbf{p}_2 \mid w_2) = (\mathbf{0} \mid 1)$. Likewise, rows I, J, and K contain special cases of the general formula given by row L. In the distance formulas at the bottom of the table, rows Q and S are special cases of rows P and R when the point $\boldsymbol{p}$ is taken to be the origin.

There are eight rows in Table 3.1 containing four pairs of formulas, indicated by a matching background colors, that are related through a concept known as *duality*. Two lines $\{\mathbf{v}_1 \mid \mathbf{m}_1\}$ and $\{\mathbf{v}_2 \mid \mathbf{m}_2\}$ are said to be *dual* to each other when their direction vectors and moment vectors are swapped so that $\mathbf{v}_2 = \mathbf{m}_1$ and $\mathbf{m}_2 = \mathbf{v}_1$. A point $(\mathbf{p} \mid w)$ and a plane $[\mathbf{n} \mid d]$ are dual to each other when the four components belonging to one are simply reinterpreted as the four components of the other so that $\mathbf{p} = \mathbf{n}$ and $w = d$. These relationships are exemplified by rows D and E, where the line in row D passes through two points, but when we swap its direction and moment, the line in row E represents the intersection between two planes having the same components as the two points. Another example of duality is demonstrated by the formulas in rows F and L, which both involve a line $\{\mathbf{v} \mid \mathbf{m}\}$. The formula in row F gives the point at which the line intersects a plane $[\mathbf{n} \mid d]$, and the formula in row L gives the dual plane containing the line and a point having the same components as the plane in row F. The two formulas are exactly the same after swapping the meanings of $\mathbf{v}$ and $\mathbf{m}$ for the line.

The geometric symmetry of the duality between points and planes is perhaps best exhibited by the pair of rows G and M and the pair of rows H and N. The first pair shows the relationship between the point closest to the origin on a line $\{\mathbf{v} \mid \mathbf{m}\}$ and the plane farthest from the origin containing the same line. The formulas are the same except for the fact that $\mathbf{v}$ and $\mathbf{m}$ are swapped. The second pair shows that the point closest to the origin on a plane is related to the plane farthest from the origin containing a point through the simple reinterpretation of the four components making up each element.

Keep in mind that geometric entities calculated with the formulas in Table 3.1 are not generally normalized, and we extend this term to include homogeneous points, which would usually end up not having a $w$ coordinate of one. To put each type of element into normalized form, which may simplify later calculations, a point $(\mathbf{p} \mid w)$ needs to be divided by its $w$ coordinate, a plane $[\mathbf{n} \mid d]$ needs to be divided by $\|\mathbf{n}\|$, and a line $\{\mathbf{v} \mid \mathbf{m}\}$ needs to be divided by $\|\mathbf{v}\|$.

In the case of a degeneracy, each formula in Table 3.1 produces a geometric element whose components are all zeros. The simplest example is attempting to construct a line from two points that are exactly the same, in which case the formula in row B produces $\{\mathbf{0}\,|\,\mathbf{0}\}$. In the more complex case arising in row J, if the point $\boldsymbol{p}$ lies on the line $\{\mathbf{v}\,|\,\mathbf{m}\}$, then there is not enough information to construct a plane, and the result is $[\mathbf{0}\,|\,0]$. Similarly, the formula in row F produces the point $(\mathbf{0}\,|\,0)$ if the line $\{\mathbf{v}\,|\,\mathbf{m}\}$ is parallel to the plane $[\mathbf{n}\,|\,d]$ because there can be no unique point of intersection.

The distance between two lines $\{\mathbf{v}_1\,|\,\mathbf{m}_1\}$ and $\{\mathbf{v}_2\,|\,\mathbf{m}_2\}$, stated in row O of the table, can be derived by considering the distance between parallel planes constructed to contain each line and the direction $\mathbf{v}$ of the other line, as shown in Figure 3.17. Using row I in Table 3.1, these two planes are given by $[\mathbf{v}_1\times\mathbf{v}_2\,|-\mathbf{v}_2\cdot\mathbf{m}_1]$ and $[\mathbf{v}_1\times\mathbf{v}_2\,|\,\mathbf{v}_1\cdot\mathbf{m}_2]$, where the second plane has been negated so that the normal vectors point in the same direction. These planes are both normalized by dividing by $\|\mathbf{v}_1\times\mathbf{v}_2\|$, after which their $w$ coordinates correspond to the perpendicular distances between the planes and the origin. Subtracting these gives us

$$d = \frac{|\mathbf{v}_1\cdot\mathbf{m}_2 + \mathbf{v}_2\cdot\mathbf{m}_1|}{\|\mathbf{v}_1\times\mathbf{v}_2\|} \tag{3.47}$$

as the distance $d$ between the planes, which is also the distance between the original lines. If this distance is zero, then the lines are coplanar and intersect at a point.

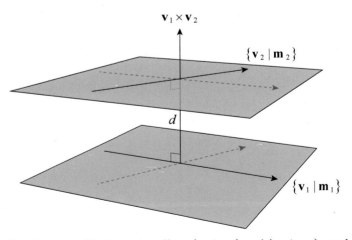

**Figure 3.17.** The distance $d$ between two lines $\{\mathbf{v}_1\,|\,\mathbf{m}_1\}$ and $\{\mathbf{v}_2\,|\,\mathbf{m}_2\}$ can be calculated by considering the parallel planes containing each line and the direction of the other.

### 3.5.3 Transforming Lines

Because Plücker coordinates contain both a difference of two points and the cross product between two points, the transformation of a line from one coordinate system to another can be somewhat tricky. As in the discussion of planes in the previous section, let $\mathbf{H}$ be a $4 \times 4$ matrix representing an affine transformation from coordinate system $A$ to coordinate system $B$ consisting of a $3 \times 3$ matrix $\mathbf{M}$ and a 3D translation vector $\mathbf{t}$, and suppose that $\{\mathbf{v}^A \mid \mathbf{m}^A\}$ is a line in coordinate system $A$ with $\mathbf{v}^A = \boldsymbol{p}_2 - \boldsymbol{p}_1$ and $\mathbf{m}^A = \boldsymbol{p}_1 \times \boldsymbol{p}_2$. Clearly, the transformed direction vector is simply given by $\mathbf{v}^B = \mathbf{M}\mathbf{v}^A$, but the transformed moment vector requires a closer look. Applying the matrix $\mathbf{H}$ to each of the points $\boldsymbol{p}_1$ and $\boldsymbol{p}_2$, the transformed points are equal to $\mathbf{M}\boldsymbol{p}_1 + \mathbf{t}$ and $\mathbf{M}\boldsymbol{p}_2 + \mathbf{t}$. The moment of the transformed line must be the cross product between these, so we have

$$\begin{aligned} \mathbf{m}^B &= \left(\mathbf{M}\boldsymbol{p}_1 + \mathbf{t}\right) \times \left(\mathbf{M}\boldsymbol{p}_2 + \mathbf{t}\right) \\ &= \left(\mathbf{M}\boldsymbol{p}_1\right) \times \left(\mathbf{M}\boldsymbol{p}_2\right) + \mathbf{t} \times \left(\mathbf{M}\boldsymbol{p}_2\right) - \mathbf{t} \times \left(\mathbf{M}\boldsymbol{p}_1\right). \end{aligned} \tag{3.48}$$

The cross product $\left(\mathbf{M}\boldsymbol{p}_1\right) \times \left(\mathbf{M}\boldsymbol{p}_2\right)$ transforms under a $3 \times 3$ matrix $\mathbf{M}$ according to Equation (3.14), and the cross products involving the translation $\mathbf{t}$ can be combined into one cross product that operates on $\mathbf{v}^A$. This lets us write

$$\mathbf{m}^B = \mathbf{m}^A \operatorname{adj}(\mathbf{M}) + \mathbf{t} \times \left(\mathbf{M}\mathbf{v}^A\right), \tag{3.49}$$

where we are treating $\mathbf{m}^A$ and $\mathbf{m}^B$ as row vectors. The complete affine transformation of a line from coordinate system $A$ to coordinate system $B$ is thus given by

$$\boxed{\left\{\mathbf{v}^B \mid \mathbf{m}^B\right\} = \left\{\mathbf{M}\mathbf{v}^A \mid \mathbf{m}^A \operatorname{adj}(\mathbf{M}) + \mathbf{t} \times \left(\mathbf{M}\mathbf{v}^A\right)\right\}.} \tag{3.50}$$

This formula is implemented in its strict form in Listing 3.11. As usual, the calculation of the adjugate of $\mathbf{M}$ can be avoided if we know that $\mathbf{M}$ is orthogonal, in which case we can treat $\mathbf{m}^A$ and $\mathbf{m}^B$ as column vectors and replace $\mathbf{m}^A \operatorname{adj}(\mathbf{M})$ with $\mathbf{M}\mathbf{m}^A$.

**Listing 3.11.** This function transforms a `Line` data structure with a `Transform4D` data structure. The first line calculates the transpose of the adjugate of the upper-left $3 \times 3$ portion of `H` because `Matrix3D` structures are stored in column-major order. Later, this matrix is multiplied on the right by the moment of the line as a column vector, which is equivalent to multiplying the nontransposed matrix on the left by a row vector as done in Equation (3.50).

```
Line Transform(const Line& line, const Transform4D& H)
{
    Matrix3D adj(Cross(H[1], H[2]), Cross(H[2], H[0]), Cross(H[0], H[1]));
    const Point3D& t = H.GetTranslation();

    Vector3D v = H * line.direction;
    Vector3D m = adj * line.moment + Cross(t, v);
    return (Line(v, m));
}
```

## Exercises for Chapter 3

1.  In a closed triangle mesh having at least four vertices, what is the minimum number of triangles that must make use of any particular vertex, assuming that there are no degenerate cases in which a triangle has zero area?

2.  Let $\mathcal{L}(t) = \boldsymbol{p} + t\mathbf{v}$ be a line, and let $\boldsymbol{q}$ be an arbitrary point. Find a formula that gives the point on the line $\mathcal{L}$ that is closest to $\boldsymbol{q}$.

3.  Let $\mathcal{L}_1(t_1) = \boldsymbol{p}_1 + t_1\mathbf{v}_1$ and $\mathcal{L}_2(t_2) = \boldsymbol{p}_2 + t_2\mathbf{v}_2$ be nonparallel lines, and define the function $f(t_1, t_2) = [\mathcal{L}_2(t_2) - \mathcal{L}_1(t_1)]^2$ to be the squared distance between a point on $\mathcal{L}_1$ and a point on $\mathcal{L}_2$. Use the partial derivatives $\partial f / \partial t_1$ and $\partial f / \partial t_2$ to find the values of $t_1$ and $t_2$ at which $f$ reaches a minimum, and show that they are equivalent to the values calculated in Equation (3.24).

4.  Show that the point $\boldsymbol{p}$ calculated with Equation (3.42) is the point closest to the origin on the line where two planes intersect.

5.  Find formulas for the new components $\mathbf{n}'$ and $d'$ of a plane $[\mathbf{n} \,|\, d]$ after it has been translated by a vector $\mathbf{t}$.

6.  Find formulas for the new components $\mathbf{v}'$ and $\mathbf{m}'$ of a line $\{\mathbf{v} \,|\, \mathbf{m}\}$ after it has been translated by a vector $\mathbf{t}$.

7.  Show that $(\mathbf{v} \times \mathbf{m} \,|\, v^2)$ is the homogeneous point on the line $\{\mathbf{v} \,|\, \mathbf{m}\}$ closest to the origin by constructing a plane with normal vector $\mathbf{v}$ that contains the origin and intersecting it with $\{\mathbf{v} \,|\, \mathbf{m}\}$.

8.  Find a formula for the plane $[\mathbf{n} \,|\, d]$ containing two nonparallel lines $\{\mathbf{v}_1 \,|\, \mathbf{m}_1\}$ and $\{\mathbf{v}_2 \,|\, \mathbf{m}_2\}$ that intersect.

9.  Find a formula for the plane $[\mathbf{n} \,|\, d]$ containing two distinct parallel lines $\{\mathbf{v} \,|\, \mathbf{m}_1\}$ and $\{\mathbf{v} \,|\, \mathbf{m}_2\}$ having the same direction but different moments.

10. Let $\{\mathbf{v} \,|\, \mathbf{m}_1\}$ and $\{\mathbf{v} \,|\, \mathbf{m}_2\}$ be parallel lines having the same direction but different moments. Find a formula for the distance $d$ between these two lines by considering the triangle formed by the origin and the closest point to the origin on each line.

**11.** Let $a$ and $b$ be distinct points on a stationary line, and let $p(t)$ and $q(t)$ be functions that give points on a moving line as a function of time $t$, defined by

$$p(t) = p_0 + t\mathbf{v}_p$$
$$q(t) = q_0 + t\mathbf{v}_q,$$

where $\mathbf{v}_p$ and $\mathbf{v}_q$ are constant velocities. Find a quadratic equation in $t$ whose solutions are the times at which the two lines intersect.

**12.** Let $\{\mathbf{v}_1 \mid \mathbf{m}_1\}$ and $\{\mathbf{v}_2 \mid \mathbf{m}_2\}$ be nonparallel lines, and define $\mathbf{u} = \mathbf{v}_1 \times \mathbf{v}_2$. Find a formula for the homogeneous point on line 1 that is closest to line 2 by first constructing a plane $\mathbf{f}$ that contains line 2 and is parallel to the direction $\mathbf{u}$ and then finding the intersection between $\mathbf{f}$ and line 1.

# Chapter 4

# Advanced Algebra

The previous chapters discussed vectors, points, lines, planes, matrices, and transforms using the conventional mathematics that are most widely known throughout the field of game engine development. In several places, we gave an indication that something was a little off. The conventional mathematics didn't tell the whole story, or it caused us to misinterpret subtle concepts that could provide a more intuitive understanding if they were explained in the right way. It is now time to remedy this situation by presenting a different kind of mathematics that is actually somewhat older but was lost to obscurity for much of its existence. This will likely require a few mental adjustments on the part of the reader, but the reward will be an understanding of a much more natural and elegant mathematical structure that can be used to engineer your virtual simulations.

Most of this chapter focuses on the discoveries of Hermann Grassmann (1809–1877), which occurred contemporaneously with Hamilton's discovery of the quaternions and slightly earlier than the independent development of Plücker coordinates. Grassmann called his mathematical breakthrough the *theory of extension*, but it is now referred to as *Grassmann algebra* in his honor or as the more generic term *exterior algebra*. The remainder of this chapter will briefly introduce *geometric algebra*, which is related to Grassmann algebra by the fact that they are both specific instances of the general concept of a *Clifford algebra*. Grassmann algebra and geometric algebra are vast topics that we cannot cover with any kind of completeness. Our goal is to present the basics and concentrate on providing a better understanding of the mathematics presented throughout the earlier chapters in this book. During this process, we will limit ourselves to Euclidean space in order to avoid mathematical generalizations that would only clutter our presentation without adding any significant practical value in the context of game engines.

# 4.1 Grassmann Algebra

In Grassmann algebra, the types of mathematical elements that arise and the operations that can be performed on them exhibit a precise symmetry. Every type of element is associated with another type of element that is naturally opposite. Directions, areas, and volumes are built up and torn down by two opposing fundamental operations. A proper understanding of Grassmann algebra requires that we give equal importance to both sides of each symmetry, and this is emphasized throughout this section as we introduce the wedge product and antiwedge product. In the next section, we will apply Grassmann algebra to four-dimensional homogeneous coordinates, where these products make it particularly easy to express certain geometric calculations.

## 4.1.1 Wedge Product

At the heart of Grassmann algebra is an operation called the *wedge product*, which like the dot product and cross product, gets its name from the symbol $\wedge$ that we use to denote it, an upward-pointing wedge. The wedge product is also known as the *exterior product*, or as Grassmann originally called it, the *progressive product*. An $n$-dimensional Grassmann algebra is constructed by starting with ordinary scalars and $n$-dimensional vectors and then defining how they are multiplied together using the wedge product. The wedge product provides a natural way to multiply vectors and other mathematical entities together in a geometrically meaningful way, and it will lead us to a deeper understanding the homogeneous representations of points, lines, and planes in 3D space.

For any product involving a scalar, either scalar times scalar or scalar times vector, the wedge product is no different from the scalar multiplication that we are familiar with from conventional mathematics. Beyond that, however, things get a little different, but the entire algebra is derived from one simple rule: any vector multiplied by itself using the wedge product is zero. That is, for any vector $\mathbf{a}$, we always have

$$\boxed{\mathbf{a} \wedge \mathbf{a} = 0.}$$
(4.1)

This rule has an important consequence that reveals itself when we consider the sum of two vectors $\mathbf{a}$ and $\mathbf{b}$. The wedge product of $\mathbf{a} + \mathbf{b}$ with itself gives us

$$(\mathbf{a} + \mathbf{b}) \wedge (\mathbf{a} + \mathbf{b}) = \mathbf{a} \wedge \mathbf{a} + \mathbf{a} \wedge \mathbf{b} + \mathbf{b} \wedge \mathbf{a} + \mathbf{b} \wedge \mathbf{b} = 0.$$
(4.2)

| Property | Description |
|---|---|
| $\mathbf{a} \wedge \mathbf{b} = -\mathbf{b} \wedge \mathbf{a}$ | Anticommutativity of the wedge product. |
| $(\mathbf{a} \wedge \mathbf{b}) \wedge \mathbf{c} = \mathbf{a} \wedge (\mathbf{b} \wedge \mathbf{c})$ | Associative law for the wedge product. |
| $\mathbf{a} \wedge (\mathbf{b} + \mathbf{c}) = \mathbf{a} \wedge \mathbf{b} + \mathbf{a} \wedge \mathbf{c}$ | Distributive laws for the wedge product. |
| $(\mathbf{a} + \mathbf{b}) \wedge \mathbf{c} = \mathbf{a} \wedge \mathbf{c} + \mathbf{b} \wedge \mathbf{c}$ | |
| $(t\mathbf{a}) \wedge \mathbf{b} = \mathbf{a} \wedge (t\mathbf{b}) = t(\mathbf{a} \wedge \mathbf{b})$ | Scalar factorization for the wedge product. |
| $s \wedge t = t \wedge s = st$ | Wedge product between scalars. |
| $s \wedge \mathbf{a} = \mathbf{a} \wedge s = s\mathbf{a}$ | Wedge product between a scalar and a vector. |

**Table 4.1.** These are the basic properties of the wedge product. The letters $\mathbf{a}$, $\mathbf{b}$, and $\mathbf{c}$ represent vectors, and the letters $s$ and $t$ represent scalar values.

The products $\mathbf{a} \wedge \mathbf{a}$ and $\mathbf{b} \wedge \mathbf{b}$ must both be zero, and that leaves us with

$$\mathbf{a} \wedge \mathbf{b} + \mathbf{b} \wedge \mathbf{a} = 0, \tag{4.3}$$

from which we conclude that

$$\boxed{\mathbf{a} \wedge \mathbf{b} = -\mathbf{b} \wedge \mathbf{a}.} \tag{4.4}$$

This establishes the property that multiplication of vectors with the wedge product is anticommutative. Reversing the order of the two factors negates the product. We should stress that we have only shown this to be true for vectors at this point, and it does not hold in general. In particular, the wedge product between scalars, being ordinary multiplication, is commutative. These facts and a few additional properties of the wedge product, when used to multiply scalars and vectors, are summarized in Table 4.1.

## 4.1.2 Bivectors

The wedge product $\mathbf{a} \wedge \mathbf{b}$ between two vectors $\mathbf{a}$ and $\mathbf{b}$ cannot be expressed in terms of scalars and vectors. It forms a new type of mathematical element called a *bivector*, and this being something outside the space of scalars and vectors is the reason why the wedge product is also called the exterior product. Whereas a vector can be thought of as a combination of a direction and a magnitude, a bivector can be thought of as a combination of an *oriented area* and a magnitude. A bivector $\mathbf{a} \wedge \mathbf{b}$ can be visualized as a parallelogram whose sides are parallel to the vectors $\mathbf{a}$ and $\mathbf{b}$, as shown in Figure 4.1. The parallelogram has an intrinsic winding direction that reflects the order of the vectors $\mathbf{a}$ and $\mathbf{b}$ in the wedge product, and this direction can be determined by following the perimeter of the parallelogram first along the direction of $\mathbf{a}$ and then along the direction of $\mathbf{b}$. If the order of the vectors is reversed, negating the result, then the winding direction is also reversed, exchanging clockwise and counterclockwise directions around the perimeter.

In order to give some quantitative substance to a bivector, we can examine the effect the wedge product has on vectors that have been decomposed into components over an orthonormal basis. We'll be working in three dimensions for now, but keep in mind that a similar analysis is valid in any number of dimensions. Let $\mathbf{e}_1$, $\mathbf{e}_2$, and $\mathbf{e}_3$ represent three mutually orthogonal unit vectors in three-dimensional space. These generic labels are intended to avoid being tied to any particular coordinate system, but we will equate them to a typical right-handed configuration of the $x$, $y$, and $z$ axes. We can write an arbitrary vector $\mathbf{a} = (a_x, a_y, a_z)$ in terms of the three basis vectors as

$$\mathbf{a} = a_x\mathbf{e}_1 + a_y\mathbf{e}_2 + a_z\mathbf{e}_3. \tag{4.5}$$

Doing this for two vectors $\mathbf{a}$ and $\mathbf{b}$ allows us to write the bivector $\mathbf{a} \wedge \mathbf{b}$ as

$$\begin{aligned}
\mathbf{a} \wedge \mathbf{b} &= (a_x\mathbf{e}_1 + a_y\mathbf{e}_2 + a_z\mathbf{e}_3) \wedge (b_x\mathbf{e}_1 + b_y\mathbf{e}_2 + b_z\mathbf{e}_3) \\
&= a_xb_y (\mathbf{e}_1 \wedge \mathbf{e}_2) + a_xb_z (\mathbf{e}_1 \wedge \mathbf{e}_3) + a_yb_x (\mathbf{e}_2 \wedge \mathbf{e}_1) \\
&\quad + a_yb_z (\mathbf{e}_2 \wedge \mathbf{e}_3) + a_zb_x (\mathbf{e}_3 \wedge \mathbf{e}_1) + a_zb_y (\mathbf{e}_3 \wedge \mathbf{e}_2),
\end{aligned} \tag{4.6}$$

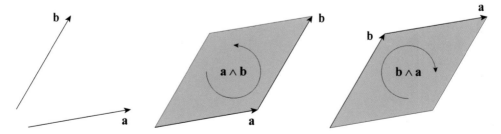

**Figure 4.1.** The bivector $\mathbf{a} \wedge \mathbf{b}$ can be visualized as a parallelogram whose sides are parallel to the vectors $\mathbf{a}$ and $\mathbf{b}$. The intrinsic winding direction follows the perimeter along the first vector in the wedge product and then along the second vector. Reversing the order of the vectors in the product also reverses the winding direction.

where each term containing the wedge product of a basis vector with itself has been dropped because it is zero. Every term in this expression contains a wedge product whose factors appear in the reverse order of the wedge product in another term, so we can negate one half of the terms and collect over common bivectors to arrive at

$$\mathbf{a} \wedge \mathbf{b} = \left( a_y b_z - a_z b_y \right) \left( \mathbf{e}_2 \wedge \mathbf{e}_3 \right) + \left( a_z b_x - a_x b_z \right) \left( \mathbf{e}_3 \wedge \mathbf{e}_1 \right)$$
$$+ \left( a_x b_y - a_y b_x \right) \left( \mathbf{e}_1 \wedge \mathbf{e}_2 \right). \tag{4.7}$$

Here, we have arranged terms in the order by which a basis vector does *not* appear in the wedge product, so the term missing $\mathbf{e}_1$ comes first, the term missing $\mathbf{e}_2$ comes second, and the term missing $\mathbf{e}_3$ comes third. This expression can be simplified no further, and it demonstrates that an arbitrary bivector in 3D space has three components over a *bivector basis* consisting of $\mathbf{e}_2 \wedge \mathbf{e}_3$, $\mathbf{e}_3 \wedge \mathbf{e}_1$, and $\mathbf{e}_1 \wedge \mathbf{e}_2$.

The three coefficients in Equation (4.7) should have a familiar ring to them. They are exactly the same values that are calculated by the cross product, which is something we defined in Section 1.5 with no explanation of its source. Now, these numbers appear as a result that was derived from a fundamental property of the wedge product. The fact that bivectors have three components is unique to three dimensions, and this similarity makes a bivector *look* like an ordinary vector, but it is indeed something different, and failing to make a distinction leads to an incomplete and inelegant picture of the mathematics. An important thing to understand is that the wedge product is defined in a manner similar to Equation (4.7) in any number of dimensions, while the cross product is confined to only three dimensions, limiting its usefulness.

Once the three coefficients in Equation (4.7) have been calculated, the resulting bivector no longer contains any information about the two vectors multiplied together to create it. The only information carried by a bivector is its orientation in space and its area. Even though we have drawn a bivector as a parallelogram in Figure 4.1, it doesn't actually possess any particular shape. In fact, there are infinitely many pairs of vectors that could be multiplied together to produce any given bivector, and they could all be drawn as different parallelograms that have the same area and lie in the same plane but don't have the same angles. There is no specific parallelogram whose shape is a fixed property of the bivector.

### 4.1.3 Trivectors

We now have an algebraic system that includes scalars, vectors, and bivectors, but this is not the end of the road, at least not in three dimensions. Let's consider the wedge product among three vectors **a**, **b**, and **c** given by

$$\mathbf{a} \wedge \mathbf{b} \wedge \mathbf{c} = \left( a_x \mathbf{e}_1 + a_y \mathbf{e}_2 + a_z \mathbf{e}_3 \right) \wedge \left( b_x \mathbf{e}_1 + b_y \mathbf{e}_2 + b_z \mathbf{e}_3 \right)$$
$$\wedge \left( c_x \mathbf{e}_1 + c_y \mathbf{e}_2 + c_z \mathbf{e}_3 \right). \tag{4.8}$$

When multiplying all of this out, remember that any term containing a repeated factor is zero, and the only parts that remain are the terms containing all three of $\mathbf{e}_1$, $\mathbf{e}_2$, and $\mathbf{e}_3$ in the six possible orders in which they can be multiplied. Fully written out, these six terms are

$$\mathbf{a} \wedge \mathbf{b} \wedge \mathbf{c} = a_x b_y c_z \left( \mathbf{e}_1 \wedge \mathbf{e}_2 \wedge \mathbf{e}_3 \right)$$
$$+ a_y b_z c_x \left( \mathbf{e}_2 \wedge \mathbf{e}_3 \wedge \mathbf{e}_1 \right)$$
$$+ a_z b_x c_y \left( \mathbf{e}_3 \wedge \mathbf{e}_1 \wedge \mathbf{e}_2 \right)$$
$$+ a_z b_y c_x \left( \mathbf{e}_3 \wedge \mathbf{e}_2 \wedge \mathbf{e}_1 \right)$$
$$+ a_y b_x c_z \left( \mathbf{e}_2 \wedge \mathbf{e}_1 \wedge \mathbf{e}_3 \right)$$
$$+ a_x b_z c_y \left( \mathbf{e}_1 \wedge \mathbf{e}_3 \wedge \mathbf{e}_2 \right). \tag{4.9}$$

We can swap the order of adjacent factors one or more times in each of the triple wedge products to make all of them equal to $\mathbf{e}_1 \wedge \mathbf{e}_2 \wedge \mathbf{e}_3$ as long as we negate the scalar coefficient each time we do it. For example, $\mathbf{e}_1 \wedge \mathbf{e}_3 \wedge \mathbf{e}_2 = -\left( \mathbf{e}_1 \wedge \mathbf{e}_2 \wedge \mathbf{e}_3 \right)$ because it requires a single swap of the last two factors, and $\mathbf{e}_3 \wedge \mathbf{e}_1 \wedge \mathbf{e}_2 = +\left( \mathbf{e}_1 \wedge \mathbf{e}_2 \wedge \mathbf{e}_3 \right)$ because it requires two swaps. After adjusting all of the terms, we can write the complete product as

$$\boxed{\begin{array}{l} \mathbf{a} \wedge \mathbf{b} \wedge \mathbf{c} = \\ \left( a_x b_y c_z + a_y b_z c_x + a_z b_x c_y - a_x b_z c_y - a_y b_x c_z - a_z b_y c_x \right) \left( \mathbf{e}_1 \wedge \mathbf{e}_2 \wedge \mathbf{e}_3 \right). \end{array}} \tag{4.10}$$

This is yet another new mathematical element called a *trivector*, which is distinct from a scalar, vector, and bivector. Notice that in three dimensions, the trivector has only one component, and it is associated with the basis trivector $\mathbf{e}_1 \wedge \mathbf{e}_2 \wedge \mathbf{e}_3$. A trivector combines an *oriented volume* and a magnitude, but the only choice we have about the orientation is whether the volume is positive or negative.

You may recognize the scalar coefficient in Equation (4.10) as the determinant of a $3 \times 3$ matrix whose columns or rows are the vectors **a**, **b**, and **c**, or you may recognize it as the scalar triple product $[\mathbf{a}, \mathbf{b}, \mathbf{c}] = (\mathbf{a} \times \mathbf{b}) \cdot \mathbf{c}$, which has the same value. Just as the wedge product $\mathbf{a} \wedge \mathbf{b}$ of two vectors has a magnitude equal to the area of the parallelogram spanned by $\mathbf{a}$ and $\mathbf{b}$, the wedge product $\mathbf{a} \wedge \mathbf{b} \wedge \mathbf{c}$ of three vectors has a magnitude equal to the volume of the parallelepiped spanned by $\mathbf{a}$, $\mathbf{b}$, and $\mathbf{c}$. In contrast to the scalar triple product, however, the triple wedge product possesses a pleasing symmetry among its factors. In higher dimensions, this can be continued to hypervolumes with greater numbers of sides by simply adding more vectors to the product. The wedge product builds higher-dimensional geometry by combining the dimensionalities of the elements on which it operates.

When three vectors $\mathbf{a}$, $\mathbf{b}$, and $\mathbf{c}$ are multiplied together with the wedge product, the absolute value of the coefficient in Equation (4.10) is always the same, but its sign depends on the order in which the vectors are multiplied. If an odd number of swaps are made to change the order from $\mathbf{a} \wedge \mathbf{b} \wedge \mathbf{c}$, then the result is negated, but if an even number of swaps are made, then nothing happens. The six possible orderings are illustrated in Figure 4.2. The three products in the top row have one sign, whichever is given by Equation (4.10) for any given inputs, and the three products in the bottom row have the opposite sign. In this figure, the vectors have a right-handed configuration so that the volumes in the top row are positive and the volumes in the bottom row are negative, but reversing any one of the vectors so that it points in the opposite direction would cause these signs to be flipped. In general, when the third vector in the product follows the right-hand rule, meaning that the right thumb points in the direction of the third vector when the fingers of the right hand curl in the winding direction of the first two vectors, the volume is positive, and otherwise, the volume is negative. The universe doesn't actually have a preference for the right-hand rule over a similar left-hand rule, however, and the sign of our calculation depends on the fact that we are choosing $\mathbf{e}_1 \wedge \mathbf{e}_2 \wedge \mathbf{e}_3$ as our trivector basis element (as opposed to some other ordering of those vectors) and that $\mathbf{e}_1$, $\mathbf{e}_2$, and $\mathbf{e}_3$ form the axes of a right-handed coordinate system.

## 4.1.4 Algebraic Structure

In three dimensions, trivectors are the limit for new mathematical entities. We cannot multiply by a fourth vector to create a *quadrivector* because the product $\mathbf{a} \wedge \mathbf{b} \wedge \mathbf{c} \wedge \mathbf{d}$ for *any* vectors $\mathbf{a}$, $\mathbf{b}$, $\mathbf{c}$, and $\mathbf{d}$ must be zero. When we expand the product, we find that every term contains a repeated factor due to the fact that it's impossible to have four linearly independent vectors in three-dimensional space. This means that the complete Grassmann algebra in three dimensions consists of elements that are scalars, vectors having three components, bivectors having three components, and trivectors having one component.

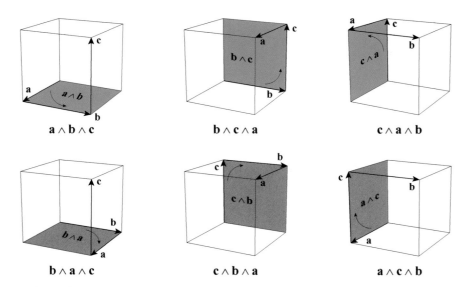

**Figure 4.2.** These are the six ways in which three vectors can be multiplied together with the wedge product to construct a trivector. The three trivectors in the top row are equal to each other, and the three trivectors in the bottom row are negated relative to the top row. In the top row, the third vector in the product satisfies the right-hand rule by pointing out of an area that is wound counterclockwise due to the order of the first two vectors in the product. The trivectors in the bottom row have the opposite sign because their third vectors point out of areas that are instead wound clockwise.

There is a combinatorial reason why it works out this way, and it has to do with how basis vectors from the set $S = \{\mathbf{e}_1, \mathbf{e}_2, \mathbf{e}_3\}$ are used by each type of element. Components of a vector each use one member of the set $S$, and there are three ways to choose one member, so vectors have three components. Components of a bivector each use two members of the set $S$, and there are three ways to choose two members, so bivectors also have three components. Finally, the component of a trivector uses all three members of the set $S$, and because there is only one way to choose all three, trivectors have only one component. Along the same line of reasoning, we can say that scalars use *no* members of the set $S$, and there is only one way to choose nothing, so scalars have one component.

To generalize, we introduce the term *k-vector* to mean the type of element whose components all correspond to some possible combination of $k$ basis vectors. The number $k$ is called the *grade* of the element. An ordinary vector is a 1-vector, a bivector is a 2-vector, a trivector is a 3-vector, and so on. Scalars have a grade of zero. Whenever a $k$-vector can be expressed as the wedge product of $k$ different 1-vectors, we call it a *k-blade*. That is, a $k$-blade is an element $\mathbf{A}$ that can be written as the product

$$\mathbf{A} = \mathbf{v}_1 \wedge \mathbf{v}_2 \wedge \cdots \wedge \mathbf{v}_k, \tag{4.11}$$

where each $\mathbf{v}_i$ is an ordinary vector. The term *blade* without the number $k$ in front of it means an element that's equal to the wedge product of some arbitrary number of 1-vectors. (The term *simple k-vector* is also used to mean the same thing as a $k$-blade in some texts.) As a notational convention, we use uppercase bold letters in this book to represent $k$-vectors whenever $k \geq 2$ to make it easier to distinguish them from 1-vectors, which are still represented by lowercase bold letters. We also use uppercase letters to represent blades of unspecified grade, even if they could be 1-blades or 0-blades.

In three dimensions or fewer, every $k$-vector is also a $k$-blade, but this is not true in higher dimensions. The simplest counterexample in four dimensions is the bivector

$$\mathbf{B} = \mathbf{e}_1 \wedge \mathbf{e}_2 + \mathbf{e}_3 \wedge \mathbf{e}_4, \tag{4.12}$$

which cannot be written as $\mathbf{B} = \mathbf{v}_1 \wedge \mathbf{v}_2$ for any vectors $\mathbf{v}_1$ and $\mathbf{v}_2$, and thus $\mathbf{B}$ is a 2-vector, but it is not a 2-blade (or equivalently, it is not a simple bivector). Elements that are not blades will have no utility in the remainder of this chapter, so it can always be assumed that every element under discussion after this point is a blade and can thus be expressed as the wedge product of some number of vectors.

We define the *grade function* $\mathrm{gr}(\mathbf{A})$ as the function that returns the grade of the blade $\mathbf{A}$. This function lets us write things like

$$\boxed{\mathrm{gr}(\mathbf{A} \wedge \mathbf{B}) = \mathrm{gr}(\mathbf{A}) + \mathrm{gr}(\mathbf{B}),} \tag{4.13}$$

which states that the grade of the wedge product between two blades $\mathbf{A}$ and $\mathbf{B}$ is the sum of the grades of $\mathbf{A}$ and $\mathbf{B}$. In order to handle the special case in which $\mathrm{gr}(\mathbf{A}) > 0$ and $\mathrm{gr}(\mathbf{B}) > 0$, but $\mathbf{A} \wedge \mathbf{B} = 0$, we must either leave $\mathrm{gr}(0)$ undefined or wave our hands and say that zero is allowed to assume any grade. It doesn't really matter, though, because we'll never use the grade function as a computational device, but only as a symbolic operation on nonzero inputs.

We mentioned earlier that anticommutativity applied to vectors under the wedge product, but not generally to other kinds of elements in the algebra. Using the grade function, we can succinctly express the condition under which two blades $\mathbf{A}$ and $\mathbf{B}$ commute as

$$\mathbf{A} \wedge \mathbf{B} = (-1)^{\mathrm{gr}(\mathbf{A})\,\mathrm{gr}(\mathbf{B})}\,\mathbf{B} \wedge \mathbf{A}. \tag{4.14}$$

This means that if either $\mathrm{gr}(\mathbf{A})$ or $\mathrm{gr}(\mathbf{B})$ is even, then $\mathbf{A}$ and $\mathbf{B}$ commute under the wedge product. Otherwise, when both grades are odd, they anticommute. The case in which $\mathbf{A}$ and $\mathbf{B}$ commute can be understood by considering the factor with an even grade as the wedge product of an even number of basis vectors. The other factor can be moved from one side of the product to the other by making an even number of transpositions and multiplying by $-1$ for each one, resulting in no overall change in sign.

In the $n$-dimensional Grassmann algebra, the number of components composing an element of grade $k$ is given by the binomial coefficient

$$\binom{n}{k} = \frac{n!}{k!\,(n-k)!} \tag{4.15}$$

because this gives the number of ways to choose $k$ items from a set of $n$ items. The binomial coefficients produce Pascal's triangle, as shown in Figure 4.3, where the row corresponding to three dimensions reads $1, 3, 3, 1$. The complete $n$-dimensional Grassmann algebra is constructed by choosing basis vectors from the set $\{\mathbf{e}_1, \mathbf{e}_2, \ldots, \mathbf{e}_n\}$ in every possible quantity and combining them in every possible way. For any given element in the algebra, a particular basis vector $\mathbf{e}_i$ is either included or excluded, so we can think of the inclusion status of the entire set of basis vectors as an $n$-bit quantity for which all $2^n$ values are allowed. This is reflected in the fact that each row of Pascal's triangle sums to the power of two corresponding to the number of dimensions.

In this book, we will explore Grassmann algebras primarily in three and four dimensions. We will not have the need to visit any higher dimensions, but we will briefly discuss some of the lower-dimensional algebras. For a side-by-side comparison, Table 4.2 lists the basis elements of each grade belonging to the Grassmann algebras in dimensions numbering zero through four. In the table, we have adopted the simplified notation $\mathbf{e}_{ab\cdots}$ in which multiple subscripts indicate the wedge product among multiple basis vectors so that, for example, $\mathbf{e}_{12} = \mathbf{e}_1 \wedge \mathbf{e}_2$ and $\mathbf{e}_{123} = \mathbf{e}_1 \wedge \mathbf{e}_2 \wedge \mathbf{e}_3$.

The zero-dimensional Grassmann algebra is nothing more than the set of real numbers because it has no basis vectors. The one-dimensional Grassmann algebra has a single basis vector $\mathbf{e}$, and every element of the entire algebra can be written as $a + b\mathbf{e}$, where $a$ and $b$ are real numbers. This algebra is known as the *dual numbers*, and it is something that we will combine with quaternions in Volume 3.

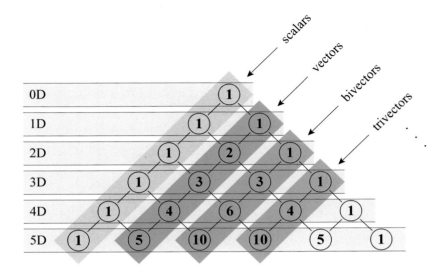

**Figure 4.3.** The number of components composing an element of grade $k$ in the $n$-dimensional Grassmann algebra is given by the binomial coefficient $\binom{n}{k}$, which produces Pascal's triangle. Each row corresponds to a particular number of dimensions, and the numbers in each row tell how many independent basis elements exist for each grade. There is always one scalar basis element and $n$ vector basis elements. The number of bivector basis elements is given by the third number in each row, the number of trivector basis elements is given by the fourth number, and so on.

In the dual numbers, the wedges are typically omitted, and a product between two elements $a + b\mathbf{e}$ and $c + d\mathbf{e}$ looks like

$$(a + b\mathbf{e})(c + d\mathbf{e}) = ac + (ad + bc)\mathbf{e},$$

where the term containing $bd$ does not appear because $\mathbf{e}^2 = 0$.

The two-dimensional Grassmann algebra contains two basis vectors $\mathbf{e}_1$ and $\mathbf{e}_2$ that correspond to the $x$ and $y$ axes, and it contains a single basis bivector $\mathbf{e}_{12}$ that corresponds to the only planar orientation possible, that of the whole 2D coordinate system. The wedge product between two 2D vectors $\mathbf{a}$ and $\mathbf{b}$ is

$$\mathbf{a} \wedge \mathbf{b} = (a_x b_y - a_y b_x)\mathbf{e}_{12}, \tag{4.16}$$

and the value of this bivector is equal to the signed area of a parallelogram whose sides are given by $\mathbf{a}$ and $\mathbf{b}$. (Exercise 1 asks for a proof.) The area is positive when $\mathbf{a}$ and $\mathbf{b}$ are wound counterclockwise about the origin and negative otherwise. Of

| Dimension | Grade | Count | Basis Element Values |
|---|---|---|---|
| **0D** | Scalar | 1 | 1 |
| **1D** | Scalar | 1 | 1 |
| | Vector | 1 | $\mathbf{e}$ |
| **2D** | Scalar | 1 | 1 |
| | Vector | 2 | $\mathbf{e}_1, \mathbf{e}_2$ |
| | Bivector | 1 | $\mathbf{e}_{12}$ |
| **3D** | Scalar | 1 | 1 |
| | Vector | 3 | $\mathbf{e}_1, \mathbf{e}_2, \mathbf{e}_3$ |
| | Bivector | 3 | $\mathbf{e}_{23}, \mathbf{e}_{31}, \mathbf{e}_{12}$ |
| | Trivector | 1 | $\mathbf{e}_{123}$ |
| **4D** | Scalar | 1 | 1 |
| | Vector | 4 | $\mathbf{e}_1, \mathbf{e}_2, \mathbf{e}_3, \mathbf{e}_4$ |
| | Bivector | 6 | $\mathbf{e}_{41}, \mathbf{e}_{42}, \mathbf{e}_{43}, \mathbf{e}_{23}, \mathbf{e}_{31}, \mathbf{e}_{12}$ |
| | Trivector | 4 | $\mathbf{e}_{234}, \mathbf{e}_{314}, \mathbf{e}_{124}, \mathbf{e}_{132}$ |
| | Quadrivector | 1 | $\mathbf{e}_{1234}$ |

**Table 4.2.** This table lists the basis elements of each grade in the $n$-dimensional Grassmann algebras for $0 \leq n \leq 4$. The total number of basis elements is always equal to $2^n$, and the number of basis elements of a particular grade $k$ is given by $\binom{n}{k}$.

course, the area of a triangle having sides given by **a** and **b** is half the value given by Equation (4.16).

The elements of the $n$-dimensional Grassmann algebra can be generalized so that the components of every grade are mixed into a single quantity called a *multivector*. For example, a multivector belonging to the three-dimensional Grassmann algebra is written as

$$a + b\mathbf{e}_1 + c\mathbf{e}_2 + d\mathbf{e}_3 + f\mathbf{e}_{23} + g\mathbf{e}_{31} + h\mathbf{e}_{12} + k\mathbf{e}_{123}. \qquad (4.17)$$

It would be possible to design a computational system in which all eight components of the 3D multivector in Equation (4.17) were always stored in memory and operations were always performed between two complete multivectors. However, this would be rather impractical and wasteful because many of the components would often be zero, and it gets even worse when we move to four-dimensional homogeneous coordinates. Furthermore, it's largely unnecessary because there is no significant geometric meaning in a quantity composed of components having different grades. In the context of Grassmann algebra, we will always be working with quantities that are purely composed of components having the same grade. (In the discussion of geometric algebra later in this chapter, however, we will have a reason to study mixed scalars and bivectors.)

The highest-grade basis element in an *n*-dimensional Grassmann algebra is called the *unit volume element*, and it is given the special symbol $\mathbf{E}_n$, defined as

$$\boxed{\mathbf{E}_n = \mathbf{e}_{12\cdots n} = \mathbf{e}_1 \wedge \mathbf{e}_2 \wedge \cdots \wedge \mathbf{e}_n.}$$ (4.18)

The unit volume element corresponds to an *n*-dimensional volume of magnitude one that involves all *n* basis vectors in the algebra. Because it has only one component, any multiple of the unit volume element is often called a *pseudoscalar* quantity. Many texts use the symbol $\mathbf{I}_n$ for the unit volume element, but this conflicts with the symbol used for the $n \times n$ identity matrix, which could appear in the same context, so we prefer $\mathbf{E}_n$ in this book.

### 4.1.5 Complements

Let us consider the basis vectors $\mathbf{e}_1$, $\mathbf{e}_2$, and $\mathbf{e}_3$ in the 3D Grassmann algebra. Each one can be multiplied on the right by the wedge product of the other two vectors in such an order that the wedge product of all three yields the volume element $\mathbf{E}_3$, as shown by

$$\mathbf{e}_1 \wedge (\mathbf{e}_2 \wedge \mathbf{e}_3) = \mathbf{E}_3$$
$$\mathbf{e}_2 \wedge (\mathbf{e}_3 \wedge \mathbf{e}_1) = \mathbf{E}_3$$
$$\mathbf{e}_3 \wedge (\mathbf{e}_1 \wedge \mathbf{e}_2) = \mathbf{E}_3.$$ (4.19)

The parentheses aren't really necessary here because the wedge product is associative, but they have been included to clarify the values by which the basis vectors are being multiplied. The bivectors $\mathbf{e}_{23}$, $\mathbf{e}_{31}$, and $\mathbf{e}_{12}$ (using the shorthand notation now) are called the *complements* of the vectors $\mathbf{e}_1$, $\mathbf{e}_2$, and $\mathbf{e}_3$, respectively.

If we instead multiply the basis vectors on the left, we get the same results, as shown by

$$(\mathbf{e}_2 \wedge \mathbf{e}_3) \wedge \mathbf{e}_1 = \mathbf{E}_3$$
$$(\mathbf{e}_3 \wedge \mathbf{e}_1) \wedge \mathbf{e}_2 = \mathbf{E}_3$$
$$(\mathbf{e}_1 \wedge \mathbf{e}_2) \wedge \mathbf{e}_3 = \mathbf{E}_3.$$ (4.20)

This demonstrates that we can consider the vectors $\mathbf{e}_1$, $\mathbf{e}_2$, and $\mathbf{e}_3$ to be the complements of the bivectors $\mathbf{e}_{23}$, $\mathbf{e}_{31}$, and $\mathbf{e}_{12}$ because multiplication on the right produces the value $\mathbf{E}_3$. In general, the complement of any blade is whatever quantity we need to multiply it by, on the right, to produce the volume element. The complement of one is the whole volume element $\mathbf{E}_3$ because $1 \wedge \mathbf{E}_3 = \mathbf{E}_3$, and the complement of $\mathbf{E}_3$ is just one because $\mathbf{E}_3 \wedge 1 = \mathbf{E}_3$. The complements of all eight basis elements in the 3D Grassmann algebra are summarized in Table 4.3.

We specify the operation of taking a complement by placing a bar above a quantity so that $\overline{\mathbf{B}}$ means the complement of $\mathbf{B}$. Using this notation, the complements of the three basis vectors and three basis bivectors can be written as follows.

$$\begin{aligned}
\overline{\mathbf{e}}_1 &= \mathbf{e}_{23} & \overline{\mathbf{e}}_{23} &= \mathbf{e}_1 \\
\overline{\mathbf{e}}_2 &= \mathbf{e}_{31} & \overline{\mathbf{e}}_{31} &= \mathbf{e}_2 \\
\overline{\mathbf{e}}_3 &= \mathbf{e}_{12} & \overline{\mathbf{e}}_{12} &= \mathbf{e}_3
\end{aligned} \tag{4.21}$$

The term "complement" is used because $\overline{\mathbf{B}}$ fills in whichever dimensions are missing from a basis element $\mathbf{B}$ in order to create the full volume element $\mathbf{E}_n$ of the $n$-dimensional Grassmann algebra. The binomial coefficients that make up Pascal's triangle exhibit a natural symmetry because the number of ways that we can choose $k$ items from a set of $n$ items is exactly equal to the number of ways that we can choose *all except k* items. When we take a complement, we are turning a $k$-dimensional element into an $(n-k)$-dimensional element by essentially inverting the spatial dimensions that are involved.

| Basis Element B | Complement $\overline{\mathbf{B}}$ |
|:---:|:---:|
| $1$ | $\mathbf{e}_1 \wedge \mathbf{e}_2 \wedge \mathbf{e}_3$ |
| $\mathbf{e}_1$ | $\mathbf{e}_2 \wedge \mathbf{e}_3$ |
| $\mathbf{e}_2$ | $\mathbf{e}_3 \wedge \mathbf{e}_1$ |
| $\mathbf{e}_3$ | $\mathbf{e}_1 \wedge \mathbf{e}_2$ |
| $\mathbf{e}_2 \wedge \mathbf{e}_3$ | $\mathbf{e}_1$ |
| $\mathbf{e}_3 \wedge \mathbf{e}_1$ | $\mathbf{e}_2$ |
| $\mathbf{e}_1 \wedge \mathbf{e}_2$ | $\mathbf{e}_3$ |
| $\mathbf{e}_1 \wedge \mathbf{e}_2 \wedge \mathbf{e}_3$ | $1$ |

**Table 4.3.** These are the complements of the eight basis elements belonging to the three-dimensional Grassmann algebra.

We've defined what the complement means for basis elements, and now to extend it to all elements of the algebra, we simply require that it is a linear operation. That is, for any scalar $s$ and $k$-blades $\mathbf{A}$ and $\mathbf{B}$, we must have

$$\overline{s\mathbf{A}} = s\overline{\mathbf{A}}$$
$$\overline{\mathbf{A} + \mathbf{B}} = \overline{\mathbf{A}} + \overline{\mathbf{B}}. \tag{4.22}$$

If we apply these rules to an arbitrary 3D vector $\mathbf{v} = x\mathbf{e}_1 + y\mathbf{e}_2 + z\mathbf{e}_3$, then we can calculate its complement as $\overline{\mathbf{v}} = x\mathbf{e}_{23} + y\mathbf{e}_{31} + z\mathbf{e}_{12}$. The complement has the same magnitude, and it can be thought of as a reinterpretation of the original components in terms of the complementary basis elements. If we multiply $\mathbf{v}$ by its complement, then we get

$$\mathbf{v} \wedge \overline{\mathbf{v}} = v^2\mathbf{E}_3, \tag{4.23}$$

and this will be an important result later in our discussion of the dot product.

The complement operation can be used in three dimensions to explicitly convert the wedge product between two vectors into the conventional cross product. That is, we can define the cross product between vectors $\mathbf{a}$ and $\mathbf{b}$ as

$$\boxed{\mathbf{a} \times \mathbf{b} = \overline{\mathbf{a} \wedge \mathbf{b}}.} \tag{4.24}$$

Each of the bivector basis elements in the wedge product is replaced by its complementary vector basis element to make the result of the cross product a vector. It is the process of taking the complement that destroys the associative property of the cross product because it occurs between successive multiplications. There is seldom any mathematical justification for preferring the artificiality of a vector resulting from the cross product over the more natural and intuitive bivector resulting from the analogous wedge product.

Although we have been careful to state that complements appear on the right side of a wedge product, it should be clear that they are commutative in three dimensions and could just as well appear on the left side of the wedge product in every case. However, this is not true for Grassmann algebras in even numbers of dimensions, so we need to make a distinction between complements that appear on the right and left sides.

The *right complement* of a basis element $\mathbf{B}$ in the $n$-dimensional Grassmann algebra is the complement that we have been discussing so far, and it is the quantity $\overline{\mathbf{B}}$ such that

$$\mathbf{B} \wedge \overline{\mathbf{B}} = \mathbf{E}_n. \tag{4.25}$$

The *left complement* of $\mathbf{B}$ is written with the bar beneath it, and it is the quantity $\underline{\mathbf{B}}$ such that

$$\underline{\mathbf{B}} \wedge \mathbf{B} = \mathbf{E}_n. \tag{4.26}$$

The left complement is also extended to all blades by the same linearity property required for the right complement in Equation (4.22).

When the number of dimensions $n$ is odd, then all right and left complements are the same, and we can simply call both of them "the complement". When $n$ is even, the right and left complement of a $k$-blade $\mathbf{A}$ are related by the equation

$$\boxed{\underline{\mathbf{A}} = (-1)^{k(n-k)}\, \overline{\mathbf{A}},} \tag{4.27}$$

and this shows that the right and left complements are equal when $k$ is even, and they are negatives when $k$ is odd. This equation gives us a way to raise or lower the bar in order to switch between right and left complement whenever it would be convenient.

The blades for which the right and left complements have different signs also have the property that they change sign when either complement is applied twice. The relationship between a $k$-blade $\mathbf{A}$ and either of its double complements is

$$\overline{\overline{\mathbf{A}}} = \underline{\underline{\mathbf{A}}} = (-1)^{k(n-k)}\, \mathbf{A}. \tag{4.28}$$

Taking mixed complements of a blade $\mathbf{A}$, a right complement and a left complement together, always restores the original blade $\mathbf{A}$, as expressed by

$$\underline{\overline{\mathbf{A}}} = \mathbf{A}. \tag{4.29}$$

This is true for all grades in all dimensions, and it doesn't matter in which order the two complements are applied, so the notation is intentionally ambiguous about whether the right or left complement is taken first.

Table 4.4 demonstrates the differences between the left and right complements as well as the negating effects of the double complement for the 16 basis elements belonging to the four-dimensional Grassmann algebra. Only the vectors and trivectors, being the elements with odd grade, exhibit the sign-alternating behavior. The scalar basis element, the six bivector basis elements, and the volume element have equal right and left complements and do not change sign when either complement is applied twice.

| Basis Element B | Complement $\overline{B}$ | Complement $\underline{B}$ | Double Complement |
|---|---|---|---|
| $1$ | $\mathbf{e}_1 \wedge \mathbf{e}_2 \wedge \mathbf{e}_3 \wedge \mathbf{e}_4$ | $\mathbf{e}_1 \wedge \mathbf{e}_2 \wedge \mathbf{e}_3 \wedge \mathbf{e}_4$ | $1$ |
| $\mathbf{e}_1$ | $\mathbf{e}_2 \wedge \mathbf{e}_3 \wedge \mathbf{e}_4$ | $-\mathbf{e}_2 \wedge \mathbf{e}_3 \wedge \mathbf{e}_4$ | $-\mathbf{e}_1$ |
| $\mathbf{e}_2$ | $\mathbf{e}_3 \wedge \mathbf{e}_1 \wedge \mathbf{e}_4$ | $-\mathbf{e}_3 \wedge \mathbf{e}_1 \wedge \mathbf{e}_4$ | $-\mathbf{e}_2$ |
| $\mathbf{e}_3$ | $\mathbf{e}_1 \wedge \mathbf{e}_2 \wedge \mathbf{e}_4$ | $-\mathbf{e}_1 \wedge \mathbf{e}_2 \wedge \mathbf{e}_4$ | $-\mathbf{e}_3$ |
| $\mathbf{e}_4$ | $\mathbf{e}_1 \wedge \mathbf{e}_3 \wedge \mathbf{e}_2$ | $-\mathbf{e}_1 \wedge \mathbf{e}_3 \wedge \mathbf{e}_2$ | $-\mathbf{e}_4$ |
| $\mathbf{e}_4 \wedge \mathbf{e}_1$ | $-\mathbf{e}_2 \wedge \mathbf{e}_3$ | $-\mathbf{e}_2 \wedge \mathbf{e}_3$ | $\mathbf{e}_4 \wedge \mathbf{e}_1$ |
| $\mathbf{e}_4 \wedge \mathbf{e}_2$ | $-\mathbf{e}_3 \wedge \mathbf{e}_1$ | $-\mathbf{e}_3 \wedge \mathbf{e}_1$ | $\mathbf{e}_4 \wedge \mathbf{e}_2$ |
| $\mathbf{e}_4 \wedge \mathbf{e}_3$ | $-\mathbf{e}_1 \wedge \mathbf{e}_2$ | $-\mathbf{e}_1 \wedge \mathbf{e}_2$ | $\mathbf{e}_4 \wedge \mathbf{e}_3$ |
| $\mathbf{e}_2 \wedge \mathbf{e}_3$ | $-\mathbf{e}_4 \wedge \mathbf{e}_1$ | $-\mathbf{e}_4 \wedge \mathbf{e}_1$ | $\mathbf{e}_2 \wedge \mathbf{e}_3$ |
| $\mathbf{e}_3 \wedge \mathbf{e}_1$ | $-\mathbf{e}_4 \wedge \mathbf{e}_2$ | $-\mathbf{e}_4 \wedge \mathbf{e}_2$ | $\mathbf{e}_3 \wedge \mathbf{e}_1$ |
| $\mathbf{e}_1 \wedge \mathbf{e}_2$ | $-\mathbf{e}_4 \wedge \mathbf{e}_3$ | $-\mathbf{e}_4 \wedge \mathbf{e}_3$ | $\mathbf{e}_1 \wedge \mathbf{e}_2$ |
| $\mathbf{e}_2 \wedge \mathbf{e}_3 \wedge \mathbf{e}_4$ | $-\mathbf{e}_1$ | $\mathbf{e}_1$ | $-\mathbf{e}_2 \wedge \mathbf{e}_3 \wedge \mathbf{e}_4$ |
| $\mathbf{e}_3 \wedge \mathbf{e}_1 \wedge \mathbf{e}_4$ | $-\mathbf{e}_2$ | $\mathbf{e}_2$ | $-\mathbf{e}_3 \wedge \mathbf{e}_1 \wedge \mathbf{e}_4$ |
| $\mathbf{e}_1 \wedge \mathbf{e}_2 \wedge \mathbf{e}_4$ | $-\mathbf{e}_3$ | $\mathbf{e}_3$ | $-\mathbf{e}_1 \wedge \mathbf{e}_2 \wedge \mathbf{e}_4$ |
| $\mathbf{e}_1 \wedge \mathbf{e}_3 \wedge \mathbf{e}_2$ | $-\mathbf{e}_4$ | $\mathbf{e}_4$ | $-\mathbf{e}_1 \wedge \mathbf{e}_3 \wedge \mathbf{e}_2$ |
| $\mathbf{e}_1 \wedge \mathbf{e}_2 \wedge \mathbf{e}_3 \wedge \mathbf{e}_4$ | $1$ | $1$ | $\mathbf{e}_1 \wedge \mathbf{e}_2 \wedge \mathbf{e}_3 \wedge \mathbf{e}_4$ |

**Table 4.4.** These are the right and left complements of the 16 basis elements belonging to the four-dimensional Grassmann algebra. The two complements for vectors and trivectors, highlighted in orange, have different signs. Vectors and trivectors also change sign when either complement operation is applied twice.

## 4.1.6 Antivectors

In the $n$-dimensional Grassmann algebra, a 1-vector and its complement, which is an $(n-1)$-vector, both have $n$ components. We give the complement of a vector the special name *antivector* because it corresponds to all of the directions in space that are perpendicular to the vector, excluding only the one direction to which the vector corresponds. An antivector is everything that a vector is not, and vice versa. They are opposites of each other and stand on equal ground with perfect symmetry. Since vectors and antivectors have the same numbers of components, a clear distinction is not always made between the two in much of the existing literature, and an antivector is often called a *pseudovector* because its transformation properties are different from an ordinary vector. However, the prefix "pseudo" tends to induce a characterization of lower status through its meaning of "false" without adding any descriptive value to the term, whereas the prefix "anti" accurately depicts an antivector as something that "opposes" its complementary vector.

Let $\mathbf{v} = v_1\mathbf{e}_1 + v_2\mathbf{e}_2 + \cdots + v_n\mathbf{e}_n$ be a vector in the $n$-dimensional Grassmann algebra. The antivector corresponding to $\mathbf{v}$ is simply its right complement, which we can express in terms of the right complements of the basis vectors $\mathbf{e}_i$ as

$$\overline{\mathbf{v}} = v_1\overline{\mathbf{e}}_1 + v_2\overline{\mathbf{e}}_2 + \cdots + v_n\overline{\mathbf{e}}_n. \tag{4.30}$$

Then, as we saw earlier in three dimensions, the wedge product between a vector $\mathbf{v}$ and its corresponding antivector $\overline{\mathbf{v}}$ is

$$\mathbf{v} \wedge \overline{\mathbf{v}} = v^2\mathbf{E}_n. \tag{4.31}$$

Using the right complement was an arbitrary choice. We could also construct an antivector in terms of the left complements of the basis vectors, and then we would write

$$\underline{\mathbf{v}} = v_1\underline{\mathbf{e}}_1 + v_2\underline{\mathbf{e}}_2 + \cdots + v_n\underline{\mathbf{e}}_n. \tag{4.32}$$

The wedge product that gives us a positive volume would then be

$$\underline{\mathbf{v}} \wedge \mathbf{v} = v^2\mathbf{E}_n. \tag{4.33}$$

In odd dimensions, there is no difference between antivectors based on right complements and antivectors based on left complements, but in even dimensions, they are negatives of each other. The distinction only matters when we explicitly convert a vector to an antivector by reinterpreting the components over the complements of the basis vectors. When an antivector is constructed by calculating the wedge product of lower-grade elements, the results are automatically interpreted with the correct signs matching the choice of $\overline{\mathbf{e}}_i$ or $\underline{\mathbf{e}}_i$ as the antivector's basis elements.

Consider the $n$-dimensional wedge product between a vector $\mathbf{a}$ and the complement of a vector $\mathbf{b}$. If we were to write this out completely as

$$\mathbf{a} \wedge \overline{\mathbf{b}} = \left(a_1\mathbf{e}_1 + a_2\mathbf{e}_2 + \cdots + a_n\mathbf{e}_n\right)\left(b_1\overline{\mathbf{e}}_1 + b_2\overline{\mathbf{e}}_2 + \cdots + b_n\overline{\mathbf{e}}_n\right) \tag{4.34}$$

and distribute the multiplication, then we would get a result that has $n^2$ terms. But only $n$ terms are nonzero, and they are the ones for which each $\mathbf{e}_i$ is matched with its complement $\overline{\mathbf{e}}_i$. The product then becomes

$$\mathbf{a} \wedge \bar{\mathbf{b}} = a_1 b_1 \mathbf{e}_1 \bar{\mathbf{e}}_1 + a_2 b_2 \mathbf{e}_2 \bar{\mathbf{e}}_2 + \cdots + a_n b_n \mathbf{e}_n \bar{\mathbf{e}}_n$$
$$= \left( a_1 b_1 + a_2 b_2 + \cdots + a_n b_n \right) \mathbf{E}_n, \tag{4.35}$$

and this demonstrates that the origin of the dot product is the wedge product between a vector and an antivector, or $(n-1)$-vector. (We could take a complement to eliminate the volume element $\mathbf{E}_n$, but the antiwedge product will provide a better alternative below.) As with the cross product, the defining formula for the dot product was given with no explanation in Section 1.5, but we have now derived it from fundamental principles in Grassmann algebra. Note that we arrive at the same result if we calculate $\underline{\mathbf{a}} \wedge \mathbf{b}$ instead of $\mathbf{a} \wedge \bar{\mathbf{b}}$, as shown by

$$\underline{\mathbf{a}} \wedge \mathbf{b} = a_1 b_1 \underline{\mathbf{e}}_1 \mathbf{e}_1 + a_2 b_2 \underline{\mathbf{e}}_2 \mathbf{e}_2 + \cdots + a_n b_n \underline{\mathbf{e}}_n \mathbf{e}_n$$
$$= \left( a_1 b_1 + a_2 b_2 + \cdots + a_n b_n \right) \mathbf{E}_n. \tag{4.36}$$

Antivectors have the property that they behave like row vectors that transform properly through multiplication on the right by the adjugate of a transformation matrix. That is, if $\mathbf{M}$ is an $n \times n$ matrix that transforms an ordinary $n$-dimensional vector $\mathbf{v}$ from one coordinate system to another through the product $\mathbf{Mv}$, then an $n$-dimensional antivector $\mathbf{a}$ is transformed through the product $\mathbf{a} \, \mathrm{adj}(\mathbf{M})$. We have already encountered this property for normal vectors and implicit planes in Chapter 3. A normal vector is really a three-dimensional antivector, which is evident when it's calculated with the cross product of two vectors that we consider to be a wedge product in disguise. A plane is really a four-dimensional antivector, and we will show how it can be constructed from the wedge product of three points in the next section.

### 4.1.7 Antiwedge Product

At the beginning of this section, we mentioned that there are two opposing fundamental operations in Grassmann algebra that exhibit a natural and precise symmetry. The wedge product has a mirror operation that we call the *antiwedge product* and denote by the symbol $\vee$, a downward-pointing wedge. Grassmann called the antiwedge product the *regressive product* to complement his progressive product, but he considered them to be different manifestations of the same *combinatorial product*, and he used the same notation for both. This made some sense in Grassmann's original work because he equated scalars with volume elements, but we have since learned that it's necessary to make an explicit distinction between the two types of products.

The antiwedge product operates on antivectors in the same way that the wedge product operates on vectors. Whereas the wedge product $\mathbf{A} \wedge \mathbf{B}$ combines the basis elements that are *present* in the factors $\mathbf{A}$ and $\mathbf{B}$, the antiwedge product $\mathbf{A} \vee \mathbf{B}$ combines the basis elements that are *absent* in the factors $\mathbf{A}$ and $\mathbf{B}$. In this way, the wedge product and antiwedge product are analogous to the union and intersection of spatial dimensions, and this feature will be put to practical use in the next section.

In a manner symmetric to the wedge product between vectors, the antiwedge product between antivectors is anticommutative. For any antivectors $\mathbf{a}$ and $\mathbf{b}$, this means that

$$\mathbf{a} \vee \mathbf{b} = -\mathbf{b} \vee \mathbf{a}, \tag{4.37}$$

and as a special case, $\mathbf{a} \vee \mathbf{a} = 0$. Note that *vectors* anticommute under the antiwedge product only in even-dimensional Grassmann algebras. This is symmetric to the fact that *antivectors* anticommute under the wedge product only in even numbers of dimensions because that's where antivectors have odd grade. The general rule for the antiwedge product between any elements $\mathbf{A}$ and $\mathbf{B}$ is

$$\mathbf{A} \vee \mathbf{B} = (-1)^{(n-\mathrm{gr}(\mathbf{A}))(n-\mathrm{gr}(\mathbf{B}))} \mathbf{B} \vee \mathbf{A}. \tag{4.38}$$

Comparing this to the rule for the wedge product given by Equation (4.14), we see that two elements commute under the antiwedge product precisely when their complements commute under the wedge product. If either $n - \mathrm{gr}(\mathbf{A})$ or $n - \mathrm{gr}(\mathbf{B})$ is even, then $\mathbf{A}$ and $\mathbf{B}$ commute under the antiwedge product.

The complements of the wedge product and antiwedge product between elements $\mathbf{A}$ and $\mathbf{B}$ obey the laws

$$\overline{\mathbf{A} \wedge \mathbf{B}} = \overline{\mathbf{A}} \vee \overline{\mathbf{B}}$$
$$\overline{\mathbf{A} \vee \mathbf{B}} = \overline{\mathbf{A}} \wedge \overline{\mathbf{B}}. \tag{4.39}$$

These correspond very exactly to De Morgan's laws from logic and set theory. (Unfortunately, the established meanings of the symbols $\wedge$ and $\vee$ in Grassmann algebra have the opposite meanings of the same symbols when used for the AND and OR operations in logic or the similar symbols $\cap$ and $\cup$ when used for intersection and union in set theory.) We can convert right complements to left complements using Equation (4.27) to obtain the similar laws

$$\mathbf{A} \wedge \mathbf{B} = \underline{\mathbf{A}} \vee \underline{\mathbf{B}}$$
$$\mathbf{A} \vee \mathbf{B} = \overline{\mathbf{A}} \wedge \overline{\mathbf{B}}. \tag{4.40}$$

After taking the left complement of both sides of the laws in Equation (4.39) and the right complement of both sides of the laws in Equation (4.40), we find that we can write either of the wedge and antiwedge products in terms of the other as

$$\mathbf{A} \wedge \mathbf{B} = \overline{\underline{\mathbf{A}} \vee \underline{\mathbf{B}}} = \underline{\overline{\mathbf{A}} \vee \overline{\mathbf{B}}}$$
$$\mathbf{A} \vee \mathbf{B} = \overline{\underline{\mathbf{A}} \wedge \underline{\mathbf{B}}} = \underline{\overline{\mathbf{A}} \wedge \overline{\mathbf{B}}}. \tag{4.41}$$

As a basic example of the antiwedge product, consider the three-dimensional antivectors $\mathbf{a} = a_x \overline{\mathbf{e}}_1 + a_y \overline{\mathbf{e}}_2 + a_z \overline{\mathbf{e}}_3$ and $\mathbf{b} = b_x \overline{\mathbf{e}}_1 + b_y \overline{\mathbf{e}}_2 + b_z \overline{\mathbf{e}}_3$. When these are multiplied with the antiwedge product, the result is expressed in terms of the complements of bivectors as

$$\mathbf{a} \vee \mathbf{b} = \left( a_y b_z - a_z b_y \right) \overline{\mathbf{e}}_{23} + \left( a_z b_x - a_x b_z \right) \overline{\mathbf{e}}_{31} + \left( a_x b_y + a_y b_x \right) \overline{\mathbf{e}}_{12}. \tag{4.42}$$

The shorthand notation $\mathbf{e}_{ij}$ continues to have the same meaning $\mathbf{e}_i \wedge \mathbf{e}_j$, but we can interpret the complement $\overline{\mathbf{e}}_{ij}$ as either $\overline{\mathbf{e}_i \wedge \mathbf{e}_j}$ or $\overline{\mathbf{e}}_i \vee \overline{\mathbf{e}}_j$ due to Equation (4.39). Evaluating the complements in the product $\mathbf{a} \vee \mathbf{b}$ gives us

$$\mathbf{a} \vee \mathbf{b} = \left( a_y b_z - a_z b_y \right) \mathbf{e}_1 + \left( a_z b_x - a_x b_z \right) \mathbf{e}_2 + \left( a_x b_y + a_y b_x \right) \mathbf{e}_3, \tag{4.43}$$

which shows that the antiwedge product between two bivectors in three dimensions yields an ordinary vector with the familiar cross product components.

Using the fact that the complement operation subtracts the grade from the number of dimensions $n$, it should now be apparent that the antiwedge product has a grade-reducing effect given by

$$\boxed{\begin{aligned} \mathrm{gr}\left( \mathbf{A} \vee \mathbf{B} \right) &= n - \left( n - \mathrm{gr}\left( \mathbf{A} \right) + n - \mathrm{gr}\left( \mathbf{B} \right) \right) \\ &= \mathrm{gr}\left( \mathbf{A} \right) + \mathrm{gr}\left( \mathbf{B} \right) - n. \end{aligned}} \tag{4.44}$$

Multiplication with the wedge product combines the number of dimensions *included* by its factors, and multiplication with the antiwedge product combines the number of dimensions *excluded* by its factors. Just as the wedge product is zero whenever the grade given by Equation (4.13) is greater than $n$, the antiwedge product is zero whenever the grade given by Equation (4.44) is less than zero.

We saw in Equation (4.35) that the wedge product between a vector $\mathbf{a}$ and the right complement of a vector $\mathbf{b}$ yielded the $n$-dimensional volume element scaled by the dot product between $\mathbf{a}$ and $\mathbf{b}$. Replacing the wedge product with the anti-wedge product changes the result to a scalar:

$$\mathbf{a} \vee \overline{\mathbf{b}} = a_1 b_1 + a_2 b_2 + \cdots + a_n b_n. \tag{4.45}$$

This is actually the right complement of Equation (4.36), as shown by

$$\mathbf{a} \vee \overline{\mathbf{b}} = \overline{\underline{\mathbf{a}} \wedge \mathbf{b}} = \left( a_1 b_1 + a_2 b_2 + \cdots + a_n b_n \right) \overline{\mathbf{E}_n}, \tag{4.46}$$

and the product $\underline{\mathbf{a}} \vee \mathbf{b}$ is similarly the left complement of Equation (4.35).

Equation (4.45) would seem to provide a valid formula for the dot product $\mathbf{a} \cdot \mathbf{b}$ in the context of Grassmann algebra, but we still need to verify that using the same formula to calculate $\mathbf{b} \cdot \mathbf{a}$ produces the same result because the dot product is commutative. If we reverse the positions of $\mathbf{a}$ and $\mathbf{b}$, then we can use Equation (4.38) to write

$$\mathbf{b} \vee \overline{\mathbf{a}} = (-1)^{n-1} \, \overline{\mathbf{a}} \vee \mathbf{b}. \tag{4.47}$$

Applying Equation (4.27) to convert the right complement to the left complement, we can rewrite this as

$$\begin{aligned} \mathbf{b} \vee \overline{\mathbf{a}} &= (-1)^{n-1} (-1)^{n-1} \, \underline{\mathbf{a}} \vee \mathbf{b} \\ &= \underline{\mathbf{a}} \vee \mathbf{b}, \end{aligned} \tag{4.48}$$

which we know is equivalent to $\mathbf{a} \vee \overline{\mathbf{b}}$. Thus, Equation (4.45) produces the same result when $\mathbf{a}$ and $\mathbf{b}$ are swapped, and we are able to define the dot product $\mathbf{a} \cdot \mathbf{b}$ with any of the equivalent formulas

$$\boxed{\mathbf{a} \cdot \mathbf{b} = \mathbf{a} \vee \overline{\mathbf{b}} = \underline{\mathbf{a}} \vee \mathbf{b} = \mathbf{b} \vee \overline{\mathbf{a}} = \underline{\mathbf{b}} \vee \mathbf{a}.} \tag{4.49}$$

These formulas generalize to operations called the left and right *interior products* when we allow the factors to be not just vectors, but elements of any grade. We will not have the opportunity to discuss interior products in detail, but see Exercises 6 and 7 for a little additional information.

# 4.2 Projective Geometry

In Section 2.6, we introduced the concept of homogeneous coordinates and explained how a 4D vector corresponds to a 3D point through projection into the subspace where $w = 1$. In Chapter 3, we also discussed homogeneous representations of lines and planes, but at the time, we were not able to characterize the geometry of either of those as the outcome of any similar projection. We now have the tools necessary to demonstrate how homogeneous points, lines, and planes are all elements of increasing grade in the 4D Grassmann algebra, and we can show how the geometry for each of them arises through the same projection into the subspace where $w = 1$.

## 4.2.1 Lines

In the same way that a point is an object spanning zero dimensions that results from the projection of a *vector* spanning one dimension, a line is an object spanning one dimension that results from the projection of a *bivector* spanning two dimensions. The wedge product between two arbitrary vectors $\mathbf{a}$ and $\mathbf{b}$ in 4D Grassmann algebra is given by

$$\mathbf{a} \wedge \mathbf{b} = (a_w b_x - a_x b_w)\mathbf{e}_{41} + (a_w b_y - a_y b_w)\mathbf{e}_{42} + (a_w b_z - a_z b_w)\mathbf{e}_{43}$$
$$+ (a_y b_z - a_z b_y)\mathbf{e}_{23} + (a_z b_x - a_x b_z)\mathbf{e}_{31} + (a_x b_y - a_y b_x)\mathbf{e}_{12}. \quad (4.50)$$

If we replace $\mathbf{a}$ and $\mathbf{b}$ with homogeneous points $p$ and $q$, having implicit $w$ coordinates of one, then this becomes

$$p \wedge q = (q_x - p_x)\mathbf{e}_{41} + (q_y - p_y)\mathbf{e}_{42} + (q_z - p_z)\mathbf{e}_{43}$$
$$+ (p_y q_z - p_z q_y)\mathbf{e}_{23} + (p_z q_x - p_x q_z)\mathbf{e}_{31} + (p_x q_y - p_y q_x)\mathbf{e}_{12}. \quad (4.51)$$

This is a bivector whose six components are precisely the Plücker coordinates that were introduced as the implicit form of a line in Section 3.5, but now these components emerge from the fundamental multiplication rules of the 4D Grassmann algebra. As shown in Figure 4.4, this bivector corresponds to an oriented plane in 4D space, and it intersects the 3D subspace where $w = 1$ at the line containing the points $p$ and $q$. In this way, a homogeneous line is a higher-dimensional analog of the homogeneous point whose projection is shown in Figure 2.9.

We can equate the notation $\{\mathbf{v} \,|\, \mathbf{m}\}$ used in Chapter 3 to a 4D bivector $\mathbf{L}$ and label the components of a line having the direction $\mathbf{v} = q - p$ and the moment $\mathbf{m} = p \times q$ as

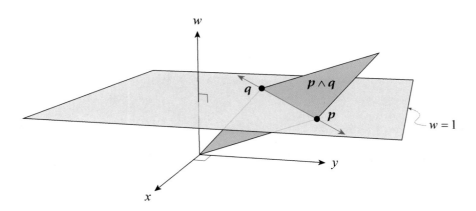

**Figure 4.4.** The 4D bivector $p \wedge q$ intersects the 3D subspace where $w = 1$ at the line determined by the homogeneous points $p$ and $q$. The $z$ axis is omitted from the figure, and it should be understood that the subspace for which $w = 1$ is not planar, but also extends in the $z$ direction.

$$\mathbf{L} = L_{vx}\mathbf{e}_{41} + L_{vy}\mathbf{e}_{42} + L_{vz}\mathbf{e}_{43} + L_{mx}\mathbf{e}_{23} + L_{my}\mathbf{e}_{31} + L_{mz}\mathbf{e}_{12}. \tag{4.52}$$

This assigns some meaning to the components of the bivector and allows us to continue regarding lines as having two three-dimensional parts. However, we can now interpret the direction $\mathbf{v}$ as a 3D vector and the moment $\mathbf{m}$ as a 3D bivector. The parts $\mathbf{v}$ and $\mathbf{m}$, when interpreting both as vectors, are always orthogonal for any 4D bivector constructed through the wedge product of any two 4D vectors (see Exercise 8). When interpreting $\mathbf{m}$ as a bivector, we can say that $\mathbf{v}$ always lies in the plane spanned by $\mathbf{m}$.

## 4.2.2 Planes

The four components of an implicit plane constitute a trivector in the 4D Grassmann algebra. A plane $\mathbf{f}$ can be constructed by calculating the triple wedge product among three homogeneous points $p$, $q$, and $r$, as in

$$\mathbf{f} = p \wedge q \wedge r. \tag{4.53}$$

This trivector intersects the subspace $w = 1$ at the plane containing the three points that were multiplied together, continuing the progression of projective geometries to the next step beyond points and lines.

A plane can also be constructed by multiplying a point and a line together, which is obvious when we consider that the wedge product between any pair of points in Equation (4.53) constructs a line that ends up being contained in the plane. In the case that we set $\mathbf{L} = q \wedge r$, the components of the plane containing $p$, $q$, and $r$ are given by

$$p \wedge \mathbf{L} = \left( L_{vy} p_z - L_{vz} p_y + L_{mx} \right) \overline{\mathbf{e}}_1 + \left( L_{vz} p_x - L_{vx} p_z + L_{my} \right) \overline{\mathbf{e}}_2$$
$$+ \left( L_{vx} p_y - L_{vy} p_x + L_{mz} \right) \overline{\mathbf{e}}_3 + \left( -L_{mx} p_x - L_{my} p_y - L_{mz} p_z \right) \overline{\mathbf{e}}_4. \quad (4.54)$$

Here, we have expressed the components in terms of the complements of the basis vectors to highlight the fact that a plane is a 4D antivector. Because $\mathbf{L}$ has an even grade, it's true that $\mathbf{L} \wedge p = p \wedge \mathbf{L}$, so it doesn't matter in which order a point and line are multiplied together.

Using the notation $[\mathbf{n} \,|\, d]$ from Chapter 3, we can express a plane as

$$p \wedge q \wedge r = n_x \overline{\mathbf{e}}_1 + n_y \overline{\mathbf{e}}_2 + n_z \overline{\mathbf{e}}_3 + d \,\overline{\mathbf{e}}_4, \quad (4.55)$$

where the normal $\mathbf{n}$ and distance to origin $d$ can be calculated with the formulas

$$\mathbf{n} = \mathbf{p} \wedge \mathbf{q} + \mathbf{q} \wedge \mathbf{r} + \mathbf{r} \wedge \mathbf{p}$$
$$d = -\overline{\mathbf{p} \wedge \mathbf{q} \wedge \mathbf{r}}. \quad (4.56)$$

These wedge products occur in three dimensions, and the points $\mathbf{p}$, $\mathbf{q}$ and $\mathbf{r}$ are written in the nonscript style to indicate that they are to be treated as 3D vectors. Both pieces of Equation (4.56) possess an elegant trinary symmetry, but neither they nor the formula in Equation (4.54) represents the most computationally efficient way of constructing a plane if we are starting with three points. The conventional methods of Chapter 3 are still the best, and we can rewrite them using the operations of Grassmann algebra as

$$\mathbf{n} = (\mathbf{q} - \mathbf{p}) \wedge (\mathbf{r} - \mathbf{p})$$
$$d = -\mathbf{n} \vee \mathbf{p} = -\mathbf{n} \vee \mathbf{q} = -\mathbf{n} \vee \mathbf{r}, \quad (4.57)$$

where the wedge and antiwedge products are still occurring in three dimensions. Any one of the three points may be used in the calculation of the distance $d$.

### 4.2.3  Join and Meet

With the homogeneous representations of points, lines, and planes in 4D Grassmann algebra, performing union and intersection operations by means of the wedge and antiwedge products is exquisitely straightforward and natural. However, our use of the words "union" and "intersection" in this context differ slightly from the ordinary geometric meaning because degenerate cases have null outcomes, as described below. For that reason, the terms *join* and *meet* are often used when referring to the respective operations of (a) combining the unshared directions of geometric objects to construct something with a greater number of dimensions and (b) retaining the shared directions of geometric objects to construct something with a lesser number of dimensions. The exact meanings of join and meet vary significantly in the literature as attempts are made to bring them in alignment with the set-theoretic meanings of union and intersection, but this is both unnecessary and unnatural. In this book, we choose the simplest definition and equate the join and meet operations exactly with the geometric results produced by the wedge and antiwedge products, respectively.

We have already encountered most of the join operations that can be considered in four dimensions. The join $p \wedge q$ between two points is given by Equation (4.51) and produces the line containing them. If the two points happen to be coincident, then no line can be determined, and the result is the line $\{0\,|\,0\}$ in which all six components of the bivector are zero. The join $p \wedge L$ between a point and a line is given by Equation (4.54) and produces the plane containing them. If the point happens to lie on the line, then no plane can be determined, and the result is the plane $[0\,|\,0]$ in which all four components of the trivector are zero. This degeneracy includes the case that a plane is constructed from three collinear points because one point will always lie on the line constructed with the other two.

The meet operations are symmetric to the join operations through the recognition that points and planes are complementary geometry objects, and the wedge and antiwedge products are complementary operations. Whereas the *wedge* product of two *points* yields the line joining them together, the *antiwedge* product of two *planes* yields the line at which they meet, or intersect. For two planes $\mathbf{f}$ and $\mathbf{g}$, represented by 4D trivectors, the meet is given by

$$\mathbf{f} \vee \mathbf{g} = (f_y g_z - f_z g_y)\mathbf{e}_{41} + (f_z g_x - f_x g_z)\mathbf{e}_{42} + (f_x g_y - f_y g_x)\mathbf{e}_{43}$$
$$+ (f_w g_x - f_x g_w)\mathbf{e}_{23} + (f_w g_y - f_y g_w)\mathbf{e}_{31} + (f_w g_z - f_z g_w)\mathbf{e}_{12}. \quad (4.58)$$

If the two planes happen to be coincident, then there is no unique line where they meet, and the result is $\{0\,|\,0\}$ as in the case of joining coincident points. If the two planes are parallel but not coincident, then the result is the line at infinity $\{\mathbf{0}\,|\,\mathbf{m}\}$ having a zero direction vector $\mathbf{v} = (0, 0, 0)$, but a nonzero moment bivector $\mathbf{m}$ that is parallel to the planes. (The vector $\overline{\mathbf{m}}$ is parallel to the planes' normal vectors.)

In a manner symmetric to the join of a point and a line, the meet of a plane $\mathbf{f}$ and a line $\mathbf{L}$ is given by

$$\mathbf{f} \vee \mathbf{L} = \left( L_{my} f_z - L_{mz} f_y + L_{vx} f_w \right) \mathbf{e}_1 + \left( L_{mz} f_x - L_{mx} f_z + L_{vy} f_w \right) \mathbf{e}_2$$
$$+ \left( L_{mx} f_y - L_{my} f_x + L_{vz} f_w \right) \mathbf{e}_3 + \left( -L_{vx} f_x - L_{vy} f_y - L_{vz} f_z \right) \mathbf{e}_4. \qquad (4.59)$$

This produces the homogeneous point at which the line intersects the plane. As with the wedge product between a point and a line, the antiwedge product between a plane and a line is commutative, but this time because $\overline{\mathbf{L}}$ has an even grade, so $\mathbf{L} \vee \mathbf{f} = \mathbf{f} \vee \mathbf{L}$. It will generally not be the case that the $w$ coordinate resulting from this operation is one, so it's necessary to divide by $w$ to obtain a projected 3D point. In the case that the line lies in the plane, there is no unique point of intersection, and the result is the point $(\mathbf{0}\,|\,0)$ having four zero components. If the line is parallel to the plane without lying in the plane, then the result is the point at infinity $(\mathbf{p}\,|\,0)$, where $\mathbf{p}$ is parallel to the direction of the line.

## 4.2.4 Line Crossing

The wedge product between two lines gives us some useful information about the distance between them and their relative orientations in space. Suppose that $\mathbf{L}_1 = \{\mathbf{v}_1 \,|\, \mathbf{m}_1\} = \boldsymbol{p}_1 \wedge \boldsymbol{q}_1$ and $\mathbf{L}_2 = \{\mathbf{v}_2 \,|\, \mathbf{m}_2\} = \boldsymbol{p}_2 \wedge \boldsymbol{q}_2$. Although it's somewhat difficult to visualize, the wedge product

$$\mathbf{L}_1 \wedge \mathbf{L}_2 = \boldsymbol{p}_1 \wedge \boldsymbol{q}_1 \wedge \boldsymbol{p}_2 \wedge \boldsymbol{q}_2 \qquad (4.60)$$

can be interpreted as the signed volume of a four-dimensional parallelotope whose sides are given by the vectors $\boldsymbol{p}_1$, $\boldsymbol{q}_1$, $\boldsymbol{p}_2$, and $\boldsymbol{q}_2$ extended to four dimensions with their implicit $w$ coordinates of one. Since all four sides have a length of one in the direction of the $w$ axis, that direction can be ignored by essentially dividing it out, leaving behind the three-dimensional parallelepiped shown in Figure 4.5. Without loss of generality, we can assume that the points $\boldsymbol{p}_1$ and $\boldsymbol{p}_2$ correspond to the points of closest approach on the two lines because sliding the points along each line (keeping the distance between $\boldsymbol{p}$ and $\boldsymbol{q}$ constant) only has the effect of skewing the parallelepiped, which does not change its volume.

The area of the base of the parallelepiped is given by $\|\mathbf{v}_1 \wedge \mathbf{v}_2\|$. If we divide $\mathbf{L}_1 \wedge \mathbf{L}_2$ by this area, then the only remaining length is the distance between the

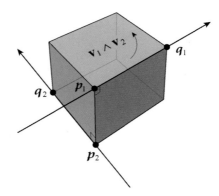

**Figure 4.5.** The distance between two lines $\mathbf{L}_1 = \boldsymbol{p}_1 \wedge \boldsymbol{q}_1$ and $\mathbf{L}_2 = \boldsymbol{p}_2 \wedge \boldsymbol{q}_2$ having directions $\mathbf{v}_1 = \boldsymbol{q}_1 - \boldsymbol{p}_1$ and $\mathbf{v}_2 = \boldsymbol{q}_2 - \boldsymbol{p}_2$ is given by the complement of the volume $\mathbf{L}_1 \wedge \mathbf{L}_2$ divided by the base area $\|\mathbf{v}_1 \wedge \mathbf{v}_2\|$.

two lines, corresponding to the magnitude of $\boldsymbol{p}_1 - \boldsymbol{p}_2$ in the figure. We are express-ing this as a multiple of the volume element $\mathbf{E}_4$, however, so we take the comple-ment of $\mathbf{L}_1 \wedge \mathbf{L}_2$ to turn it into a scalar. Thus, the formula for the signed distance $d$ between two lines is given by

$$d = \frac{\mathbf{L}_1 \vee \mathbf{L}_2}{\|\mathbf{v}_1 \wedge \mathbf{v}_2\|}, \tag{4.61}$$

where we have used the fact that

$$\overline{\mathbf{L}_1 \wedge \mathbf{L}_2} = \overline{\mathbf{L}_1} \vee \overline{\mathbf{L}_2} = \mathbf{L}_1 \vee \mathbf{L}_2 \tag{4.62}$$

for bivectors in four-dimensional space. The numerator in Equation (4.61) is the antiwedge product between two 4D bivectors, and the denominator contains the wedge product between two 3D vectors. In terms of the directions and moments of the two lines, the product $\mathbf{L}_1 \vee \mathbf{L}_2$ can be calculated as

$$\mathbf{L}_1 \vee \mathbf{L}_2 = -\mathbf{v}_1 \vee \mathbf{m}_2 - \mathbf{v}_2 \vee \mathbf{m}_1. \tag{4.63}$$

Since each direction is a vector and each moment is a bivector, this formula basi-cally amounts to a pair of dot products.

The sign of the distance $d$ given by Equation (4.61) corresponds to a crossing orientation that is mutually observed by both of the lines $\mathbf{L}_1$ and $\mathbf{L}_2$. As shown in

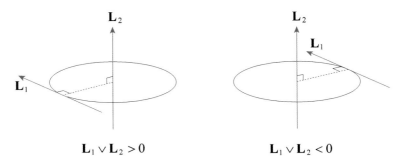

$$\mathbf{L}_1 \vee \mathbf{L}_2 > 0 \qquad\qquad \mathbf{L}_1 \vee \mathbf{L}_2 < 0$$

**Figure 4.6.** The sign of the antiwedge product $\mathbf{L}_1 \vee \mathbf{L}_2$ corresponds to the crossing orientation of the lines $\mathbf{L}_1$ and $\mathbf{L}_2$. The sign is positive when the lines are wound clockwise around each other, and it is negative when they are wound counterclockwise around each other.

Figure 4.6, if the antiwedge product $\mathbf{L}_1 \vee \mathbf{L}_2$ is positive, then the direction of each line is wound clockwise around the other. Conversely, if $\mathbf{L}_1 \vee \mathbf{L}_2$ is negative, then the winding is counterclockwise.

The crossing orientation can be used as a test to determine on which side one line passes another. As a practical example, consider a triangle whose edges are wound in a counterclockwise direction, and suppose that we need to determine whether a ray passes through the interior of the triangle. After calculating the antiwedge products between the ray and three lines corresponding to each of the triangle's edges, we know that the ray hits the triangle if all three products are positive and misses if any one of the products is negative.

## 4.2.5 Plane Distance

The wedge product $\boldsymbol{p} \wedge \mathbf{f}$ between a point $\boldsymbol{p}$ and a plane $\mathbf{f} = [\mathbf{n} \mid d]$ brings about another situation in which we have the signed volume of a four-dimensional parallelotope. Suppose that the plane is given by the wedge product of three points $\boldsymbol{q}_0$, $\boldsymbol{q}_1$, and $\boldsymbol{q}_2$. As in the case of two lines multiplied together, we can ignore the dimension corresponding to the $w$ axis because the parallelotope spans a length of one in that direction and all of the points lie in the $w = 1$ subspace. The value of $\boldsymbol{p} \wedge \mathbf{f}$ can then be interpreted as the volume of the parallelepiped whose sides are $\boldsymbol{q}_1 - \boldsymbol{q}_0$, $\boldsymbol{q}_2 - \boldsymbol{q}_0$, and $\boldsymbol{p} - \boldsymbol{q}_0$.

The plane's normal $\mathbf{n}$ is a 3D bivector quantity that's given by

$$\mathbf{n} = (\boldsymbol{q}_1 - \boldsymbol{q}_0) \wedge (\boldsymbol{q}_2 - \boldsymbol{q}_0), \tag{4.64}$$

and the magnitude of this bivector is the area of the parallelepiped's base. If we divide by $\|\mathbf{n}\|$, then the remaining length corresponds to the perpendicular distance between the base and the point $\boldsymbol{p}$, but it is expressed as a multiple of the volume element $\mathbf{E}_4$, so we take the complement of $\boldsymbol{p} \wedge \mathbf{f}$. Thus, the formula for the signed distance $d$ between a point and a plane is given by

$$d = \frac{\boldsymbol{p} \vee \mathbf{f}}{\|\mathbf{n}\|}, \tag{4.65}$$

where we have used the fact that

$$\underline{\boldsymbol{p} \wedge \mathbf{f}} = \underline{\boldsymbol{p}} \vee \underline{\mathbf{f}} = \boldsymbol{p} \vee \mathbf{f} \tag{4.66}$$

when $\boldsymbol{p}$ is a vector and $\mathbf{f}$ is an antivector.

The quantity $\boldsymbol{p} \vee \mathbf{f}$ is equivalent to the dot product $\underline{\mathbf{f}} \cdot \boldsymbol{p}$ discussed throughout Section 3.4, where the left complement has been taken to turn $\mathbf{f}$ into an ordinary vector. However, the dot product is commutative, but the antiwedge product anticommutes as $\boldsymbol{p} \vee \mathbf{f} = -\mathbf{f} \vee \boldsymbol{p}$. Since the components of $\mathbf{f}$ are expressed in terms of the right complements of the basis vectors, the quantity $\boldsymbol{p} \vee \mathbf{f}$ corresponds to the formula $\mathbf{a} \vee \overline{\mathbf{b}}$ given for the dot product in Equation (4.49). In order to calculate the same dot product with $\mathbf{f}$ appearing as the first factor, the components would need to be expressed in terms of the left complements to match the formula $\underline{\mathbf{a}} \vee \mathbf{b}$. The technically correct formulas for calculating $\underline{\mathbf{f}} \cdot \boldsymbol{p}$ are thus given by

$$\underline{\mathbf{f}} \cdot \boldsymbol{p} = \boldsymbol{p} \vee \mathbf{f} = \underline{\underline{\mathbf{f}}} \vee \boldsymbol{p}. \tag{4.67}$$

The double complement cancels the negation due to swapping the factors. Both results are equal to the quantity $f_x p_x + f_y p_y + f_z p_z + f_w$ that we're already familiar with from Chapter 3.

## 4.2.6 Summary and Implementation

Table 4.5 lists the elements of grades one, two, and three in 4D Grassmann algebra and shows that they correspond to geometric objects having intrinsic dimensionalities one less than their grades. A vector of grade one has four components, and it corresponds to a zero-dimensional point. A bivector of grade two has six components, and it corresponds to a one-dimensional line. A trivector of grade three, which is also an antivector, has four components, and it corresponds to a two-dimensional plane.

| Element | Geometric Meaning | Projection |
|---------|-------------------|------------|
| Vector | Point $(\mathbf{p}\,|\,w) = p_x\mathbf{e}_1 + p_y\mathbf{e}_2 + p_z\mathbf{e}_3 + w\mathbf{e}_4$ | $w = 1$ |
| Bivector | Line $\{\mathbf{v}\,|\,\mathbf{m}\} = v_x\mathbf{e}_{41} + v_y\mathbf{e}_{42} + v_z\mathbf{e}_{43} + m_x\mathbf{e}_{23} + m_y\mathbf{e}_{31} + m_z\mathbf{e}_{12}$ | $\|\mathbf{v}\| = 1$ |
| Trivector | Plane $[\mathbf{n}\,|\,d] = n_x\overline{\mathbf{e}}_1 + n_y\overline{\mathbf{e}}_2 + n_z\overline{\mathbf{e}}_3 + d\,\overline{\mathbf{e}}_4$ | $\|\mathbf{n}\| = 1$ |

**Table 4.5.** Vectors, bivectors, and trivectors having grades one, two, and three, correspond to points, lines, and planes having dimensionality zero, one, and two. Each type of geometry is projected into 3D space when the components including the basis vector $\mathbf{e}_4$ collectively have a magnitude of one.

The table also lists the conditions under which each type of geometry is considered to have been projected into 3D space. For a point $(\mathbf{p}\,|\,w)$, the $w$ coordinate has to be one. For a line $\{\mathbf{v}\,|\,\mathbf{m}\}$, the magnitude of the direction $\mathbf{v}$ has to be one. And for a plane $[\mathbf{n}\,|\,d]$, the magnitude of the normal $\mathbf{n}$ has to be one. In general, these correspond to the components of each type of geometry that contain the basis vector $\mathbf{e}_4$, which can collectively be thought of as the geometry's weight. For the geometry to be projected, or for the weight to be normalized, the part that extends into the $w$ direction must have a magnitude of one. For a point, this part is simply the $w$ coordinate. For a line, this part is the set of components corresponding to the basis bivectors $\mathbf{e}_{41}$, $\mathbf{e}_{42}$, and $\mathbf{e}_{43}$. For a plane, this part is the set of components corresponding to the basis antivectors $\overline{\mathbf{e}}_1$, $\overline{\mathbf{e}}_2$, and $\overline{\mathbf{e}}_3$ because these are the components that don't *exclude* the basis vector $\mathbf{e}_4$.

All of the geometric operations discussed in this section are summarized in Table 4.6. The wedge product corresponds to a join operation and builds geometry of higher dimensionality by combining smaller objects. The antiwedge product corresponds to a meet operation and extracts geometry of lower dimensionality by intersecting larger objects. Products between two lines or between a point and a plane calculate signed distances between those types of geometries.

The operations listed in Table 4.6 are implemented by the code in Listing 4.1. Points, lines, and planes are represented by the `Point3D`, `Line`, and `Plane` data structures introduced earlier in this book. We make use of overloaded ^ operators because this symbol conveniently resembles the wedge product. We employ the same symbol for the antiwedge product as well because it is never the case that we need both the wedge product and the antiwedge product for the same inputs. Either one of the operations is identically zero or the two operations produce a scalar and volume element having the same sign and magnitude.

Unfortunately, the ^ operator has a very low evaluation precedence among operators in C++, even lower than the relational operators, so it is rather ill-suited in this respect for the role of infix multiplication. It's necessary to surround each wedge or antiwedge product with parentheses to prevent operations from occurring in the wrong order. For example, the expression a ^ b < c ^ d would be interpreted by the compiler as a ^ (b < c) ^ d, so you would have to write (a ^ b) < (c ^ d) to get the correct result.

| Formula | Description | Special Cases |
|---------|-------------|---------------|
| $p \wedge q$ | Line containing points $p$ and $q$. | $\{\mathbf{0} \mid \mathbf{0}\}$ if $p$ and $q$ are coincident. |
| $p \wedge q \wedge r$ | Plane containing points $p$, $q$, and $r$. | $[\mathbf{0} \mid 0]$ if all three points are collinear. |
| $p \wedge \mathbf{L}$, $\mathbf{L} \wedge p$ | Plane containing line $\mathbf{L}$ and point $p$. | $[\mathbf{0} \mid 0]$ if $p$ lies on the line $\mathbf{L}$. |
| $\mathbf{f} \vee \mathbf{g}$ | Line where planes $\mathbf{f}$ and $\mathbf{g}$ intersect. | $\{\mathbf{0} \mid \mathbf{0}\}$ if $\mathbf{f}$ and $\mathbf{g}$ are coincident. $\{\mathbf{0} \mid \mathbf{m}\}$ if $\mathbf{f}$ and $\mathbf{g}$ are parallel but not coincident. |
| $\mathbf{f} \vee \mathbf{g} \vee \mathbf{h}$ | Point where planes $\mathbf{f}$, $\mathbf{g}$, and $\mathbf{h}$ intersect. | $(\mathbf{0} \mid 0)$ if any two planes are coincident or all three planes are parallel. $(\mathbf{p} \mid 0)$ if planes all intersect at parallel lines. |
| $\mathbf{f} \vee \mathbf{L}$, $\mathbf{L} \vee \mathbf{f}$ | Point where line $\mathbf{L}$ intersects plane $\mathbf{f}$. | $(\mathbf{0} \mid 0)$ if $\mathbf{L}$ lies in the plane $\mathbf{f}$. $(\mathbf{p} \mid 0)$ if $\mathbf{L}$ is parallel to $\mathbf{f}$ but does not lie in $\mathbf{f}$. |
| $\mathbf{L}_1 \vee \mathbf{L}_2$ | Signed distance between lines $\mathbf{L}_1 = \{\mathbf{v}_1 \mid \mathbf{m}_1\}$ and $\mathbf{L}_2 = \{\mathbf{v}_2 \mid \mathbf{m}_2\}$ scaled by $\|\mathbf{v}_1 \wedge \mathbf{v}_2\|$. | Zero if $\mathbf{L}_1$ and $\mathbf{L}_2$ are coplanar. |
| $p \vee \mathbf{f}$, $-\mathbf{f} \vee p$ | Signed distance between point $p$ and plane $\mathbf{f} = [\mathbf{n} \mid d]$ scaled by $\|\mathbf{n}\|$. | Zero if $p$ lies in the plane $\mathbf{f}$. |

**Table 4.6.** These are the operations carried out by the wedge product and antiwedge product when applied to vectors (points), bivectors (lines), and trivectors (planes) in the 4D Grassmann algebra.

**Listing 4.1.** These overloaded operators implement the wedge and antiwedge products among points, lines, and planes.

```
inline Line operator ^(const Point3D& p, const Point3D& q)
{
    return (Line(q.x - p.x, q.y - p.y, q.z - p.z,
      p.y * q.z - p.z * q.y, p.z * q.x - p.x * q.z, p.x * q.y - p.y * q.x));
}

inline Line operator ^(const Plane& f, const Plane& g)
{
    return (Line(f.y * g.z - f.z * g.y,
                f.z * g.x - f.x * g.z,
                f.x * g.y - f.y * g.x,
                g.x * f.w - f.x * g.w,
                g.y * f.w - f.y * g.w,
                g.z * f.w - f.z * g.w));
}

inline Plane operator ^(const Line& L, const Point3D& p)
{
    return (Plane(L.direction.y * p.z - L.direction.z * p.y + L.moment.x,
                L.direction.z * p.x - L.direction.x * p.z + L.moment.y,
                L.direction.x * p.y - L.direction.y * p.x + L.moment.z,
                -L.moment.x * p.x - L.moment.y * p.y - L.moment.z * p.z));
}

inline Plane operator ^(const Point3D& p, const Line& L)
{
    return (L ^ p);
}

inline Vector4D operator ^(const Line& L, const Plane& f)
{
    return (Vector4D(
            L.moment.y * f.z - L.moment.z * f.y + L.direction.x * f.w,
            L.moment.z * f.x - L.moment.x * f.z + L.direction.y * f.w,
            L.moment.x * f.y - L.moment.y * f.x + L.direction.z * f.w,
            -L.direction.x * f.x - L.direction.y * f.y - L.direction.z * f.z));
}
```

```
inline Vector4D operator ^(const Plane& f, const Line& L)
{
    return (L ^ f);
}

inline float operator ^(const Line& L1, const Line& L2)
{
    return (-(Dot(L1.direction, L2.moment) + Dot(L2.direction, L1.moment)));
}

inline float operator ^(const Point3D& p, const Plane& f)
{
    return (p.x * f.x + p.y * f.y + p.z * f.z + f.w);
}

inline float operator ^(const Plane& f, const Point3D& p)
{
    return (-(p ^ f));
}
```

## 4.3 Matrix Inverses

Grassmann algebra is able to provide some insights into the calculation of matrix inverses. In Section 1.7, we learned the importance of determinants and saw how a matrix inverse could be calculated with the cofactor matrix, which is composed of the determinants of smaller matrices. The wedge product of $n$ vectors yields a volume element whose sign and magnitude are precisely equal to the determinant of an $n \times n$ matrix whose columns are those $n$ vectors. They both represent the same hypervolume of an $n$-dimensional parallelotope. This equivalency allows us to formulate the inverse of a matrix in terms of nothing other than wedge products among its columns.

Let $\mathbf{c}_0, \mathbf{c}_1, \ldots, \mathbf{c}_{n-1}$ be the $n$ columns of an $n \times n$ matrix $\mathbf{M}$. The determinant $D$ of $\mathbf{M}$ is given by

$$D = \underline{\mathbf{c}_0 \wedge \mathbf{c}_1 \wedge \cdots \wedge \mathbf{c}_{n-1}} = \underline{\mathbf{c}}_0 \vee \underline{\mathbf{c}}_1 \vee \cdots \vee \underline{\mathbf{c}}_{n-1}, \qquad (4.68)$$

where we have taken the complement of the wedge product to produce a scalar quantity. (The left complement was chosen because it will be the more convenient option for the other parts of the inverse.) If we think about the way that all of the components of the columns are multiplied together in this product, we come to the realization that it's equivalent to the Leibniz formula given by Equation (1.75), but for the transpose of $\mathbf{M}$. Every term contains a product of $n$ factors, one from each column, corresponding to a unique permutation of the vector components.

The wedge product of any subset of $n-1$ columns of the matrix $\mathbf{M}$ creates an antivector that, when multiplied by the remaining column and complemented, produces the determinant $D$ after a possible sign flip to account for the ordering. This suggests that row $i$ of $D\mathbf{M}^{-1}$ should be composed of the wedge product of every column of $\mathbf{M}$ *except* column $i$. This causes the row's wedge product with the column vector $\mathbf{c}_i$ to yield the complement of the determinant $D$, and it causes the row's wedge product with any other column to yield zero.

The $(i, j)$ entry (where indexes are zero-based) of the matrix product $\mathbf{M}^{-1}\mathbf{M}$ is given by the dot product between row $i$ of $\mathbf{M}^{-1}$, which we assign the name $\mathbf{r}_i$, and column $j$ of $\mathbf{M}$, which has already been named $\mathbf{c}_j$. Selecting the formula

$$\mathbf{r}_i \cdot \mathbf{c}_j = \underline{\mathbf{c}_j} \vee \mathbf{r}_i \qquad (4.69)$$

in Equation (4.49) for the dot product makes it clear that the value of $\mathbf{r}_i$ must be given by

$$\mathbf{r}_i = \frac{(-1)^i}{D} \bigwedge_{k \neq i} \mathbf{c}_k \qquad (4.70)$$

in order to produce the entries of the identity matrix. The wedge product runs over all columns except column $i$, and the factor $(-1)^i$ accounts for an even or odd permutation of the columns. (If we had chosen to use right complements, then this factor would depend on the dimensionality $n$.)

The simplest application of Equation (4.70) is the calculation of the inverse of a $2 \times 2$ matrix whose columns are the vectors $\mathbf{a}$ and $\mathbf{b}$. The determinant is $D = \mathbf{a} \wedge \mathbf{b}$, and the rows of the inverse are simply given by $\mathbf{r}_0 = \underline{\mathbf{b}}/D$ and $\mathbf{r}_1 = -\underline{\mathbf{a}}/D$. Writing this out completely, we have

$$\begin{bmatrix} \uparrow & \uparrow \\ \mathbf{a} & \mathbf{b} \\ \downarrow & \downarrow \end{bmatrix}^{-1} = \frac{1}{\mathbf{a} \wedge \mathbf{b}} \begin{bmatrix} \underline{\mathbf{b}} \\ -\underline{\mathbf{a}} \end{bmatrix} = \frac{1}{a_x b_y - a_y b_x} \begin{bmatrix} b_y & -b_x \\ -a_y & a_x \end{bmatrix}, \qquad (4.71)$$

and this is equivalent to the formula given by Equation (1.93).

The inverse of a $3 \times 3$ matrix whose columns are the vectors $\mathbf{a}$, $\mathbf{b}$, and $\mathbf{c}$ can now be written as

$$\begin{bmatrix} \uparrow & \uparrow & \uparrow \\ \mathbf{a} & \mathbf{b} & \mathbf{c} \\ \downarrow & \downarrow & \downarrow \end{bmatrix}^{-1} = \frac{1}{\mathbf{a} \wedge \mathbf{b} \wedge \mathbf{c}} \begin{bmatrix} \mathbf{b} \wedge \mathbf{c} \\ -\mathbf{a} \wedge \mathbf{c} \\ \mathbf{a} \wedge \mathbf{b} \end{bmatrix}, \tag{4.72}$$

and this is equivalent to the formula given by Equation (1.95), but with the cross products and scalar triple product replaced by wedge products.

In Equation (1.99), we gave an interesting formula for the inverse of a $4 \times 4$ matrix, and its origin is now revealed as the four-dimensional application of Equation (4.70) given by

$$\begin{bmatrix} \uparrow & \uparrow & \uparrow & \uparrow \\ \mathbf{a} & \mathbf{b} & \mathbf{c} & \mathbf{d} \\ \downarrow & \downarrow & \downarrow & \downarrow \end{bmatrix}^{-1} = \frac{1}{\mathbf{a} \wedge \mathbf{b} \wedge \mathbf{c} \wedge \mathbf{d}} \begin{bmatrix} \mathbf{b} \wedge \mathbf{c} \wedge \mathbf{d} \\ -\mathbf{a} \wedge \mathbf{c} \wedge \mathbf{d} \\ \mathbf{a} \wedge \mathbf{b} \wedge \mathbf{d} \\ -\mathbf{a} \wedge \mathbf{b} \wedge \mathbf{c} \end{bmatrix}. \tag{4.73}$$

In Chapter 1, we had to use 3D vectors $\mathbf{a}$, $\mathbf{b}$, $\mathbf{c}$, and $\mathbf{d}$ because only the cross product provided the type of multiplication that we needed, and it is limited to three dimensions. With our knowledge of the wedge product, which has no such limitation, we can use 4D vectors and avoid separate names for the entries in the fourth row.

We can demonstrate the equivalence between Equation (4.73) and Equation (1.99) by first calculating $\mathbf{a} \wedge \mathbf{b}$ and $\mathbf{c} \wedge \mathbf{d}$ as

$$\mathbf{a} \wedge \mathbf{b} = u_x \mathbf{e}_{41} + u_y \mathbf{e}_{42} + u_z \mathbf{e}_{43} + s_x \mathbf{e}_{23} + s_y \mathbf{e}_{31} + s_z \mathbf{e}_{12}$$
$$\mathbf{c} \wedge \mathbf{d} = v_x \mathbf{e}_{41} + v_y \mathbf{e}_{42} + v_z \mathbf{e}_{43} + t_x \mathbf{e}_{23} + t_y \mathbf{e}_{31} + t_z \mathbf{e}_{12}. \tag{4.74}$$

The quantities $\mathbf{u}$ and $\mathbf{v}$ are 3D vectors given by

$$\mathbf{u} = a_w \mathbf{b}_{xyz} - b_w \mathbf{a}_{xyz}$$
$$\mathbf{v} = c_w \mathbf{d}_{xyz} - d_w \mathbf{c}_{xyz}, \tag{4.75}$$

where the notation $\mathbf{a}_{xyz}$ means the 3D vector $(a_x, a_y, a_z)$ without the $w$ component. The quantities $\mathbf{s}$ and $\mathbf{t}$ are 3D bivectors given by

$$\mathbf{s} = \mathbf{a}_{xyz} \wedge \mathbf{b}_{xyz}$$
$$\mathbf{t} = \mathbf{c}_{xyz} \wedge \mathbf{d}_{xyz}. \tag{4.76}$$

The values of $\mathbf{s}$, $\mathbf{t}$, $\mathbf{u}$, and $\mathbf{v}$ correspond to the coefficients given by Equation (4.50) for the wedge product of two 4D vectors. The determinant of the matrix is

$$D = \left(\mathbf{a} \wedge \mathbf{b}\right) \wedge \left(\mathbf{c} \wedge \mathbf{d}\right) = -\mathbf{u} \vee \mathbf{t} - \mathbf{v} \vee \mathbf{s}, \tag{4.77}$$

where we have applied the antiwedge product of two 4D bivectors given by Equation (4.63). Because both terms are an antiwedge product between a vector and antivector, the dot product formulas in Equation (4.49) apply, and the determinant can be written as $D = -\underline{\mathbf{s}} \cdot \mathbf{v} - \underline{\mathbf{t}} \cdot \mathbf{u}$ after some rearrangement. The vectors $\mathbf{u}$ and $\mathbf{v}$ were negated in Chapter 1 to make these terms positive. All four rows of the inverse are given by the wedge product between one of the columns of the original matrix and one of the bivectors calculated in Equation (4.74). Using the notation $\left[\mathbf{n} \,|\, d\right]$ for a 4D antivector, the rows can be expressed as

$$
\begin{aligned}
\mathbf{r}_0 &= \phantom{-}(1/D)\left[\mathbf{v} \wedge \mathbf{b} + b_w\mathbf{t} \,|\, -\mathbf{b} \vee \mathbf{t}\right] \\
\mathbf{r}_1 &= -(1/D)\left[\mathbf{v} \wedge \mathbf{a} + a_w\mathbf{t} \,|\, -\mathbf{a} \vee \mathbf{t}\right] \\
\mathbf{r}_2 &= \phantom{-}(1/D)\left[\mathbf{u} \wedge \mathbf{d} + d_w\mathbf{s} \,|\, -\mathbf{d} \vee \mathbf{s}\right] \\
\mathbf{r}_3 &= -(1/D)\left[\mathbf{u} \wedge \mathbf{c} + c_w\mathbf{s} \,|\, -\mathbf{c} \vee \mathbf{s}\right],
\end{aligned}
\tag{4.78}
$$

and the values inside the brackets are the same that appear inside the matrix in Equation (1.99) after multiplying by the negative one in the odd-numbered rows and accounting for the opposite signs of $\mathbf{u}$ and $\mathbf{v}$.

## 4.4 Geometric Algebra

There is a more general set of algebras called Clifford algebras that are built up from scalars and vectors much like Grassmann algebra is. A Clifford algebra has bivectors, trivectors, and all of the other elements of the same grades that appear in Grassmann algebra for a particular number of dimensions. The difference is that the basis vectors $\mathbf{e}_i$ are not required to square to zero. In $n$-dimensional Euclidean space, we may choose whether $e_i^2 = 0$, $e_i^2 = 1$, or $e_i^2 = -1$ for each $i$ with $1 \leq i \leq n$, and those choices determine the structure of the algebra. It is still true that the *basis* vectors anticommute, but that is no longer a property of all vectors in the algebra. Grassmann algebra is the special case in which $e_i^2 = 0$ for every $i$. In this section, we provide a short introduction to *geometric algebra*, which is the Clifford algebra in which $e_i^2 = 1$ for every $i$, and we show how the quaternions are actually part of the 3D geometric algebra. In Volume 3, we will discuss the *dual quaternions*, which are part of the 4D Clifford algebra in which $e_1^2 = e_2^2 = e_3^2 = 1$ and $e_4^2 = 0$.

### 4.4.1 Geometric Product

The *geometric product* is a type of multiplication discovered by William Kingdon Clifford (1845–1879) in his work to unify the quaternion product discovered by Hamilton and the wedge product discovered by Grassmann. The geometric product is written as juxtaposition without any multiplication symbol so that the geometric product between two quantities $\mathbf{a}$ and $\mathbf{b}$ is simply denoted by $\mathbf{ab}$. The wedge product is actually included in the geometric product, but as a whole, the geometric product contains additional pieces that make it behave differently. Whereas the defining characteristic of the wedge product given by Equation (4.1) states that any vector multiplied by itself must be zero, the geometric product has the property

$$\boxed{\mathbf{aa} = \mathbf{a} \cdot \mathbf{a}} \tag{4.79}$$

for any vector $\mathbf{a}$, where the product on the left is the geometric product, and the product on the right is the ordinary dot product.

If we consider the geometric product of a sum of two vectors $\mathbf{a}$ and $\mathbf{b}$, as we did for the wedge product, then we have the equality

$$(\mathbf{a} + \mathbf{b})(\mathbf{a} + \mathbf{b}) = (\mathbf{a} + \mathbf{b}) \cdot (\mathbf{a} + \mathbf{b}). \tag{4.80}$$

Expanding both sides of this equation independently gives us

$$\mathbf{aa} + \mathbf{ab} + \mathbf{ba} + \mathbf{bb} = \mathbf{a} \cdot \mathbf{a} + 2\,\mathbf{a} \cdot \mathbf{b} + \mathbf{b} \cdot \mathbf{b}, \tag{4.81}$$

where we have used the fact that the dot product is commutative. The products $\mathbf{aa}$ and $\mathbf{bb}$ on the left side cancel the products $\mathbf{a} \cdot \mathbf{a}$ and $\mathbf{b} \cdot \mathbf{b}$ on the right side, and we are left with

$$\mathbf{ab} + \mathbf{ba} = 2\,\mathbf{a} \cdot \mathbf{b} \tag{4.82}$$

as a fundamental property of the geometric product.

For a set of orthonormal basis vectors $\mathbf{e}_1, \mathbf{e}_2, \ldots, \mathbf{e}_n$, the dot products satisfy

$$\mathbf{e}_i \cdot \mathbf{e}_j = \begin{cases} 1, & \text{if } i = j; \\ 0, & \text{if } i \neq j. \end{cases} \tag{4.83}$$

Plugging distinct basis vectors into Equation (4.82) therefore gives us

$$\mathbf{e}_i \mathbf{e}_j + \mathbf{e}_j \mathbf{e}_i = 0, \tag{4.84}$$

from which we deduce the same anticommutativity property,

$$\boxed{\mathbf{e}_i\mathbf{e}_j = -\mathbf{e}_j\mathbf{e}_i,} \tag{4.85}$$

that we had for the wedge product. It's important to understand, however, that we have established this only for basis vectors, and the property does not generally hold for all pairs of vectors in the algebra.

We can now form a complete picture of what the geometric product does when two vectors are multiplied together. As an example case, we consider two arbitrary 3D vectors $\mathbf{a} = a_x\mathbf{e}_1 + a_y\mathbf{e}_2 + a_z\mathbf{e}_3$ and $\mathbf{b} = b_x\mathbf{e}_1 + b_y\mathbf{e}_2 + b_z\mathbf{e}_3$. The geometric product $\mathbf{ab}$ is given by

$$\left(a_x\mathbf{e}_1 + a_y\mathbf{e}_2 + a_z\mathbf{e}_3\right)\left(b_x\mathbf{e}_1 + b_y\mathbf{e}_2 + b_z\mathbf{e}_3\right) = a_xb_x\mathbf{e}_1\mathbf{e}_1 + a_yb_y\mathbf{e}_2\mathbf{e}_2 + a_zb_z\mathbf{e}_3\mathbf{e}_3$$
$$+ \left(a_yb_z - a_zb_y\right)\mathbf{e}_2\mathbf{e}_3 + \left(a_zb_x - a_xb_z\right)\mathbf{e}_3\mathbf{e}_1 + \left(a_xb_y - a_yb_x\right)\mathbf{e}_1\mathbf{e}_2. \tag{4.86}$$

Each product of a basis vector with itself is just one, and the terms containing the product of two distinct basis vectors have exactly the same coefficients as those given by the wedge product. We come to the conclusion that the geometric product between two vectors can be written as

$$\boxed{\mathbf{ab} = \mathbf{a}\cdot\mathbf{b} + \mathbf{a}\wedge\mathbf{b},} \tag{4.87}$$

which is a multivector containing both a scalar part having grade zero and a bivector part having grade two.

Equation (4.87) applies only to vectors, and there are generally more parts created through the geometric product $\mathbf{AB}$ between two blades $\mathbf{A}$ and $\mathbf{B}$ having arbitrary grades. Each of these parts can have a grade $g$ within the limits set by

$$\left|\mathrm{gr}\left(\mathbf{A}\right) - \mathrm{gr}\left(\mathbf{B}\right)\right| \le g \le \mathrm{gr}\left(\mathbf{A}\right) + \mathrm{gr}\left(\mathbf{B}\right), \tag{4.88}$$

but $g$ must differ from either end of this range by an even number. The reason for this is that any piece of the geometric product that yields something of a grade lower than the upper limit does so because the a particular basis vector in one factor is paired with the same basis vector in the other factor, and the two eliminate each other when they multiply to produce one.

If we solve Equation (4.82) for $\mathbf{a}\cdot\mathbf{b}$ and substitute it in Equation (4.87), then we obtain the pair of relationships

$$\mathbf{a}\cdot\mathbf{b} = \tfrac{1}{2}\left(\mathbf{ab} + \mathbf{ba}\right)$$
$$\mathbf{a}\wedge\mathbf{b} = \tfrac{1}{2}\left(\mathbf{ab} - \mathbf{ba}\right). \tag{4.89}$$

These equations highlight the fact that the geometric product yields both commutative and anticommutative components, represented by the dot product and the wedge product. The geometric product is completely commutative only when the vectors $\mathbf{a}$ and $\mathbf{b}$ are parallel because that's when the wedge product is zero. Otherwise, solving the second equation for $\mathbf{ba}$ tells us that

$$\mathbf{ba} = \mathbf{ab} - 2\,\mathbf{a} \wedge \mathbf{b}. \tag{4.90}$$

The geometric product is completely anticommutative only when the vectors $\mathbf{a}$ and $\mathbf{b}$ are perpendicular because that's when the dot product is zero. When $\mathbf{a}$ and $\mathbf{b}$ are neither parallel nor perpendicular, their geometric product contains a mixture of commutative and anticommutative parts.

## 4.4.2 Vector Division

Under the geometric product, a nonzero vector $\mathbf{v}$ has a simple inverse given by

$$\mathbf{v}^{-1} = \frac{\mathbf{v}}{v^2}, \tag{4.91}$$

and this is due to the fact that the product $\mathbf{vv}$ is equal to the scalar quantity $v^2$. The inverse allows us to investigate what it means to divide by a vector. For two vectors $\mathbf{a}$ and $\mathbf{b}$, the quotient $\mathbf{a}/\mathbf{b}$, which has the same meaning as $\mathbf{ab}^{-1}$, must be the quantity $\mathbf{c}$ such that $\mathbf{a} = \mathbf{cb}$. Thus, we can write the equation

$$\mathbf{a} = \frac{\mathbf{a}}{\mathbf{b}}\mathbf{b} = \frac{\mathbf{ab}}{b^2}\mathbf{b}. \tag{4.92}$$

When we expand the product $\mathbf{ab}$ with Equation (4.87), we get

$$\mathbf{a} = \frac{\mathbf{a} \cdot \mathbf{b}}{b^2}\mathbf{b} + \frac{\mathbf{a} \wedge \mathbf{b}}{b^2}\mathbf{b}. \tag{4.93}$$

The first term is exactly the projection of $\mathbf{a}$ onto $\mathbf{b}$ given by Equation (1.62), and this means that the second term must be the rejection of $\mathbf{a}$ from $\mathbf{b}$. We can therefore formulate the projection and rejection operations as

$$\mathbf{a}_{\parallel \mathbf{b}} = \frac{\mathbf{a} \cdot \mathbf{b}}{\mathbf{b}}$$

$$\mathbf{a}_{\perp \mathbf{b}} = \frac{\mathbf{a} \wedge \mathbf{b}}{\mathbf{b}}. \tag{4.94}$$

The division of a bivector by a vector in the formula for the rejection is interesting because it illustrates the difference in the information contained in the purely bivector result of the wedge product $\mathbf{a} \wedge \mathbf{b}$ and the mixed scalar and bivector result of the geometric product $\mathbf{ab}$. We've mentioned before that a bivector contains no information about its shape, so given a bivector $\mathbf{G} = \mathbf{a} \wedge \mathbf{b}$, we cannot expect to be able to recover the particular vector $\mathbf{a}$ originally used in the wedge product when we compute the quotient $\mathbf{G}/\mathbf{b}$ because there are infinitely many possibilities. However, in the case that $\mathbf{G} = \mathbf{ab}$, where the geometric product appears in place of the wedge product, the scalar part in the result carries additional information about the angle between $\mathbf{a}$ and $\mathbf{b}$ through the cosine associated with the dot product. This turns an amorphous bivector into a parallelogram having a definite restriction on the shapes it can assume. The magnitude and orientation of the vectors composing the sides of the parallelogram are still undetermined by $\mathbf{G}$, but as soon as we actually specify one vector $\mathbf{b}$, the other vector $\mathbf{a}$ can always be recovered. The vector given by $\mathbf{G}/\mathbf{b}$ is the unique vector $\mathbf{a}$ possessing the proper magnitude and forming the necessary angle with $\mathbf{b}$ such that $\mathbf{G} = \mathbf{ab}$.

In the case that $\mathbf{G} = \mathbf{a} \wedge \mathbf{b}$, the zero scalar part, corresponding to the cosine of the angle between sides of the parallelogram, is interpreted as meaning that $\mathbf{G}$ represents an oriented area whose shape must have right angles. Thus, dividing $\mathbf{G}$ by $\mathbf{b}$ yields a vector $\mathbf{r}$ that is orthogonal to $\mathbf{b}$ such that $\mathbf{G} = \mathbf{rb} = \mathbf{r} \wedge \mathbf{b}$. For $\mathbf{r} \wedge \mathbf{b}$ to produce the same area as $\mathbf{a} \wedge \mathbf{b}$, $\mathbf{r}$ must be the rejection of $\mathbf{a}$ from $\mathbf{b}$, as shown in Figure 4.7.

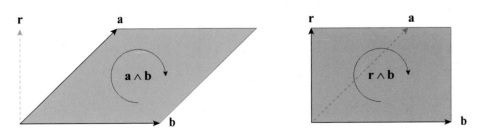

**Figure 4.7.** The bivectors $\mathbf{a} \wedge \mathbf{b}$ and $\mathbf{r} \wedge \mathbf{b}$ have the same area when $\mathbf{r}$ is the rejection of $\mathbf{a}$ from $\mathbf{b}$. Because its zero scalar part enforces a right angle, the wedge product $\mathbf{a} \wedge \mathbf{b}$ behaves like the geometric product $\mathbf{rb}$, and thus $\mathbf{r}$ is produced by $(\mathbf{a} \wedge \mathbf{b})/\mathbf{b}$.

### 4.4.3 Rotors

Suppose that **a** and **v** are vectors, and set $\mathbf{G} = \mathbf{av}$. If we divide $\mathbf{G}$ by **v**, then we get **a** right back, and that is not interesting. However, if we instead divide $\mathbf{G}$ by **a**, then something important happens. As shown in Figure 4.8, the quantity $\mathbf{G}/\mathbf{a}$ must be equal to some value $\mathbf{v}'$ such that $\mathbf{v}'\mathbf{a} = \mathbf{G}$, which means that

$$\mathbf{v}' = \mathbf{ava}^{-1}. \tag{4.95}$$

When we decompose $\mathbf{v}'$ into its scalar and bivector parts and compare it to the projection and rejection of **v** with respect to **a**, we see that

$$\begin{aligned}
\mathbf{v}' &= \frac{\mathbf{a} \cdot \mathbf{v}}{\mathbf{a}} + \frac{\mathbf{a} \wedge \mathbf{v}}{\mathbf{a}} \\
&= \frac{\mathbf{v} \cdot \mathbf{a}}{\mathbf{a}} - \frac{\mathbf{v} \wedge \mathbf{a}}{\mathbf{a}} \\
&= \mathbf{v}_{\|\mathbf{a}} - \mathbf{v}_{\perp\mathbf{a}}.
\end{aligned} \tag{4.96}$$

This is precisely the formula for the reflection across the vector **a** that was given by Equation (2.25). We called it an involution in Chapter 2 because in any odd number of dimensions, it's really a 180-degree rotation about **a**. In Figure 4.8, it's clear that the product of the reflected vector $\mathbf{v}'$ with **a** yields a quantity having the same shape and size as the product of **a** with the original vector **v**.

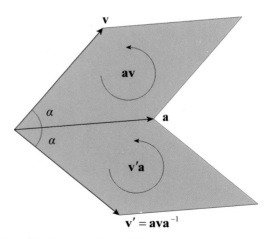

**Figure 4.8.** The vector $\mathbf{v}'$ is the reflection of the vector **v** across the vector **a**. Because $\mathbf{v}'$ is the same length as **v** and makes the same angle with **a** as **v** does, the geometric product $\mathbf{v}'\mathbf{a}$ yields the same scalar and bivector as the geometric product **av**.

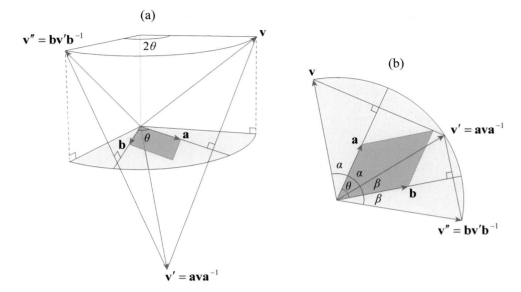

**Figure 4.9.** A vector $\mathbf{v}$ is rotated through the angle $2\theta$ by the rotor $\mathbf{ba}$, represented by the green parallelogram. (a) The reflection across the vector $\mathbf{a}$ transforms $\mathbf{v}$ into $\mathbf{v}'$, and the second reflection across the vector $\mathbf{b}$ transforms $\mathbf{v}'$ into $\mathbf{v}''$. (b) In the plane determined by $\mathbf{b} \wedge \mathbf{a}$, the two reflections combine to form a rotation through the angle $2\alpha + 2\beta$ from $\mathbf{a}$ to $\mathbf{b}$, where $\alpha$ is the angle between $\mathbf{a}$ and $\mathbf{v}$, and $\beta$ is the angle between $\mathbf{b}$ and $\mathbf{v}'$.

Let's now consider what happens when a reflection across a vector $\mathbf{a}$ is followed by another reflection across a vector $\mathbf{b}$. The first reflection transforms an arbitrary vector $\mathbf{v}$ into a new vector $\mathbf{v}'$ through the formula $\mathbf{v}' = \mathbf{ava}^{-1}$. The second reflection transforms $\mathbf{v}'$ into another new vector $\mathbf{v}''$ through the formula

$$\mathbf{v}'' = \mathbf{bv}'\mathbf{b}^{-1} = \mathbf{bava}^{-1}\mathbf{b}^{-1}. \tag{4.97}$$

These two steps are illustrated in Figure 4.9. If we set $\mathbf{R} = \mathbf{ba}$, then we can write

$$\boxed{\mathbf{v}'' = \mathbf{RvR}^{-1}} \tag{4.98}$$

after recognizing that $(\mathbf{ba})^{-1} = \mathbf{a}^{-1}\mathbf{b}^{-1}$. The bivector part of $\mathbf{R}$ is oriented in the plane determined by the vectors $\mathbf{a}$ and $\mathbf{b}$. As shown in Figure 4.9(a), the component of $\mathbf{v}$ perpendicular to this plane is negated by the first reflection, but is then negated again by the second reflection, so it does not change under the full transformation given by Equation (4.98).

The effect of the transformation on the other component of **v** is shown in Figure 4.9(b). For the sake of simplicity, we assume that **v** lies in the plane with the understanding that the following explanation otherwise applies to only the component of **v** that is parallel to the plane. The first reflection moves **v** to a new direction **v′** making an angle $2\alpha$ with **v**, where $\alpha$ is the angle between **a** and **v**. The second reflection then moves **v′** to a new direction **v″** making an angle $2\beta$ with **v′**, where $\beta$ is the angle between **b** and **v′**. As shown in the figure, the angle $\theta$ between the vectors **a** and **b** is equal to $\alpha + \beta$, and we can conclude that the two reflections combine to form a rotation through the angle $2\theta$.

The quantity $\mathbf{R} = \mathbf{ba}$ is called a *rotor*, and the sandwich product given by Equation (4.98) rotates vectors through an angle $2\theta$ in the direction from **a** to **b** parallel to the bivector $\mathbf{b} \wedge \mathbf{a}$, where $\theta$ is the angle between **a** and **b**. Note that the direction of rotation is the opposite of the winding direction associated with the bivector $\mathbf{b} \wedge \mathbf{a}$. For this reason, a rotor **R** is typically written as

$$\mathbf{R} = \mathbf{a} \cdot \mathbf{b} - \mathbf{a} \wedge \mathbf{b}, \tag{4.99}$$

which also follows from Equation (4.90). Although we have only considered the effect of rotors on vectors, we can deduce that rotors apply the same rotations to all higher-grade elements as well because for any two vectors **u** and **v**, we have

$$\mathbf{R}(\mathbf{uv})\mathbf{R}^{-1} = \left(\mathbf{RuR}^{-1}\right)\left(\mathbf{RvR}^{-1}\right). \tag{4.100}$$

Our description of rotors so far is valid in any number of dimensions, but it is usually 3D space that matters to us. In three dimensions, the wedge product $\mathbf{a} \wedge \mathbf{b}$ can be interpreted as the complement of an axis of rotation given by $\mathbf{a} \times \mathbf{b}$. If **a** and **b** have unit length, then Equation (4.99) can be written as

$$\mathbf{R} = \cos\theta - \sin\theta\,\bar{\mathbf{n}}, \tag{4.101}$$

where **n** is a unit vector pointing in the same direction as $\mathbf{a} \times \mathbf{b}$. This rotates through an angle of $2\theta$, so a rotor that rotates through an angle $\theta$ is given by

$$\boxed{\mathbf{R} = \cos\frac{\theta}{2} - \left(\sin\frac{\theta}{2}\right)\bar{\mathbf{n}}.} \tag{4.102}$$

Upon comparison with Equation (2.61), it's now clear that rotors in three dimensions are equivalent to the set of quaternions. Due to the subtraction of the bivector part in Equation (4.102), the imaginary units $i, j,$ and $k$ are equated with the negated basis elements for bivectors so that

$$i = \mathbf{e}_{32}, j = \mathbf{e}_{13}, k = \mathbf{e}_{21}. \tag{4.103}$$

As we mentioned in Chapter 2, it wasn't quite correct to call a quaternion the sum of a scalar part and a vector part, and we now know that a quaternion is really the sum of a scalar part and *bivector* part. Whenever we calculated the sandwich product $\mathbf{q}\mathbf{v}\mathbf{q}^*$ to rotate a vector $\mathbf{v}$ with a quaternion $\mathbf{q}$, we were actually treating $\mathbf{v}$ as a bivector, which works in three dimensions because it has the same number of components as a vector. The use of the quaternion conjugate arises from the fact that the inverse of $\mathbf{ba}$ is just $\mathbf{ab}$ when $\mathbf{a}$ and $\mathbf{b}$ have unit length, and reversing the order of the factors in the geometric product of two vectors has the effect of negating the bivector part of the result. (This is generalized as the concept of the *reverse* operator in Exercise 13.)

## 4.5 Conclusion

The goal of this chapter has been to provide deeper insights into much of the mathematics presented in Chapters 1, 2, and 3 by demonstrating how various conventional concepts with seemingly disparate origins fit neatly together in the more general settings of Grassmann algebra and geometric algebra. Many of the specific mathematical tools covered earlier in this book are listed in Table 4.7 alongside their replacements within the topics covered throughout this final chapter.

| Conventional Concept | Grassmann / Geometric Algebra Concept |
|---|---|
| Cross product $\mathbf{a} \times \mathbf{b}$ of two 3D vectors. | Wedge product $\mathbf{a} \wedge \mathbf{b}$ of two 3D vectors. |
| Scalar triple product $[\mathbf{a}, \mathbf{b}, \mathbf{c}]$ of three 3D vectors. | Wedge product $\mathbf{a} \wedge \mathbf{b} \wedge \mathbf{c}$ of three 3D vectors. |
| Dot product $\mathbf{a} \cdot \mathbf{b}$ of two vectors. | Antiwedge product $\mathbf{a} \vee \overline{\mathbf{b}}$ or $\underline{\mathbf{a}} \vee \mathbf{b}$ of vector and antivector. |
| Implicit plane $[\mathbf{n} \mid d]$. | Antivector $n_x \overline{\mathbf{e}}_1 + n_y \overline{\mathbf{e}}_2 + n_z \overline{\mathbf{e}}_3 + d\overline{\mathbf{e}}_4$ in 4D projective space. |
| Implicit line $\{\mathbf{v} \mid \mathbf{m}\}$ in Plücker coordinates. | Bivector $v_x \mathbf{e}_{41} + v_y \mathbf{e}_{42} + v_z \mathbf{e}_{43} + m_x \mathbf{e}_{23} + m_y \mathbf{e}_{31} + m_z \mathbf{e}_{12}$ in 4D projective space. |
| Quaternion $\mathbf{q} = xi + yj + zk + w$. | Even-grade multivector $w - x\mathbf{e}_{23} - y\mathbf{e}_{31} - z\mathbf{e}_{12}$ in 3D geometric algebra. |

**Table 4.7.** This table summarizes the mathematical concepts covered in earlier chapters that have natural replacements within Grassmann algebra or geometric algebra.

## Exercises for Chapter 4

1.  Prove that the area of a parallelogram whose sides are given by the 2D vectors **a** and **b**, shown in Figure 4.10, is equal to $a_x b_y - a_y b_x$ by calculating the areas of regions $A$, $B$, and $C$ using only the components of **a** and **b**.

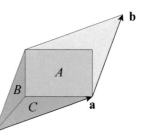

**Figure 4.10.** The parallelogram used in Exercise 1.

2.  Let **A** and **B** be blades in an $n$-dimensional Grassmann algebra. Under what conditions is it true that $\overline{\mathbf{A}} \wedge \overline{\mathbf{B}} \neq \underline{\mathbf{A}} \wedge \underline{\mathbf{B}}$?

3.  Prove that all $(n-1)$-vectors are $(n-1)$-blades for $n \geq 4$ by showing that the sum of any two $(n-1)$-blades must also be an $(n-1)$-blade.

4.  In four dimensions or higher, prove that a 2-vector **A** is a 2-blade if and only if $\mathbf{A} \wedge \mathbf{A} = 0$.

5.  Show that Equation (4.40) can be derived from Equation (4.39) and vice versa, demonstrating that one version of the laws implies the other version.

6.  Show that all of the equalities in Equation (4.49) still hold true if **a** and **b** are replaced by $k$-blades **A** and **B** having any grade $k$. This defines an *inner product* between arbitrary blades of the same grade. Furthermore, show that

    $$\mathbf{A} \cdot \mathbf{B} = \overline{\mathbf{A}} \cdot \overline{\mathbf{B}} = \underline{\mathbf{A}} \cdot \underline{\mathbf{B}}.$$

7.  Define $\mathbf{A} \dashv \mathbf{B} = \underline{\mathbf{A}} \vee \mathbf{B}$ to be the *left interior product* between any blades **A** and **B** that don't necessarily have the same grade. Prove that

    $$\mathbf{A} \dashv (\mathbf{B} \dashv \mathbf{C}) = (\mathbf{A} \wedge \mathbf{B}) \dashv \mathbf{C}.$$

8. Consider the bivector resulting from the wedge product between two 4D vectors **a** and **b**, as shown in Equation (4.50). Referring to this result in the form of Equation (4.52), show that the 3D vectors $(L_{vx}, L_{vy}, L_{vz})$ and $(L_{mx}, L_{my}, L_{mz})$ are always orthogonal.

9. For any three noncollinear points $p$, $q$, and $r$, prove that Equation (4.56) is equivalent to the trivector produced by $p \wedge q \wedge r$.

10. Show that the components of $p \vee \bar{\mathbf{e}}_4$, $\mathbf{L} \vee \bar{\mathbf{e}}_4$, and $\mathbf{f} \vee \bar{\mathbf{e}}_4$ that are not identically zero are exactly those that need to be normalized in order to project the point $p$, line **L**, and plane **f** into 3D space.

11. Find a formula for the fourth row (having a row index of 3) of the inverse of a $7 \times 7$ matrix whose columns are given by the 7D vectors **a**, **b**, **c**, **d**, **f**, **g**, and **h**.

12. Show that for any unit vector **v**, the quantity $(1 + \mathbf{v})/2$ is idempotent under the geometric product. (A quantity $a$ is called *idempotent* if $a^2 = a$.)

13. The *reverse* of a $k$-blade $\mathbf{A} = \mathbf{v}_1 \wedge \mathbf{v}_2 \wedge \cdots \wedge \mathbf{v}_k$ is the $k$-blade $\tilde{\mathbf{A}}$ produced by multiplying all of the factors $\mathbf{v}_i$ in reverse order so that $\tilde{\mathbf{A}} = \mathbf{v}_k \wedge \mathbf{v}_{k-1} \wedge \cdots \wedge \mathbf{v}_1$. Find a function $f(k)$ such that $\tilde{\mathbf{A}} = (-1)^{f(k)} \mathbf{A}$.

14. Let **L** be a line having direction vector **v** and moment bivector **m**. Show that $\mathbf{m}/\mathbf{v}$, using vector division under the geometric product, is the vector extending from the origin to the point on **L** closest to the origin.

15. Show that the set of all multivectors having only even-graded parts in an $n$-dimensional geometric algebra is closed under multiplication. That is, for any two multivectors of the form $\mathbf{A}_1 + \mathbf{A}_2 + \cdots$, where each $\mathbf{A}_i$ is a blade of even grade, show that their geometric product has the same form. This subset is called the *even subalgebra*.

16. Prove that the even subalgebra of the three-dimensional geometric algebra is isomorphic to the two-dimensional Clifford algebra in which $e_1^2 = e_2^2 = -1$.

# Index

Made in the USA
Columbia, SC
22 July 2019